# MANAGING
## PROJECT RISK

### Best Practices
### for Architects and
### Related Professionals

James B. Atkins, FAIA, FKIA
and Grant A. Simpson, FAIA

**WILEY**

John Wiley & Sons, Inc.

This book is printed on acid-free paper. ∞

Copyright © 2008 by James B. Atkins and Grant A. Simpson
All rights reserved

Published by John Wiley & Sons, Inc., Hoboken, New Jersey
Published simultaneously in Canada

For general information about our other products and services, please contact our Customer Care
Department within the United States at (800) 762-2974, outside the United States at (317) 572-3993 or
fax (317) 572-4002.

Wiley also publishes its books in a variety of electronic formats. Some content that appears in print may
not be available in electronic books. For more information about Wiley products, visit our web site at
www.wiley.com.

*Library of Congress Cataloging-in-Publication Data:*

ISBN: 978-0-470-27381-4 (cloth)

Printed in the United States of America

10  9  8  7  6  5  4  3  2  1

# Contents

## Chapter 1
## Fundamentals   |   1

## Chapter 2
## Clients   |   39

# Chapter 3

## Power and Proficiency | 63

# Chapter 4

## Essentials | 99

# Chapter 5

## Applications | 139

# Chapter 6

## The Architects' Lament | **189**

# Chapter 7

## Introspection | **211**

# Foreword

By Douglas Gordon, Hon. AIA, Executive editor, and
Stephanie Stubbs, Assoc. AIA, Managing editor, *AIArchitect*

Over the decades, dozens of potential contributors have come to us offering to write this series of articles or that. Some would actually write an article, maybe two, then lose interest or run out of ideas. And when an AIA committee comes up with the idea that its members will write a column, we never say "no." And, almost invariably, when we invite such a series, nothing materializes.

So it was in 2004 when we met Jim Atkins and (a bit later) Grant Simpson, who—at the instigation of an AIA committee—said they had some ideas for a risk management series. With a slight sense of trepidation, we agreed and set up a meeting. That first sit-down was markedly different from any before or since, though. At the outset, the authors presented us with the first article, fully written (a reprint from *Texas Architect*, "A Loss Cause") and a full year's worth of article titles and a submission schedule. The draft of the second article came soon thereafter.

In the coming months, we became believers. These two very busy architects working at the top levels within and with some of the largest firms in the country were delivering their monthly risk management medicine—always laced with spoonfuls of sugar in the form of tongue-in-cheek humor—on time every time. What luxury it is to work with such tireless, knowledgeable, informative people. But it gets better . . .

Being electronic, we are able to track the readership of every article that runs in *AIArchitect*, and we do. It didn't take long to notice that every time we ran a Simpson/Atkins article, they had the highest article hit rate for the week (often for the month). To this day, that phenomenon continues.

We did hear some criticism, too, of course—from lawyers. Interestingly, the lawyers found the articles too anecdotal, with no citations, limited case law, and oversimplification of complex legal issues, for instance. Whenever they delve into the level of detail that these articles do, apparently, it was in law reviews, not architectural periodicals.

So, it seems, what draws the lawyerly ire is the very reason practicing architects keep asking for more. Atkins and Simpson were telling the story from the architect's perspective. They have both been through litigation, arbitration, and mediation. They have conferred with the sharpest legal minds in the field of construction law, and they understand the finer points of that sometimes arcane discipline. They also recognize that few other architects do. They chose their mission to spread the word, as they are wont to write: "Be careful out there."

These two writers have sustained their momentum for more than two years, and keep promising more. In the meantime, anecdotally but continually, we hear from principals of firms large and small that they want printed copies of the articles to pass around for all their firm associates to read. The next step, then, which we had all been contemplating all along, actually, was self-evident. It is the book you are holding right now.

Read it. Enjoy it. Learn from it.

# Preface

*Managing Project Risk: Best Practices for Architects and Related Professionals* is composed of a series of articles that we had originally written over a three-year period for *AIArchitect* online at AIA.org, with a small handful initially published in *Texas Architect* magazine. It is intended to provoke thought and provide information that the design professional can apply in delivery of services. This book should be utilized with the understanding that we, both practicing architects, are in no way providing legal advice or services or any other type of expert consultation regarding specific conditions or situations. The reader must also understand that the laws, codes, and documents referenced herein periodically change and their authority should be confirmed prior to reliance or use.

The practice issues, conditions, and situations cited in this book are relevant studies and commentary of how specific situations on actual projects have been effectively administered by design professionals. However, all projects are unique and specific situations may require actions or approaches that significantly differ from those cited or suggested in this book. Further, actions taken and decisions made in certain situations may require the advice of legal counsel or special consultants.

It is also important that the reader understand that laws vary from state to state and that professional practices may vary depending on the geographical location and size or type of your practice and the project. In addition, the reader should seek the advice of a competent lawyer with expertise in the defense of design professionals should matters proceed to the claim or dispute resolution stage.

# Acknowledgments

We are very grateful to The American Institute of Architects, particularly Jay Stephens, Esq., and Douglas E. Gordon, Hon. AIA, who cleared the path and enabled the article series to be born and to flourish. Jay's leadership on the AIA Risk Management Committee supported our efforts to do the series, and Doug's talented edits and nourishing support gave life to our messages in *AIArchitect*. The talented editing and production work of Stephanie Stubbs, Assoc. AIA, enabled our series to shine brightly. We have both learned and grown from the guidance of Joseph A. Demkin, AIA, who taught us the benefits of good editing and critical review.

Our appreciation also goes to Stephen Sharpe, executive editor of *Texas Architect* magazine, who published our first coauthored work and came up with good titles. Our articles would not have come to you in book form without the able leadership and direction of John Czarnecki, Assoc. AIA, with John Wiley & Sons.

**Jim Atkins:** I am indebted to my business partners at HKS Architects for their many years of support and encouragement. Special thanks go to mentor and friend, Ronald L. Skaggs, FAIA. My growth as an architect was profoundly shaped by three late great mentors: my father, C. B. Atkins, who taught me to work hard and not fear adversity; my professor and friend, Ernest L. Buckley, PE, PhD, who encouraged me to write and speak; and an old-style contractor, Hap Padgett, who showed me how buildings can and should be constructed.

Finally, I am grateful to my daughter, Ashley, for her eternal love and support, and my ultimate gratitude goes to my wife, Sook Kim, PhD, for allowing these articles to steal me away from her all those nights and weekends. This book would not have been possible without her loving support, understanding, and encouragement.

**Grant Simpson:** I am indebted to several important mentors who shaped my career. Joe Moore, homebuilder, who let me work summers during high school and college, building the things I drew; the wise old chief draftsmen from the '70s, Robert Reynolds, Arthur Stone, William Echols, Terry Garrett, and Bob Jackson, who taught me more about construction documents than anyone else could; Ronald M. Brame, FAIA, from whom I learned, during my 22 years with HKS, that architecture is a business; and my friend Lance K. Josal, AIA, who invited me to help out with project delivery at RTKL.

I am grateful to my two sons, Andrew and Austin, who, in the midst of innocence and their unconditional love and concern for me, asked me in the early fall of 2003, as we made our morning commute to school, if I was ever going to work again, and to my grandfather, Clyde W. Wilkerson, the wisest man I've ever known. Finally, I am most grateful to Tina, my wife and loving companion of 37 years. Her patience is without limits, and she nurtures and tolerates me endlessly.

# Introduction

The articles that compose this publication are a product of our experiences as project managers and group leaders over many years. As we entered the profession in the late 1970s, the two of us began to encounter the issues we would later discuss with architects as copresenters at AIA events and write about together. As we debated, presented, and published our works, we began to realize that many of the most contested topics were not represented well in the literature that was available. When these issues were addressed, they tended to be superficial, watered down, or off the mark entirely.

In 2003, while working together on a large litigation that made rude, rhetorical, and disingenuous claims against an architect, we decided it was time to address some of the basic issues such as the realities of errors and omissions and the concept of betterment. Our decision led us to writing the article "A Loss Cause" that was initially published in 2004 by *Texas Architect* magazine and later republished by AIA.org's *AIArchitect* as one of its "Best Practices" topics. Discussions with *AIArchitect* regarding future topics resulted in the "Best Practices in Risk Management" monthly series. The *AIArchitect* readership responded with much praise and some criticism, leading us to augment, temper, and strengthen our messages, our opinions, and our resolve.

The elements of our approach to practice cover many areas in risk management—from the fundamentals to client issues to the essentials that we believe necessary to survive in today's challenging work environment. We include applications from our personal experience to accompany traditional AIA-based project management to strengthen and enhance this well-established industry standard. We are introspective, observing and questioning our actions in an effort to keep our path true and within the best-practices arena. We continuously sound our best-practice ideas to a network of professionals across the country that supports us with beneficial advice and commentary. The group includes prominent architects, lawyers, and insurance specialists with direct and extensive experience in the topics we address. We occasionally look backward, lamenting the loss of the way things once were, but we learn and use these past events to keep our expectations and projections of the future in context.

The topics in this book reference both the 2007 and the 1997 AIA documents. Claims adjudication often takes many years due to lengthy or nonexistent statutes of limitation and repose and our somewhat glacial legal system. A significant number of disputes pending in litigation today involve contracts written using both the 1987 and 1997 AIA document editions. Although the 2007 AIA document revisions are now available, some practitioners will continue to use the 1997 document family that they are familiar with for as long as they remain available. However, in an attempt to fulfill the needs of readers, we have references to both revisions. This publication is intended to not only present the reader with sound risk management suggestions but also to help give context to professional practice and provide supplemental assistance to the references and resources currently available for the practitioner. It is not so much a book of directions as it is a collection of opinions derived from our experiences. We hope to provoke thought and provide information that you can apply in your approach to architecture. We also hope that you benefit from this information and you use this publication as a handy reference. We sincerely invite your debate, because by questioning and arguing the issues, we grow together. There is no substance to the phrase "ask a stupid question," because the angst of regretting a question asked is much preferred over ignorance.

Many of our readers and supporters have asked how we continue to come up with informative, stimulating, and relevant topics to address. The problem we face is not in finding new topics, but in choosing from the many ways we architects get into trouble not only in practice but also from the fantastic ways plaintiffs' lawyers spin the alleged wrongdoings of architects. From this great source we find the few topics we have time to write about.

We admonish you to wisely balance your risks with your rewards, cherish that shingle on the front door while having fun and finding fulfillment along the way, and please, as we note at the end of every article, don't forget to be careful out there.

# Chapter 1

## Fundamentals

## The Importance of Risk Management: Its Key Role in Professional Service Delivery

This introductory article for the series was actually our second article written as a team. We felt it important that the series lead-off piece convey the overall message of the integral part risk management plays in our daily work. The operative word in this article is "attitude." Risk management is a way that we think about work that affects many things we do each day. We also touch on some topics we will be addressing in later articles, and for the first time we close with our now familiar monthly departure line, "be careful out there."

> There is no security on this earth, only opportunity.
> —General Douglas MacArthur

Risk management is not a standard course in architecture school. It is not a topic on the Architect Registration Examination. Yet there are many seminars on the subject presented each year at the AIA Convention, and professional publications address the topic frequently. The AIA Risk Management Committee is one of the two most funded committees in the Institute.

Unfortunately, many architects believe risk management is a remote activity and should be discharged by the "technical guys" in the back room, out of sight of clients. Our profession is actually heavily influenced by risk management, yet there are no checklists or descriptive processes. Why is it so enigmatic? Why is it so important? Why should we be concerned with something so distant from architecture? Or is it so distant?

Only in the last 30 years have we had to worry about our risks. It all began about the time the request for information (RFI) appeared on the scene. Up until then contractors didn't write down the questions they asked the architect. They didn't keep track of what their questions were or how they were answered. They were only concerned with building the project, collecting their fee, and moving on to the next job.

Today, as you know, things are quite different. Our documents are scrutinized in excruciating detail for conflicting, duplicated, or missing information. The RFI process has become a struggle, with architects considering their answers to be "supplemental instructions" and contractors often claiming them to be added scope. RFIs and submittal tracking logs are now viewed as the contractor's primary tools for making a case against the architect. As architects, we are condemned if we don't answer any and all questions quickly or correctly. We are also condemned if we answer correctly, with the presumption that the question was necessary because the drawings were deficient in some way.

The result has been an alarming increase in claims and litigation against architects. This has threatened the existence of many insurance providers, and premiums and deductibles have risen as they attempt to stay alive. Meanwhile, insurance companies and defense lawyers are preaching risk management. They tell us to proceed with great caution, and they warn against project types of higher risk.

## It's an attitude

Risk management is not so much a subject as an attitude. It is more an approach to business than it is a part of business. Achieving success in architecture in today's treacherous industry is dependent upon how you apply relevant risk management as you go about providing your professional services.

Our topics will cover essentials such as good contracts and effective documentation. We will look at the risks that arise from our plans and specifications and the minefield of construction administration liabilities. We will review high-risk areas in project delivery, such as the broadly misunderstood aspects of fast track and the varying expectations of construction management. We will also examine risks associated with the contractor's work responsibilities and how easily the architect can assume them if not prepared and knowledgeable. In virtually every article, we will examine the benefits of communicating with and understanding your clients and their expectations of your performance.

> The trouble with law is lawyers.
>
> —Clarence Darrow

## How did things get this way?

First, let's look at how we got into this fine mess. What happened to cause the contractor to start worrying more about keeping score than keeping in budget and on schedule? What caused us to start dissecting words and using those cover-your-assets phrases?

The worm began to turn back in the '50s when the courts ruled that you could sue someone although you were not contracted with them. The contractual relationship, known in legal terms as *privity*, ceased to be an absolute requirement for filing suit, and architects began to experience the joys of being served with legal papers. The climate quickly changed for architects from never being involved in lawsuits to almost always being involved.

As a result, architects began to worry more about semantics than about their services. Inspection and supervision gave way to observation and just being generally familiar with the work. Any certifications that were made had to be based on the "best of our knowledge, information, and belief." Architects had to start dancing with the legal aspects of their services because they were becoming targets in claims and legal actions.

## Insurance plays a role

But architects didn't really become a viable target for claims until they acquired professional liability insurance. The insurance policy gave the plaintiffs a measurable goal for claim damage awards. Professional liability insurance was created for architects and engineers by Victor O. Schinnerer in 1957 to protect against a very real threat. But one has to wonder if the policy itself has become the desired target. Could this response to a need have actually helped to seal our fate?

Claims against design professionals typically allege negligence—that is, a negligent act or failure to act by the architect in the performance of professional services. In today's design industry everyone keeps score. Contractors want additional general conditions costs if the architect fails to act quickly enough, and owners want to be compensated for anything that is added to the job after the contract is signed. This has grown out of the perception that almost everything is the architect's fault. Any error or omission or duplication is perceived as caused in some way by the design professional. This topic is explored in "A Loss Cause: Drawing Discrepancies and Ensuing Damages" in Chapter 4. If you have ever been involved in a lawsuit, you have experienced firsthand that every mistake that can be divined from your services will be cited as evidence of a "pattern of negligence."

> They say that nobody is perfect. Then they tell you practice makes perfect.
> I wish they'd make up their minds.
> —Winston Churchill

## Nobody's perfect

This raises the question: Why do they perceive us to be the perpetrator? Why is it that for years the architect was never thought to be at fault, and now it is automatically assumed? The accepted definition of "Standard of Care" does not contain the word perfection—not for architects and not for any other profession. So how have contractors and owners come to demand such performance? Standard of Care as addressed in AIA Document B503, 2007, Guide for Amendments to AIA Owner-Architect Agreements, emphasizes that "The law . . . does not expect architects to provide perfect or flawless services or to guarantee or warrant the results of their services." Nevertheless, the topic warns architects that "Use of words or phrases such as 'highest,' 'best,' or 'most qualified' in relation to the Architect's standard of care, increases to extreme levels the standard of performance expected of the Architect."

Perhaps architects have brought some of their trouble on themselves with lofty representations that have altered expectations. But there is also a marked demand and expectation for perfect services that prevails in the industry. Clients want architects to sign "redraw at the architect's sole expense" and "time is of the essence" clauses in contracts, and they frequently demand "100 percent complete" or "fully coordinated" construction documents. This has come about in part because architects do not concern themselves enough with what the general public thinks and knows about realities in their profession. Architects who practice as if they can do no wrong will likely create the same expectation from those with whom they do business.

So risk management in architecture is much more than just playing it safe by documenting decisions and securing a good contract. It is also about education, enlightenment, communications, and relationships. It is partly about improving your product delivery, but it also includes demanding the full measure of the obligations of others. These practice adaptations are necessary if we are to overcome the risk challenges that face us.

## A good start

A good place to start is in your own shop. How good is your documentation? What's in your laptop? E-mail has become perilous, and the trail that we leave behind us can be condemning. When you think of documentation, you must think in terms of your complete body of services. Remember, people are now keeping score on not only what you do but also when you do it and how fast. It is a lot like keeping a diary. In fact, many architects keep a personal journal of their projects that much resembles a diary. They document decisions, events, discussions, and any other information that chronicles the project delivery. We address the essentials of a project journal in detail in "To Document or Not to Document" later in this Chapter in Chapter 1.

A reasonable risk management objective is to have everyone in your office keeping records in a similar manner and with the same thoroughness. This will make training easier, and it will enable data research should you need your records for defending yourself. Your records should be clear and easy to understand. Remember that the person reviewing them later will likely not be an architect, so try to refrain from terminology and jargon that the layperson will not understand. You should also be careful to avoid self-criticism in project-related correspondence. At any given time, on any given project, we are likely to take actions that we could have done better, and there is no reason to make a case against yourself by identifying and emphasizing your shortcomings.

The "story" of the design and construction of a project is told primarily through meeting reports, site observation reports, and communicating correspondence such as letters, memoranda, and e-mails. Therefore, it is essential that you manage these media to the greatest extent possible. In addition to the site observation report, it is important that you also manage the project meeting report. After all, they are essentially tools for reporting project progress to the owner. If you issue the report, you will be able to recount the events as you have experienced them, and if you do not issue the report, you will likely read results or opinions that do not coincide with your own. If your contract or your project organizational structure does not allow you to issue the project meeting report, it will be necessary for you to rebut in writing each and every issue and event that is not consistent with your experiences and understandings. Rebuttal is a laborious process that too frequently falls through the cracks of a busy schedule.

## Managing communications and the 24-hour rule

Letters, memoranda, and e-mails must also be managed effectively. Though seemingly ludicrous, a good rule to follow is not to put anything in writing that you do not want to see projected on a screen in a courtroom. This includes criticism of yourself and your consultants, documentation of any breaches of responsibility, and any unprofessional actions or behavior. When managing sensitive subjects, it is usually a good idea to wait a while after you have written on the subject before sending it to someone. This is known as the 24-hour rule. This allows you time to cool down and think over the appropriateness of your response. An abrupt or rude e-mail "missile" cannot be recovered once it has been fired.

It is also important to administer your project management activities effectively through your spoken words and actions on the job. To achieve this goal, you should think of risk management as an integral part of the project management process. Ideally, this is done without affecting the outward appearance of your management activities. However, if you are too heavy-handed with your risk management behavior and activities, it could do more harm than good with your relationships and your effectiveness. It takes time and work to develop a balance that is effective without being inefficient or damaging.

As mentioned earlier, your success in managing your risks within your project will depend to a great extent on the understanding and perception of others. Owners, contractors, and subcontractors all bring to the table their own expectations of what architects are responsible for. Therefore, it can be greatly beneficial if the owner and contractor fully understand what your contracted services are and how you are required to do them. This may require frequent explanations and much patience because many aspects of architecture services are not generally well understood.

> What we think, we become.
>
> —Gautama Buddha, born 563 BC

## A new way of thinking

The only way that you can truly eliminate risk in the practice of architecture is to close your practice, shutter the doors, and go home. If we practice as architects, we must take risks, and the objective becomes a balancing act. We must balance our risks with our rewards. The more we can control our professional risks without adversely affecting the level and quality of our services, the more successful we will be. The new way of thinking we espouse involves developing a reasonable attitude about effective risk management.

Effective risk management goes beyond what we were taught in architecture school. It is an influence on our practice that we must cultivate and accomplish effectively. It is a departure from the traditional design-draw-build process that we have been striving to perform throughout our careers. The many aspects of risk management that affect what we do as architects must be integrated into our practice so as to maintain our effectiveness and efficiency while still protecting ourselves from the threats and agendas that other parties continue to assert on our profession.

Many of the articles in this book will address the critical aspects of risk management as they relate to the many areas and activities of architecture practice. Our goal is to provide insights into how you can reduce your risks and increase your successes through constructive modifications to your project delivery process. The ultimate accomplishment will be to improve your professional practice technique as you do what you set out to do—practice architecture, make a little money along the way, and, hopefully, have a little fun doing it. Meanwhile, be careful out there.

# Risk Management Basics: Essentials for Maintaining an Effective Risk Program

I n this article, we address what a claim is and, drawing from our own experiences over many years, we outline a "quick response plan" for responding to and dealing with claims. Our intention is to give experienced managers a guide for managing claims, and for the uninitiated, we offer a glimpse of what to expect. We close with suggestions for hanging on to your client through the fray to avoid losing something much more valuable than the money sometimes paid to settle a single dispute—future business.

> Expect the best, plan for the worst, and prepare to be surprised.
> —Dennis Waitley

You don't have to practice architecture very long before you encounter challenges to your work. These may come in the form of a simple disagreement over your opinions or the performance of your services, or they may come as a direct demand for compensation for alleged damages caused by your actions. Nevertheless, you will find that you are judged not only by what you do, but when, how fast, and why you do it. And the services you provide will be scrutinized by other professionals who almost certainly will disagree with your actions.

To understand this challenging process and defend yourself through it better, it is helpful to understand what a claim is: the vehicle for launching an effort to recover alleged damages. We are protected from claims against our services by our professional liability insurance policy. These policies typically have deductibles that you must pay up front to activate coverage; they contain policy limits, which are the monetary amounts that the policy provides; and they have rules for preserving the coverage, to which you must conform to keep your coverage intact.

Professional liability insurance policies are known as *claims-made* policies. That is, policy coverage is triggered when you give notice that a claim has been made against you, and you are protected by the policy that is in effect at the time of the claim. This differs from your automobile insurance policy, which is triggered by the date the injury to a person or property occurs. Injuries done through professional services can be caused by an act or a failure to act. These can be caused by a design that may prove to be defective over an extended period of time. The claims-made process is used by insurers because of the potential difficulties in determining the date of origin of the action that precipitated the injury.

Since the claim triggers the policy coverage, it is important that a claim be defined to the extent that it can be sufficiently recognized. Accordingly, in most circumstances, an event must include three necessary elements for it to be considered a claim:

1. **An identifiable injury to a person or property.** If injury cannot be proven, legally there is no cause for claim.
2. **An allegation of wrongdoing.** It must be alleged that you caused the damages by your actions.
3. **A demand for money or services.** This is sometimes referred to as "damages," and it is intended as compensation for the alleged injury.

Under the terms and conditions of the typical insurance policy, however, insurance companies are generally content to acknowledge a claim against you if only the first two elements exist.

It is important that you respond quickly and appropriately when a claim is made. Your insurance company may require you to report claims on "first knowledge," and there are advantages that you have when a claim is first made that may not sustain over time. Therefore, it is advisable to develop a quick response plan that you can initiate immediately when a claim is made.

## Seven steps to a quick response plan

1. **Report the claim to your insurer in accordance with the notice requirements of your professional liability insurance policy.** Policies have specific claims-reporting procedures, and you should become aware of your policy requirements and give notice to your insurer accordingly. Although insurance companies may accept a verbal notice of claim, it is advisable to document your notice in writing so that there will be no misunderstanding later.
2. **Retain legal counsel and request that they represent your firm in the claim.** If you do not know a lawyer who specializes in architect and engineer errors and omissions defense, your insurance company will provide you with a "panel" attorney. This is a lawyer who has been preselected by your insurance company based on qualifications. If you wish to use counsel that has not been preapproved by your insurance company, you must get your insurer's prior consent.

Lawyers with experience in architect E&O defense are relatively rare, so it is important that you secure your representation early before someone beats you to the punch.

3. **Visit the project site, if appropriate. Gather necessary information and document relevant conditions.** Conditions that give rise to claims often mysteriously disappear or are corrected within a short time following an incident. It is wise to take photographs, make notes, and gather documents relating to the claim or circumstance while they are available. If necessary, have a third-party expert inspect the conditions and, in some cases, file a report. At a minimum, your own photographs can be beneficial. Wherever possible, you should coordinate these efforts with your legal counsel or insurer.

4. **Retain an expert acceptable to your legal counsel and/or insurance provider.** For a claimant to prove that you have breached your professional duty, that party must generally hire an expert witness who has appropriate credentials. Likewise, for you to defend against the expert's testimony, you will need a similar expert. In some cases, it may be appropriate for you or a member of your firm to serve as an expert in defense of the claim. If you do not know an architect who is qualified to be your expert, your legal counsel or your insurer can help you find one.

5. **Assemble your project team and plan how you will manage the claim within your office.** Someone in your office must be in charge of the claims management activities. These can include:

   1. Assembling in-house documents
   2. Reviewing in-house documents
   3. Reviewing documents in other offices (owner, contractor, subcontractors, subconsultants)
   4. Developing a written chronology of events that led up to the claim
   5. Communicating with the insurance claims supervisor, your legal counsel, and your experts
   6. Attending depositions
   7. Giving depositions
   8. Making your documents available for review by others
   9. Being the "corporate representative" for your firm in legal proceedings.

Designate who will serve as the primary contact within your office. If this person did not work on the project, he or she will need the assistance of project team members for knowledge of facts and to review and manage documents. People who worked on the project that have since left your firm must be contacted to obtain their knowledge of facts. You should maintain a good relationship with them even if you have to pay for their time spent giving testimony or providing information.

6. **Contact subconsultants and advise them of the claim.** Your consultants will be required to defend claims made against their portion

of the work, and it is important that they follow a response plan as well. You must be certain that their insurance carrier is involved early to ensure that they are managing their portion of the claim effectively.

7. **Assemble your documents, develop the chronology, and organize your defense effort.** One of the greatest expenses in claims management is the expenditure of personnel time. A large, complicated claim can absorb many labor hours that otherwise would be billable, and usually these expenses cannot be counted against your deductible. The more efficient you are with your claims management effort, the less it will cost you in time.

A nickel ain't worth a dime anymore.

—Yogi Berra

## Nuisance value

There can be times when you have been sued on a project and you did no wrong. Your insurance policy is a juicy target, and you may have been named in the lawsuit just because you worked on the project.

The following scenario is an example of what you may encounter.

You have been sued. You did nothing wrong. Your counsel and your insurance claims supervisor have reviewed your case, and they have determined that it will cost $25,000 to defend, including expert witness costs, time for depositions, preparation for trial, and the trial itself. These costs do not include your time or your coworkers' time.

Your lawyer has recommended that you offer $15,000 to settle out of the case early. You realize that you can save the $10,000 plus the extensive personnel time required for claims management. This settlement number is known as the *nuisance value* of the case. It is a bitter pill to take because you are paying money when you did no wrong, but it is less bitter than the alternative of weathering a protracted and expensive legal action. There may be instances such as this when the nuisance value is a good deal compared to the inevitable legal costs. The point is that you should not let your knowledge and belief that you are "in the right" overcome a wise business decision.

## It won't just go away

For many architects, just the potential threat of a problem or a lawsuit causes them to retreat into their shell and hope the matter will just go away. However, clients or contractors who believe they have been harmed by your actions seldom follow this course. For this reason, it is imperative that you keep lines of communications open with the parties, no matter how painful and intimidating it may be. Since claims rarely materialize without warning, a wise and effective claims management technique is to discuss and remain involved with any issues a party may have that could potentially lead to a formal claim. This preventive project management technique should be a part of your work habit rather than just being your risk management reaction.

In discussing disputed issues with a potential claimant, be sure to review possible early actions or remedies with your insurance carrier representatives and solicit their advice on how to carry on the discussions. It is typically forbidden for you to admit fault or agree to pay a sum of money to avoid a claim without the prior knowledge and approval of your carrier. With that said, claims can sometimes be avoided by talking the matter out and making some form of concession, monetary or otherwise. If the claim turns out to be unavoidable, at least you and the offended party will have comfort in knowing that you tried.

> I don't build in order to have clients. I have clients in order to build.
>
> —Ayn Rand

## Saving Private Client

The greatest loss that you can experience from a claim is the loss of a repeat client. Firms that depend upon repeat clients, such as developers or large corporations, can be devastated. Therefore, in many cases, it is important that, above all else, you must save the client. Many large clients have their own claims to deal with and they understand what you are going through and the defensive decisions that you are making. However, claims are often very emotional, and your client may choose to believe that you are now their enemy.

To counter this possibility, follow the rules of client care. They are quite simple, to the point of common sense. If you are managing your projects effectively, you may already be following most of them. The rules are:

1. **Frequent contact.** Call the client as soon as you are served legal papers. It may be difficult at first to stroke a mad dog, but think about the future. Good client contact during a claim can also go a long way toward an early and more beneficial settlement.
2. **Be candid.** Don't play games with your client. Sure it's war, but tricks will only get you in trouble and cause them to distrust you. In this case, honesty is the best policy.
3. **Join forces.** If at all possible, mount a joint defense. If the claimant happens to be the contractor, it may be logical to join up with the owner. Defense costs can be shared, and you are both in the trench together shoulder to shoulder; war buddies ready to do another project. By the way, it is also advisable to join forces with your consultants for the same reasons.
4. **Be reassuring.** Emphasize to the client that you are not running from the problem and that you will uphold your rightful obligations. Don't forget that you cannot admit fault or offer money without the prior consent of your insurance carrier. Such actions can void insurance coverage in some cases.

5. **Don't hold a grudge.** What good is it to pay money and save the client through a difficult claims process if you are going to stay ticked off over it? If the client senses that you are harboring ill feelings, they may choose to work with someone else. Get over it and move on.

## For old times' sake

After the battle is over and the smoke has cleared, it is time to get back to business. It is also important to remember the words of George Santayana, "Those who cannot learn from history are doomed to repeat it." It is wise to remember all of the players and the parts they played in the claim.

If any of your consultants hid under a rock when things got tough, you must ask yourself if you want to work with them again. It is only right that they defend their professional actions. Consultants should be encouraged to understand two basic rules. First, if you get sued, you will sue them for their part. They can count on it. Second, if they hang in there with you, you will be more likely to feel comfortable working with them again.

When it comes to contractors, it is our opinion, after 30-odd years in the business, that there are two kinds of contractors in the industry: those who want to make money constructing buildings and those who want to make money taking names and making claims. These are two distinct groups because of the two distinct mindsets.

When it comes to owners, it is a little more complicated. As you begin to plan your claims defense, the first question that you must ask yourself is whether or not you expect to work with this client in the future. Future work is the ultimate claims resolution technique. Spending money to make more money is simply not as painful as just spending money. Remember, this is business. If future work is in the cards, then you must consider whether the future work will make up for the loss. Fees for small jobs may never offset a healthy deductible expense. The objective is to make your decision early, and then either do everything possible to save the client or go ahead and declare Armageddon.

> Prevention is always less expensive than cure.
>
> —Kofi Annan

## An ounce of prevention . . .

Hopefully, these claims management basics will be beneficial to you should you encounter the big C down the road. You may wish to share this information with your loyal consultants so that they can benefit as well. There is one paragraph that you may wish to share with your contractor friends, if you are so inclined.

As we said in the previous article, claims management is not a course in architecture school. Many consider it to be foreign to the practice of architecture. But, instead, it is a real threat that you will most likely encounter if you continue to practice architecture. A little information and preparation will go a long way toward assisting you in defending claims, and it is wise to become thoroughly familiar with the claims process.

Meanwhile, be careful out there.

# To Document or Not to Document: Basic Documentation Requirements

In this article we point out that documentation is not only the best recourse for defending actions and decisions; but it can also be an effective management tool. While many may look upon it as cumbersome drudgery, intelligent design services should include an adequate measure of documentation. We feel that the real power in this article is the message that a little bit of documentation can be very effective and go a long way.

> The discipline of the written word punishes both stupidity and dishonesty.
>
> —John Steinbeck

Many architects think of documentation as an irritation that encroaches on their design efforts. They view documentation as a task of drudgery forced on them by the "technical guys" or the "lawyers." Actually, documentation is as integral to architecture as are sketchbooks, renderings, construction drawings, and change orders. It is not a new concept, as history reveals that Leonardo da Vinci kept detailed notebooks in the 15th century.

The review of documentation in this article ranges from simple, hand-written "to-do lists" kept only for the purpose of organizing one's work-day to more complex contracts that have significant legal implications. All of these forms of documentation with which architects interact and are required to create, manage, and maintain form a necessary part of the culture and practice of architecture. For some architects, documentation is a naturally occurring habit; for others, it is a burden that is often resisted and sometimes avoided altogether.

Over the past quarter century, the sheer quantity of documentation generated through the design process has grown significantly. Projects that required only a few file boxes in the 1980s result in many times that amount today. Documentation has become a time-consuming endeavor in the design and construction process that must be understood and managed.

## A management tool

Effective documentation habits are a necessary and valuable management tool, and the sometimes perilous path to a successful project always requires good, solid project management. Moreover, good project management always requires clear communication and careful coordination. From concise contracts that define the obligations of the parties involved in a project to meeting agendas and meeting notes that facilitate effective project meetings, documentation is the essential fabric of project management.

The most effective managers develop personal documentation habits that incorporate it into their daily work. Documentation is not drudgery to them because it is essential to the way they manage their projects. Writing a meeting report, making handwritten notes, or sending a client a contract proposal becomes second nature to their design activities. On the other hand, attending a meeting without an agenda, or making a site visit without preparing a field observation report, creates angst for the effective manager. This is counter to the smooth flow of communications and information on a successful project moreso than concerns about risks.

## Selective amnesia

Owners sometimes forget that they have made a critical design decision, such as authorizing the designer to proceed to the next phase of services. Contractors have been known to forget that they have advised the designer that a minor change in the work will have no cost or schedule impact. Consultants can forget that they agreed to have their drawings ready to issue by a certain date. Proactive documentation of decisions and reminders of commitments made by team members are essential management requirements and a definite advantage over the alternative of proving the facts after the fact without the fax (or letter, a request for information, or other written documentation) in hand.

> The deepest sin of the human mind is to believe things without evidence.
>
> —Thomas Henry Huxley

## The need for tangible evidence

Another practical use of documentation counters more sinister activities. It has been established that disputes and claims typically are resolved by the most intact and explicit documentation. In short, he or she who has the best documentation usually wins. This quantitative and qualitative advantage of documentation in claims management has no doubt increased the overall amount of paper that typically is generated on a project.

During the design and construction process, many communications affecting time and cost are exchanged. Affirmative documentation, such as phase completion sign-offs, authorizations to proceed, site observation reports, meeting reports, and schedules, are efficient tools of management that facilitate a more efficient and effective project delivery.

As we move closer to "paperless project" methods, such as the building information model (BIM), which consists of data manipulated through 3D parametric modeling, this need for tangible evidence by our legal industry eventually may diminish. However, for now, documentation will remain the hallmark of good project management.

## Types and adequacy of documentation

Documentation can take many forms. Because it can be generated by those who make decisions and those who react to those decisions, some forms of documentation by necessity must be more compelling than others.

Different individuals develop different habits for making and maintaining documentation. Just as there are messy desks and there are clean desks, there will be managers who produce clear, pristine documentation, and others who will keep files of ragged notes on whatever paper is at hand. Accordingly, the range of documentation considered to be adequate varies from almost nothing at all to an archive of properly filed and fully executed documents. Below are a few examples.

*Agreements:* Contracts are the basic vehicle by which the obligations of the parties to a legal agreement are set forth. Contracts can take many forms. When given a choice, the following are listed from most preferred to least.

↑ *Most Preferred*
- A fully executed AIA standard form of agreement
- A fully executed, customized agreement referencing AIA A201 General Conditions of the Contract for Construction and/or other AIA documents
- A letter of agreement referencing an applicable AIA form contract
- A confirming memorandum sent to the other party, but not signed and returned
- An oral understanding with no substantiating documentation

↓ *Least Preferred*

Although recognized by law as binding in many (although not all) states, oral agreements are disputable and difficult to substantiate, due to the lack of documentation. The old joke rings true when you consider that "oral agreements aren't worth the paper they're written on."

*Approvals, notices and phase completion sign-offs:* These are forms of documentation that can be generated by the owner, the contractor, or the architect. The AIA documents contain many instances where such actions are required. The preferences for these types of documents are, again, listed from most preferred to least.

↑ *Most Preferred*
- A formal letter acknowledged in writing by the approving party
- Confirming correspondence, letter, or e-mail sent by the party seeking approval to the approving party
- An oral notice, approval, or understanding with an oral acknowledgment

↓ *Least Preferred*

*Meeting Reports and Memos* Some architects do not prepare meeting reports, and they believe they are a waste of time. If an architect attending a meeting does not prepare notes from his or her observations during the meeting—no matter how informal—we believe there is no justification for attending the meeting. Meeting notes are most effectively used as a project management tool if they are issued to the project team in a timely manner. Reporting need not be a burdensome endeavor and can be useful in several formats.

↑ *Most Preferred*

- A formal typed report, with a list of attendees, recounting in narrative form the discussions and decisions made during the meeting—this form of report is issued with attachments of all handouts reviewed during the meeting and generally contains an "aging statement" indicating that it is assumed that the attendee agrees with the statements therein if he or she does not respond within a certain period of time
- A formal typed report in "action item" format, generally continued from a prior meeting, containing many items, with only items of new discussion documented—this form also typically contains an aging statement
- Handwritten notations, often with attendees' initials in lieu of names, describing the discussions and decisions made during the meeting
- A memo or e-mail listing summary bullet points
- A handwritten note

↓ *Least Preferred*

As was observed in the first article of this book, the meeting report is essentially a tool for reporting project progress to the owner. If you issue the report, you will be able to recount the events as you experienced them. If you do not issue the report, you will likely read results or opinions that do not coincide with your own. If your contract or your project organizational structure does not allow you to issue the project meeting report, it will be necessary for you to rebut in writing each and every issue and event that is not consistent with your experiences and understandings. Rebuttal is a laborious process that too frequently falls through the cracks of a busy schedule.

> Don't get it right, just get it written.
>
> —James Thurber

## Acknowledgment

A complete documentation process consists of two parts. The first part is the creation of a particular document to chronicle a decision, understanding, or event. The second part of documentation is to acknowledge that a particular document was sent or received or to confirm a decision or an act. There are four fundamental issues in acknowledging documentation. Make sure:

- You can identify your document and that you have retained a copy in your files.
- You have a record of when the document was prepared.
- You have a record of when the document was distributed.
- The receiving party received the document.

The nature of informal options for communication and documentation can be challenging when proving these four points, especially in proving that you sent the documentation and the other party received and agreed with it. In the event of a dispute where you have no documented acknowledgment, you can sometimes solve the problem if you can find the recepient's copy in his or her files during the legal "discovery"process. However, a formal documented acknowledgment is preferred to a passive acknowledgment in all cases.

Registered mail or other forms of "return receipt" are effective in establishing acknowledgment of your correspondence. In any case, some form of receipt record is the only way to be assured that the other party is in receipt of the document. Simply knowing that they received the message is no guarantee that they understand or agree with it.

### E-mail records

Because e-mail is a primary medium for communications today, it is worth mentioning that e-mail can be an effective means of documenting information in the actual format or as the distribution method. You must remember, however, not to copy or store your e-mail before it is sent. You generally must copy or store from the "sent" file in order to have the date included. Also remember that your e-mail records do not *necessarily* go away by pushing the Delete button.

### Identification

For your documentation to be relevant to your project, it must reference the project in some way. Architects typically accomplish this through the use of a project name and number. The name may have limitations if the project contains multiple phases. Therefore, a unique project number is more effective. Make sure all documents, either sent or received, identify a project name or a project number. Documentation that cannot be identified as relating to a specific project and event is useless.

### Father Time

The basic rule for establishing when a document was prepared, sent, or received is simply to place a date on everything. You should date all documents you prepare as an integral part of the format of the document. You should date all documents that you receive with a handwritten notation or a date stamp. Documentation will not be effective if it cannot be placed in the context of the project schedule.

### Transmittals

Transmittal forms or letters are useful for documenting quantities such as multiple drawings or submittals. Rather than prepare an enclosure letter for each item, you can use a transmittal form to indicate many items and the actions taken such as approvals or reviews. Be sure to include the date sent and appropriate project identification on all transmittals.

Transmittal letters can also be useful in describing why a bundle of mixed items have been issued. For example, a roll of drawings with different dates might be transmitted for purposes of making a building permit submittal and may be transmitted on a date that is different from the one shown on the drawings.

## Journals

A very important part of being an effective design professional, whether you are a manager or a designer, is keeping a journal or sketchbook. Journals and sketchbooks present opportunities that cannot be supplanted by other forms of record keeping, including personal history and fulfillment. Journals provide a contemporaneous trail through the daily activities of your practice. They place your work, thoughts, and ideas in time and context. They provide a venue for keeping notes as well as business artifacts such as business cards. A journal provides a convenient palette for sketches as well.

The modern equivalent of the journal may be considered to be a handheld personal digital assistant (PDA). These devices record schedules, schedule archives, and contemporaneous notes, and can even send e-mail at an architect's fingertips.

## The restaurant napkin

No discourse on documentation can be complete without giving proper attention and recognition to the classic design canvas, the restaurant napkin. The folklore of great designs and ideas created over the dining table is without limit. But the real point is that when it comes to documentation, something is better than nothing. When the defining moment comes, and your PDA or journal is not handy, grab anything—a business card, a scrap of paper, or a restaurant napkin—and chronicle the event or decision at hand.

Never write a letter if you can help it, and never destroy one!
—Sir John A. Macdonald

# Conclusion

This ugly duckling called documentation will always be a part of our professional design services. Diligence and consistency in attending to the necessities of effective documentation are necessary to be successful in our practice. Documentation must follow the basic rules that it be identifiable, dated, acknowledged, and retained. It is a tool that we simply cannot afford to do without.

Documentation can be viewed as a burdensome drudgery or it can become a part of the way we work. Effective project managers typically develop a routine for documenting their projects so that documentation becomes a useful habit that is as easy as filing or making copies. But like it or not, documentation is an essential part of the fabric of effective project management. And effective project management that results in successful projects is always the best form of risk management.

We'll leave you with a final thought: be careful out there.

# Another Fine Mess—The Onerous Contract, Part 1: Risk Management *after* the Agreement Is Signed

F or most architects, discussing the finer points of contracts is much like watching paint dry, but for those of us that live among the words that bind us, there can be excitement at every clause. Our message in this piece is intended to alert the reader to words and phrases that can turn around and bite us after we have signed on the line. Although we may have agreed to the clause, there is no reason why we cannot initiate risk management efforts to minimize a bad potential outcome. We must admit that occasionally in our careers, there have been times when we could hear Oliver Hardy's voice as we stared at killer agreed-upon contracted language, "Here's another fine mess you've gotten yourself into!"

> Oh, now I've got myself into an awful mess: I wish I were sitting quietly at home.
>
> —Thornton Wilder

The primary objective in contracting for professional services is to negotiate a fair agreement with provisions that are reasonable and in accordance with acceptable practice standards. AIA standard forms of agreement are available to guide us in this effort. Other available resources are your insurance agent and a legal counsel with experience in representing architects. Your insurance agent can assist you in finding appropriate legal representation when needed. Mindful of the risks so prevalent in our business, we do our best to negotiate a contract that will protect us and allow us to serve our client appropriately while providing an adequate fee for the time spent.

However, there are times when we encounter clients with requirements that go beyond our reasonable abilities and limitations. Their contract demands exceed the level of service that we feel is within acceptable professional limits. We reach that point in the negotiation process where our better judgment tells us that we should walk away; where the risk appears to be disproportionate to the reward. We come to the conclusion that the client's proposed terms are so onerous that the deal is just not worth doing.

That is, until other considerations enter the picture. Perceived rewards entice us to venture into the rocky realms of increased risk. We know better, but the temptation is great. Perhaps it is an opportunity to enter a new market or earn the business of a national client who can bring us continuing work. It may be as simple as just needing the work to keep our people busy. We wipe the perspiration from our foreheads and take a deep breath as we sign on the dotted line. We shake hands with the client and head back to the office hoping for the best, wondering what we can do to manage this "fine mess" that we have knowingly brought upon ourselves.

This article will touch on the options available for risk management when we are faced with unreasonable demands or if we have already agreed to a tough contract. Since risk management is about balancing the risk with the reward, there are times when increased risks may appear to be worth the chance. These options may not be cure-alls, but taking positive and responsive actions is far better than doing nothing at all.

## The contractual playing field

The chances we take when contracting for services can be treacherous, and the AIA has provided us with documents that offer much protection. AIA documents have been available for more than 100 years, and they have proved to be reliable industry standards of practice. The AIA aggressively manages the document content, constantly monitoring the way the documents are used and responding with appropriate revisions.

For example, when case law was established through a ruling in the court declaring that supervision was an activity that exceeded the reasonable expectation of the architect's duties during construction, the more appropriate term, *observation*, was employed to make contractual requirements more acceptable. When the architect's authority to stop the work was viewed as an action with unbalanced risk implications, it was removed from the documents.

When AIA documents are used, they can provide reasonable protection for the design professional. It is when more stringent and onerous conditions are introduced that the architect's risks can rise above the rewards consistent with market-driven fees.

Both public and private entities occasionally present take-it-or-leave-it contracts that impose a higher standard of care than is normally required of a design professional. Public clients usually control large amounts of work; we must endure their contracts if we want the job. Also, private owners with a national and worldwide presence often force contract conditions with unyielding parameters.

Unreasonable requirements, such as payment for betterment, or value added, as well as absolute defense indemnities for any and all claims, should be considered to be deal-killing conditions in contract negotiations. Unfortunately, on occasion, these are accepted by architects in service contracts because of a lack of awareness or due to perceived necessity. As a result, design professionals sometimes take a chance in the hopes of a successful outcome.

> A common danger unites even the bitterest enemies.
>
> —Aristotle

## Dangerous liaisons

Although many onerous contractual requirements may appear to be somewhat benign, they could have more serious implications. For example, *inspecting* the work connotes a more thorough review and determination of conformance. Also, *certification of payment application backup documentation* goes well beyond the requirement to be "generally familiar with the work" in that it requires a knowledge of the work that only the contractor typically has.

Some contract requirements are more obvious and threaten with more certainty, offering the unscrupulous owner a basis for filing claims against the design professional. For example, requirements such as *certifying work conformance* can make the architect responsible for the completeness and accuracy of the work. Agreeing to produce *100 percent complete documents* carries an obligation that cannot be fulfilled under the design professional's ordinary powers. Also, *guaranteeing the design will not exceed a maximum limit of cost* of construction can cause architects to become an uncompensated funding source for the owner, and can cause them to redesign until the project is within the budget. This can be an open-ended liability.

Nevertheless, these requirements are frequently demanded in contract negotiations, and they should not be agreed to unless the reward is worth the risk to be taken.

## Protective actions

Although you may have agreed to an onerous contract condition, it does not mean that you must acquiesce. There are alternatives that can be undertaken to mitigate and manage difficult requirements. They may not provide complete resolution, but they will at least improve your chances of success.

It is important to note that a formal change order is not the only alternative for changing the course of a contract. Changes can be effected in the form of oral agreements and written understandings.

## Silent acknowledgment

There is also the issue of silent acknowledgment. If you document a change in the conditions of your service agreement with your client in writing, and no response to the contrary is given in writing, the change may be determined to be enforceable and have credibility.

For example, your contract requires you to be present on the jobsite one day per week. You realize that the contractor only meets at the site on alternate Tuesdays, and visiting the site for two days every two weeks provides better service to the project. This represents an "average" of one day per week. You send a letter to the client advising of the change, and you receive no response. Months later, after the project is completed, the client complains that you did not provide the site visitation services defined in your contract. The client refuses to pay your final invoice and demands a refund to cover the services the client claims you did not provide. You forward the client a copy of the letter, noting the client's failure to respond with an objection to the adjusted visitation schedule.

While this may not guarantee exoneration from the client's accusation, nevertheless, it provides you with a reasonable position for rebuttal.

## Alternatives to onerous contract requirements

Listed below are difficult contract requirements, and some general notions for how to deal with them.

**Inspections, not observations.** There are only two inspections required of the architect by AIA documents during construction: at substantial completion and at final completion. If the contract wording requires you to "inspect" the work during each site visit, your obligation for determining if the work conforms to your design documents can be greatly increased over the normal standard of care.

**Certifying the contractor's work.** Although the architect certifies the contractor's application for payment, the normal standard of care for architectural design services does not include certifying the contractor's work.

**100 percent complete design documents.** Do not affix the notation, "100 Percent Complete Documents," or any other quantitative representation on your drawings. Instead, include descriptive notations, such as "Issued for Construction," or "Issued for Schematic Design Review."

**Guaranteeing budget conformance.** It is not reasonable for the architect to be made solely responsible for a project condition over which he or she does not have authority or control.

**Review and approval of payment application backup.** The architect is required in AIA Owner-Architect agreements to "determine in general if the Work observed . . . when fully completed, will be in accordance with the Contract Documents." This is not a requirement to check each and every detail in the contractor's application for payment.

**Unreasonable deadlines for submittal and RFI review.** The design professional has both the right and the obligation to take the appropriate amount of time necessary to review submittals or answer questions.

**Indemnities and hold-harmless agreements.** These clauses offer a guaranteed protection that may be prohibited by the terms and conditions of your professional liability insurance policy.

**Deletion of construction phase services.** Owners sometimes ask architects to delete construction phase services from their work. Because the architect typically contracts to issue a certificate of substantial completion at the end of the project, it is difficult, if not impossible, for the architect to know if the project has been constructed substantially in accordance with the drawings and specifications if he or she has not visited the site and reviewed the work during construction.

> Status Quo, you know, that is Latin for "the mess we're in."
>
> —Ronald Reagan

## Conclusion

We may not always succeed in negotiating a contract that is in complete alignment with our preferred services approach. Opportunities and rewards may sometimes lure us into treacherous contractual conditions. Our chosen "business decision" may be to agree to contract wording that places us at a higher risk than we typically accept. We may find ourselves in another fine mess that challenges us.

We must remember that although the ink may be dry, the opportunities for effective risk management remain. There are actions that can be taken to improve our exposure and possibly mitigate onerous requirements altogether. The important thing to keep in mind is to never give up. Many contingent actions can be taken throughout the project to improve your risk exposure and the chance for a successful project. Do not forget that a component of successful projects typically includes a satisfied client.

We must take risks if we are to do business, but opportunities for improvement will always persist. Stay on top of your negotiations and stay close to your clients. And if you find yourself in another onerous contract, take advantage of the opportunities and resources available for minimizing your risks and improving your chances for success.

And while you're at it, be careful out there.

# Another Fine Mess—The Onerous Contract, Part 2

Recapping from Part I: Mindful of the risks so prevalent in our business, we do our best to negotiate a contract that will protect us and allow us to serve our client appropriately while providing an adequate fee for the time spent. However, there are times when we encounter clients with requirements that go beyond our reasonable abilities and limitations. "Another Fine Mess: The Onerous Contract, Part 1" explored some options available for risk management when we are faced with unreasonable demands or if we have already agreed to a tough contract. The options that follow expand on some of those ideas. The options that we explore in this article may not be cure-alls, but taking positive and responsive actions is far better than doing nothing at all.

> To find a form that accommodates the mess, that is the task of the artist now.
>
> —Samuel Beckett

## Site inspections

*Black's Law Dictionary* states, "Inspection . . . has broader meaning than just looking (observation), and means to examine carefully or critically, investigate, and test officially." During negotiations, it is advisable to review the AIA Contract Documents B101-2007 and A201-2007 site observation duties with the client and explain the differences between observation and inspection. If you elect to agree to "inspect," then you should propose a fee commensurate with the time involved with the additional duties and increased risks.

If you have such a requirement in your contract, in the absence of specifically defined requirements for your "inspections," you can attempt to establish the standard of care that you will meet by:

1. Reporting your site observations on a form such as AIA Document G711, Architect's Field Report, which references "observations" rather than "inspections."

2. Including in your report the qualification: "Inspections performed by the architect under this contract have been conducted under the limited conditions as described by site observations in AIA Document A201, General Conditions of the Contract for Construction, as referenced in the Owner-Architect Agreement.
3. Arranging to discuss the subject of inspections versus observations in a project meeting and include the description provided in AIA Document A201 in the meeting minutes. Do this even if the client or contractor objects to your position during the discussion.

If you are working from an AIA document such as B101-2007 or A201-2007, you have a greater chance of your services conforming to "a reasonable standard of care" as established in part by the AIA family of documents for practitioners.

## Certifying the contractor's work

Although the architect certifies the contractor's application for payment, the standard of care for architectural design services typically does not include certifying the contractor's work. AIA document A201-2007 clearly states in paragraph 3.3.1, with similar language in A201-1997, that the contractor is solely responsible for their work and the work of the subcontractors:

> The Contractor shall be solely responsible for, and have control over, construction means, methods, techniques, sequences and procedures and for coordinating all portions of the Work under the Contract. . .

Certification of the contractor's work by the architect could be interpreted to represent that the architect has confirmed that the work is in strict accordance with the contract documents and is complete. Such certification may cause the architect to be held responsible for the contractor's incomplete, incorrect, or defective work.

During contract negotiations it is beneficial to help the client understand that although the architect will be responsible for his or her own acts and omissions, it is not a guarantor of the work performed by others. AIA document B101-2007 states in paragraph 3.6.1.2:

> The Architect shall be responsible for the Architect's negligent acts or omissions, but shall not have control over or charge of, and shall not be responsible for, acts or omissions of the Contractor, or of any other persons or entities performing portions of the Work.

If you fail in this endeavor or discover that your contract includes an onerous certification, you can attempt to establish a reasonable standard of care for your services *after the fact* as follows:

1. Your professional liability insurance agent may tell you that you are not covered under your insurance policy when providing such

absolute certifications. If so, you should advise your client of this fact and attempt to negotiate a compromise.

2. Inform your client that your certification is for "substantial" conformance to the contract documents as defined in AIA Document A201.
3. If your client persists in demanding that you certify the contractor's work, ask your professional liability insurance agent to contact the client and explain the potential owner liabilities of this action.
4. Consider adding the following qualification to your certificates of substantial completion:

This certification is not a representation that the contractor's work is correct or complete, but it is consistent with the architect's responsibilities as stated in AIA Document A201 as referenced in the Owner-Architect Agreement.

## 100 percent complete design documents

Contract documents are conceptual as defined in the AIA documents and, by definition, they cannot be 100 percent complete. This issue is explored in "A Loss Cause: Drawing Discrepancies and Ensuing Damages" in Chapter 4.

Most contracts appear to anticipate, and it is common in the industry for many architects to refer to the status of their documents as a "percentage of completion." This industry habit is an effort to objectively quantify what is an inherently subjective process. There is no industry-standard definition for what constitutes "completion" for the design or construction document phases of architectural services.

Such objective measurements of subjective issues tend to go without adequate discussion during contract negotiations. Architects, when negotiating an agreement, are often unwilling to engage in conflict on this issue because everyone knows that sooner or later the documents will be considered "complete." If you should agree to a contract containing this requirement, try the following:

1. Do not affix the notation "100 Percent Complete Documents" or any other quantitative representation on your drawings. Instead, include descriptive notations, such as "Issued for Construction" or "Issued for Schematic Design Review."
2. Discuss the issue openly in a project meeting, explaining that no industry definition exists and that it is impossible for documents to be 100 percent complete. Record your discussion in the meeting report.
3. Meet with the client and explain the conceptual realities of design documents. "Drawing the Line: Why the Architect's Documents Cannot Be Used for Construction" in Chapter 4 will address the conceptual nature of construction documents in greater detail. Record your conversations in a meeting report.
4. If you are still not getting through, ask your insurance agent to contact the client and explain the conceptual realities and limitations of design documents.

> If you want a guarantee, buy a toaster.
>
> —Clint Eastwood

## Guaranteeing budget conformance

Some clients may ask you to guarantee that your documents express a design concept that can be constructed within a specific project budget. Supplementary clauses such as "redesigning the project to conform to budget constraints" are sometimes imposed. It is not reasonable for the architect to be made solely responsible for a project condition over which they do not have authority or control.

Owners often mistakenly believe that the architect not only has ultimate control of project costs, but that their pursuit of design excellence is such that they will jeopardize the project budget with their efforts to have their way. During contract negotiations you must candidly explain to owners the relationship between time, cost, and quality. This issue is addressed in *The Architect's Handbook of Professional Practice,* 14th Edition, in an article entitled, "Maintaining Design Quality." Essentially, this concept states that an owner may expect to control two of the three components—time, cost, or quality—but not all three.

Owners have no doubt derived their mistaken beliefs about the architect's control over the budget because many of the requirements for the design are expressed in the architect's instruments of service. The reality is that owners, contractors, and designers all affect the time, cost, and quality on a project. Of the members of this team, the constructors are better positioned to be knowledgeable about costs and to offer advice as to when design changes should be implemented to meet budgets.

During negotiations, try to explain to the owner that you will not nickel-and-dime them for minor revisions in assisting with managing the budget, but you cannot be responsible for major changes when those changes are not consistent with prior owner approvals.

For example, an owner desires an arching barrel vaulted roof on his new villa. Estimates skyrocket, and the owner demands that you redesign with a flat roof. That demand is not consistent with prior program requirements and approvals, and it will require the architect to experience severe fee penalties. If, on the other hand, the project exceeds a predetermined budget, and the client asks you to change the specification from copper roofing to painted metal, it would probably be a wise business decision to make this minor change at your own expense.

As a rule, the design professional should *never agree* to be responsible for the cost of construction in excess of a budget. If the client resists and represents this requirement to be a deal breaker, you should walk away from the commission, no matter how grand it may be.

In the event that you have onerous budget clauses in your contract, try the following:

1. Firmly establish the owner's program requirements. Document all program discussions thoroughly in letters, memoranda, or meeting reports.

2. Firmly establish the basis for the owner's budget, including the source, date, and quality of cost data.
3. Notify the owner if you perceive a discrepancy between the program requirements and the budget. If you believe the budget is deficient for the desired program, give the owner definitive notification of this belief. Provide the owner with reasonable solutions for resolving the discrepancy, such as a reduction of program requirements or an increased budget.
4. Do not proceed with designs for which you have notified an owner a discrepancy exists without a firm direction from the owner that resolves the discrepancy. If you do proceed, you may risk setting the expectation that the discrepancy has been resolved.
5. Document all such resolutions in writing.

This subject could be reviewed in much greater detail, and it merits a great deal of brainstorming and discussion with the owner and the contractor.

## Review and approval of payment application backup

The architect is required in AIA owner-architect agreements to "determine in general if the Work observed . . . when fully completed, will be in accordance with the Contract Documents." This is not a requirement to check each and every detail in the contractor's application for payment. Payment application backup on large projects can involve hundreds of pages of documentation, and any detailed review and approval of this information should probably be done through an audit by an accountant.

In errors and omissions claims, owners often allege that the architect has inflicted damage upon them by approving payment to a contractor for erroneous or incomplete work. This is often due to a lack of understanding by the owner as to the architect's responsibilities for reviewing and certifying a contractor's application for payment. To avoid this misunderstanding, it can be beneficial to help the owner understand the specific review requirements during contract negotiations.

Suggested negotiation points are as follows:

1. The architect does not make detailed inspections and is thus not in a position to know the specific conditions of the work for which the contractor has requested payment
2. The architect does not guarantee the contractor's performance of the work
3. The contractor is responsible for their own actions.

Nevertheless, if you should have the requirement to make a detailed review of the contractor's payment application backup in your contract, you may try the following:

- If appropriate in the context of your contract terms, remind your client in writing that you are only required to determine "in general" if the work is in conformance with the contract documents. This does not include a comprehensive review, approval, or audit of the supporting data submitted by the contractor.

- Advise the client that you are not an accountant and that you are not qualified to review and evaluate such accounting data.
- Use AIA Document G702, Application and Certificate for Payment, which states the limitation that "the Architect certifies to the Owner that to the best of the Architect's knowledge, information, and belief."
- Request a change in services from the owner stating that the services of a professional accountant are required to discharge the responsibility for backup review under the terms of your contract.

> I love deadlines. I like the whooshing sound they make as they fly by.
> —Douglas Adams

## Unreasonable deadlines for submittal and RFI review

The review of submittals by the designer can be time-consuming if they are complex or submitted untimely or in an unreasonable sequence. RFIs often take time to review and resolve. Contractors use extended review time to claim delay and subsequently ask for additional general conditions costs. Nevertheless, the design professional has both the right and the obligation to take the appropriate amount of time necessary to review submittals or answer questions. A201-2007 provides for a reasonable review time in paragraph 3.10.2. Similar language can be found in A201-1997:

> The Contractor shall prepare a submittal schedule . . . for the Architect's approval.

A201-2007 gives the architect the significant authority to determine review time in paragraph 4.2.7. Similar language can be found in A201-1997:

> The Architect's action will be taken, in accordance with the submittal schedule approved by the Architect or, in the absence of an approved submittal schedule, with reasonable promptness while allowing sufficient time in the Architect's professional judgment to permit adequate review.

If you must agree in your contract to specific review periods, or in the event that your contract contains the requirement that submittals and RFIs be reviewed and responded to in a short interval of time, consider the following alternatives:

- Inform your client in writing that review times vary with the size of the submittal and that you will endeavor to respond to these documents within the average number of days required in the contract.

- If you are using MASTERSPEC specifications or other documents that require a submittal schedule, request the submittal schedule from the contractor to confirm that the contractor has scheduled reasonable and adequate review time for each submittal. If necessary, demand in writing that the contractor provide a submittal schedule for your approval. Since you are allowed in MASTERSPEC and AIA contracts to agree to this schedule, advise the contractor if the time allotted is inadequate and unreasonable.
- Monitor the submittal schedule and determine if the contractor has met their obligations for sequencing and timing to fit your review availability. Advise during construction meetings if the contractor is not meeting their schedule and document in writing if deviations or nonconformance is evident.
- Advise the owner that AIA Document B101, in Article 4.3.2.1, allows for a Change in Services to increase the architect's fee for, "Reviewing of a Contractor's submittal out of sequence from the submittal schedule agreed to by the Architect." While you may not be able to negotiate additional fees, you can use the clause as leverage in negotiating reasonable review times. In addition, AIA Document B503-2007, Guide for Amendments to AIA Owner-Architect Agreements, which is provided free to AIA members on the AIA website, provides language for the review of multiple submittals.

## Indemnities and hold-harmless agreements

Indemnities and hold-harmless agreements in contracts must be approached with caution. You should always consult with your attorney and your insurance company before you accept any indemnity or hold-harmless agreement. These clauses offer a guaranteed protection that may be prohibited by the terms and conditions of your professional liability insurance policy. However, mutual indemnities between the client and architect for damages caused by their own actions are common.

## Deletion of construction phase services

Owners sometimes ask architects to delete construction phase services from their work. Since the architect typically contracts to issue a certificate of substantial completion at the end of the project, it is difficult if not impossible for the architect to know if the project has been constructed substantially in accordance with the drawings and specifications if the architect has not visited the site and reviewed the work during construction.

Many states mandate that construction administration must be performed by a licensed architect because some state licensing boards recognize the need for professional review to determine conformance. It is important that you retain this important phase of services in your contract so that your ability to determine conformance and completion will not be impaired.

If you have prepared construction documents and a separate architect is retained to perform construction phase services on your design, you could be at a disadvantage in that you will not have the opportunity to discover discrepancies before they are constructed. The primary responsibility of the general contractor is to plan and coordinate the work in advance, and the primary objective of the architect during construction should be to resolve any conflicts or complications ahead of time. Design professionals who provide construction phase services on the work of others often have less liability and thus may be less proactive in discovering problems.

If you are asked to delete this phase of work from your services, consider the following actions:

- Explaining the importance of the benefits of a single architect and your vested interest in finding and resolving discrepancies.
- Visiting the site anyway to review conformance generally. If you cannot visit the site and develop a comfort level with construction conformance, under no circumstances should you issue a certificate of substantial completion or any other certification.
- Asking your insurance agent to contact the owner to explain the benefits of including construction administration with basic services utilizing the same architect.

It's not the tragedies that kill us, it's the messes.

—Dorothy Parker

## Conclusion

We must take risks if we are to do business, but opportunities for improvement will always exist. Stay on top of your negotiations, and stay close to your clients. And if you find yourself in another onerous contract, take advantage of the opportunities and resources available for minimizing your risks and improving your chances for success.

And while you're at it, be careful out there.

# Free Fall: Working without a Contract

All architects that we know have worked for some period of time without a contract, and it is likely that this practice will continue undisturbed. But given the risks involved with such behavior, we felt that we should point out cautions and offer suggestions for managing them. The 2007 revisions to the AIA documents have provided five new owner-architect contracts to choose from, and now it should be easier for the practitioner to find and execute one that meets their needs. We note that even the notorious letter agreement qualifies as a type of scope documentation, and the act of memorializing services you are required to provide your client cannot be overemphasized.

A verbal contract isn't worth the paper it's printed on.

—Samuel Goldwin

Have you ever provided design services without a contract? If your answer is "no," it is likely that you are somewhat new to the profession of architecture. Most architects have provided professional services without executing a contract at some time in their career. It is gratifying to receive a commission, and we tend to want to get the work going and worry about the contractual stuff later. It does not help that contracts are more complicated these days. Owners and their lawyers often negotiate tough conditions. Getting the contract executed often takes time and requires advice from our insurance agent or our lawyer.

Design services can range from brief studies and evaluations to full basic services. Although common in the industry, it is risky to document services on small projects with letter agreements. It is convenient to keep a template on our hard drive and fill in the blanks, sending it to the client quickly. Abbreviated letter agreements, however, often do not provide sufficient protection against the perils inherent in today's practice.

On larger projects, we have become accustomed to lengthy negotiation periods, and we tend to go about work without the feeling of urgency that is warranted in getting a contract executed. Contract negotiation is viewed by many architects to be an adversarial process that they would like to avoid. When those monthly checks begin to arrive from the owner, optimism can take over, and we may disregard getting the final contract executed altogether.

Meanwhile, the risks inherent in architecture practice are greater than they have ever been. A fair and balanced contract is essential if we want to protect ourselves adequately. When we work without a contract, we are like the aerialist high above the ground, walking the high wire with no safety net below. All will be fine as long as everything goes as planned. However, should things go awry, our professional and financial health could be threatened.

This article will explore the dangers of working without a contract and the safeguards that well-executed service agreements can provide. It will address the importance of effective contracts management, including suggestions for setting up a contracts management program in your firm. Included are suggestions on what to do in difficult situations, such as when clients refuse to sign the contract.

## What do contracts do?

Among other things, contracts establish a documented record of what services we are going to provide for the fee that we earn. Such documentation is necessary to help avoid disputes in the services scope and avoid misunderstandings. The following paragraphs address some important parts of a contract.

**Identification of parties.** It is important that individuals and companies doing business together be accurately identified in the agreement. Not only is this necessary to make sure that the agreement forms a binding contract between the right parties, but it is also necessary to help avoid potential problems in communications. It is wise for the name of the owner's designated representative to be listed as the primary contact so as to allow one source of communications.

**Scope of services.** Architectural design can encompass many things. There are basic services that are typically provided for projects; however, the expectation of the result of those services can vary greatly. The contract, if properly written, can define services in a way that will help prevent misunderstanding. When services are adequately defined in the contract, there is less confusion regarding subsequent "additional services" for which the architect will expect to be paid.

**Compensation.** The fee basis as well as the sequence and conditions for making payment are typically defined including hourly rates for services later added to the agreement. This should help avoid misunderstandings and simplify payment for additional services beyond basic services.

**Termination.** Contracts should also provide options and conditions for contract termination, including fair payment for work performed through the termination date. Some owners include terms requiring the architect to surrender ownership and copyrights to drawings and other instruments of service. An appropriately written termination clause can stipulate that ownership transfer will not occur until the architect has received payment for this work. These conditions can decrease the chance of wrongful termination claims and hopefully provide an organized transition.

**General conditions.** Another important component of a contract is to establish a uniform set of general conditions of the contract for construction. These conditions set out the duties and responsibilities of the parties during the construction phase and help reduce confusion. AIA Document A201, General Conditions of the Contract for Construction, is the document most commonly used for this purpose.

When the architect negotiates a basic services agreement, A201 is typically referenced as the general conditions document, as in B101-2007, Section 3.6.1.1. However, when the contractor and owner negotiate their contract, they sometimes agree on different general conditions or they modify A201 from its original form. Since the architect's agreement is usually executed first, the architect should compare the two general conditions (including any supplemental conditions to the construction contract) to determine if the requirements placed on the architect are consistent. It is advisable to explain to the owner the value in maintaining the close interrelationship between A201, if used, and the other AIA documents that may be used on the project. The AIA documents consistently relate to each other, within each document family, and changes in one document can adversely affect others.

If you are using AIA agreements B101-2007, B102-2007 or B103-2007, you are contractually obligated only for the contract conditions in the A201–2007 as originally published by the AIA, provided that it is the general conditions document referenced, but you will still need to know if the owner and contractor have modified it. For example, the owner and contractor may have agreed to specific general conditions changes in their contract which will lead them to expect a different level of service than your agreement requires. Some owners and contractors view their agreements as confidential. Should the owner or contractor refuse to provide you a copy of the owner-contractor agreement and general conditions, which is unfortunately a more frequent occurrence in today's practice, it will be impossible to know whether the owner has modified the contract conditions you are to administer under your agreement. In this instance, you should attempt to explain to the owner that your contract requirements must conform to that of the contractor's, or one or both of you may not be able to deliver the contracted services.

One option is to send the owner a blank copy of the AIA Owner-Contractor form that pertains to the way the project is contracted. For example, if the project is a lump-sum contract, you would use AIA Document A101–2007, Standard Form of Agreement Between Owner and Contractor where the basis of payment is a Stipulated Sum. Include with it a copy of A201–2007, General Conditions of the Contract for Construction, as referenced in the agreement.

Remind the owner that you have requested a copy of the executed owner-contractor agreement with general conditions, and advise them that unless they indicate otherwise, you are assuming that the enclosed documents represent the way that they expect you to perform services for administration of the contract for construction. These actions often result in a copy of the executed agreement sent by return mail, but if not, you at least have informed the owner of your contracted scope of services. If this effort fails, you should consult with your lawyer or insurance agent for assistance. If you do nothing, your actions could be called into question because of conditions within an owner-contractor agreement that conflict with your service agreement.

Moreover, AIA Owner-Architect Agreements B101-2007 and B103-2007 require the owner to provide the architect a copy of the executed agreement between the owner and the contractor, including the general conditions of the contract for construction.

## Responsive actions to non-standard contracts

The AIA documents help set the industry standard for how we practice architecture, and when they remain intact, we can generally go about our work, business as usual. However, significant changes to the documents by clients are becoming more prevalent. The result could be an agreement that does not include requirements and conditions that conform to commonly accepted standards of architecture practice and that give us reasonable protection. Should this occur, following are some actions that can be taken to attempt to rectify the difficult issues:

**No architect signature on change order.** *The general conditions in the owner-contractor agreement have been modified and no longer require the architect's signature on change orders.* In this case, the architect should advise the owner that changes to the contract without the architect's knowledge or consent could prevent their awareness of the project scope and could prevent them from determining the date or dates of substantial completion or assessing final completion.

**Waiver of warranty to architect.** *The owner was persuaded to waive the contractor's warranty to the architect guaranteeing work conformance.* A201–2007, Section 3.5, and A201-1997, Section 3.5.1 state:

> The Contractor warrants to the Owner and Architect that . . . the Work will conform to the requirements of the Contract Documents. . . .

The architect should advise the owner that deleting this requirement will make it difficult, if not impossible, for the architect to certify payments or certify substantial completion, conditions that are often unacceptable to lenders. The architect relies on the contractor's warranty that work put in place will be in conformance whether or not the architect is on site and observes the work. The issue of substantial completion is covered in detail in "Substantial Completion, Where Art Thou? A Challenging and Elusive Milestone" in Chapter 5.

**Submittals redefined as contract documents.** *The owner has agreed to a contractor demand that the owner-contractor agreement define submittals to be contract documents.* For good reason, A201 states that shop drawings and submittals are not contract documents. The architect should explain to the owner that if the contractor's submittals are defined as contract documents, the contractor can change the contract scope and thus manipulate the value of the project. This is explored further in Chapter 5, "According to Hoyle: The Submittal Process."

Clearly, it is a disadvantage to the owner to allow contract requirements to be altered by the contractor's submittals. If the owner agrees to have submittals defined as contract documents, the architect could add an explanatory note to each submittal explaining that they have been prepared by the contractor who is solely responsible for their content, and the architect's review action makes no representations as to their accuracy or completeness.

> I'm up on the tightwire, flanked by life and the funeral pyre.
> —Leon Russell, Carny, 1972

## Steadying the high wire

Such changes in the contract are usually made because the owner does not understand the issues, and dialogue with the owner often helps. However, if the owner refuses to address discrepancies between the agreement with the contractor and the agreement with the architect, the architect should consider advising the owner in writing as to how its services will be impacted.

Hopefully, this notice will cause a desire to coordinate the construction contract with the owner-architect agreement, including the applicable general conditions. If not, the architect must decide if the added risk is worth the agreed-upon professional fee. The most effective way to manage these issues is to resolve them during negotiation of the owner-architect agreement.

## Your contracts management program

Ideally all professional services should be performed under a written contract. It can be helpful to develop a contracts management program to increase the chances that some form of contract is executed on all projects. A contracts management program can be beneficial to the sole practitioner as much as to the larger firm. One could be developed along the following lines:

**Standard owner-architect agreements.** Develop a standard marked-up agreement for each type of services you perform. This can range from a letter agreement to a full-service contract, depending upon the services to be provided.

When applicable, as in the case of a full-service owner-architect agreement, choose an AIA form of agreement that best suits your needs, and modify it to meet the needs of your practice. If you think it necessary to modify agreement terms, consult your lawyer and your professional liability insurance agent for assistance. The agent should have access to resources such as insurance company in-house lawyers and panel counsel who may be able to provide assistance in developing the specific contract wording. Your standard markup may not survive negotiations completely intact, but at least you will have established a contractual position for the initiation of discussions.

**Atypical conditions.** Another key element of your contracts management program can be to develop a process for determining "atypical contract conditions" and communicating them to your project team. When an agreement is negotiated with an owner, there are often some conditions that vary from standard AIA language. Conditions that vary from the AIA language should be highlighted and communicated to the team.

For example, in the AIA Document B101-2007, the number of architect's site visits is left for the architect to negotiate with the owner. Should you negotiate a contract that stipulates, "The architect will visit the project fifty times during construction at intervals not to exceed one time per week," the project team must be made aware of this strict requirement so that someone can substitute for the construction administrator when that person is ill or on vacation. Do not forget that, in this instance, site visits requested in excess of the stipulated number can be billed as an additional service to your contract.

For more information about dealing with difficult contract requirements such as these, refer to "Another Fine Mess: The Onerous Contract" earlier in this chapter.

**Outside reviews.** Another important aspect of your program should be structured reviews of unfamiliar or difficult contract clauses by a competent outside source. Experienced construction lawyers can be retained for this purpose, or your professional liability insurance company may provide this service as a part of your policy support. If paying a fee for this service concerns you, remember that the money spent to avoid a claim is frequently a fraction of the amount required to defend against one.

**Contracts management policies.** In a larger firm, it is a good idea to establish policies for maintaining consistency and managing risk. The following suggestions may be useful in developing your contracts management policies:

- **Letter agreements.** If your firm uses letter agreements, develop a consistent format and determine to what extent professional services will be performed with this approach. Require your associates to convert the letter agreement to a formal owner-architect agreement should the project proceed beyond some pre-established preliminary phase.
- **Deal breakers.** Consult with your insurance agent or legal counsel to identify contract clauses and conditions with risks that exceed available rewards. You may also wish to have your agent or lawyer assist you in explaining these issues to a client when they arise. Be alert for new deal breakers when negotiating and check with your agent or lawyer when in doubt. Some firms include potential deal breaker clauses as a part of their "go/no go" decision-making process.
- **Outside contract reviews.** Establish a policy for when a proposed agreement should be reviewed by an outside source. Lawyer-generated and extensively marked-up AIA documents often deserve scrutiny. Unusual certifications that go beyond those addressed by AIA documents should definitely be targeted.
- **Consultant agreements.** It is important to establish a protocol for executing your architect-consultant agreements after the owner-architect agreement is signed. Some practitioners believe it is acceptable to work with consultants with only a letter agreement. However, the requirements in the owner-architect agreement must be passed through to the consultant for the architect to have adequate contractual protection. AIA Document C401-2007, Standard Form of Agreement Between Architect and Consultant, tracks the AIA owner-architect agreements and is available for this purpose.
- **Additional services.** It is important to establish the method by which you will contract for additional services. There are options available in the AIA family of documents, including AIA Document G606–2000, Amendment to the Professional Services Agreement, which can be used to modify an existing owner-architect agreement.

## Execution of the agreement

Agreements are not finalized until the terms and conditions are agreed upon by both parties in writing. Absent a signed agreement, the contract may be disputed.

There may be occasions when contract negotiation is held up by the owner. For instance, suppose you have traded drafts and made your revisions, and the owner-architect agreement is in the owner's possession. Weeks and months have passed, and there is no return draft. Your queries to the owner remain unanswered. It appears that the owner does not intend to finalize the agreement.

Although the most recent draft agreement exchanged between the parties may support credibility, it could just as likely serve to show that the parties did not agree on its provisions. Other actions can be taken to assist in confirming the owner's acceptance. Communicate with the owner by a traceable means such as certified letter or e-mail advising that you are providing services according to your last draft agreement unless they advise you to the contrary. While this may not show the owner's acceptance of the contract to the degree a signature would, it is nonetheless better than taking no action and hoping for the best.

Again, many architects view contract negotiations and getting contracts signed as inherently adversarial activities. You should view these activities as due diligence aimed at positioning your project for success.

## Additional services

Another area where owners are often reluctant to sign agreements is additional services. Agreements often require the owner's written acceptance in advance, but with the time-driven activities inherent in design and construction, it is often difficult to get a signed approval before you do the work.

A helpful recourse can be to send a confirming communication advising that you are assuming that the owner agrees unless notice to the contrary is received within a given period. You should confirm that the additional services are appropriate and have been requested before taking this action.

For more information on our views about the types and adequacy of documentation, refer to "To Document or Not to Document: Basic Documentation Requirements," earlier in this chapter.

## Initiating your contracts management program

Adequately enforcing these policies and procedures in your firm will require monitoring and management. It can be helpful to create a contracts management file to help bring order to the process. The file should contain copies of all signed agreements, the complete history of any unsigned agreements, transmittal records if no agreement has been signed, and logs indicating the status of additional service agreements and consultant agreements.

If the file is initiated at the onset of the project, it can be a helpful management tool throughout the phases of service. If your project management should transition from one person or department to another, the file can assist in maintaining continuity on the project and communicating important contract status information. It can also serve as a way to communicate with your bookkeeper or accountant to facilitate effective invoicing.

I'm fallin'
I'm fallin'
fall, fall, fall, fall

—Alicia Keys

## The safety net

The negotiation and execution of contracts has become more difficult over the years. The number of nonstandard or lawyer-generated agreements could likely increase. It is also likely that the complexity and the physical size of the average contract may increase. Even if building information modeling and the promise of integrated project delivery brings us a more cooperative, less litigious process, if we wish to maintain a reasonable balance of risk and reward, we must manage our contract negotiation and execution as efficiently as possible. Effective contracts management is as important as providing effective design services because risks must be managed and fees must be collected if we expect to achieve success.

When you sit down at the negotiation table and check your list of deal breakers, bear in mind that the draft agreement in front of you will become your safety net. The effectiveness of that net will be determined by the effectiveness of your actions and decisions in negotiating the agreement and its conditions. Be mindful that when agreement is reached and you begin your services, should you encounter problems and slip from the high wire, a fair and balanced agreement can help stop your free fall.

As you ponder putting off until tomorrow calling your client about the status of the contract, and as you teeter and sway on the high wire, don't look down, and always, remember to be careful out there.

# Chapter 2

## Clients

## Love Me Tender: Maintaining the Client Relationship

This article to some extent picks up where our introspective article "Who Are You? Defining the Architect" in Chapter 7 leaves off. We believe that a necessary part of maintaining a client's loyalty is making sure that the client knows and remembers who you are. Repeat clients pose a low risk in that they keep hiring you because they believe in you. And good friends don't often sue each other. In situations like this, a dozen roses is a cheap investment!

Summary: Since our clients are our greatest assets, there is no better way to assess our practice than to discuss the architect-client relationship. Architects covet repeat clients, for they represent love, loyalty, and low marketing costs. Repeat clients do not require expensive wining and dining. They trust and value you enough that they just call you up and tell you they want you to do another project; and, by the way, the kick-off meeting is tomorrow.

> Love me tender,
> Love me sweet,
> Never let me go.
>
> —Elvis Presley, 1956

What must you do to enjoy this wonderful benefit? You only have to endear yourself to them through great service, on-time deliverables, and, most of all, convince them that you will give them what they want, when they want it, and in a way that fulfills their every wish and need. It's a simple task, eh?

It may be simple, but it is not easy. The hardest part for most practitioners is in understanding the process. Maintaining the client relationship can be a fine art. It takes your entire crew to meet expectations and deftly deliver. One disappointing employee action and you may be out of the hunt. But when the process works, it is a wonderful thing. There are firms that have rates of over 90 percent in repeat clients due to their client maintenance process. Ninety percent is pretty amazing, right? Well, maybe, but it is more a matter of human nature. We are all consumers of goods and services, and our behavior regarding service delivery is quite consistent. We want the people we turn to for products and services to set realistic goals, we want them to keep our best interest at heart, and we want them to deliver their product or service as promised. No more, no less. In this respect, our clients are just like we are.

This article will examine the art of maintaining the client relationship. It will explore what it takes to convince an owner that you should be his or her one and only architect. But such a position is not easy to come by. It is borne out of service behavior that leaves no doubts or hesitation. If you desire this status, it is a discipline that you must passionately pursue with your total effort and stamina. And, if you are successful in your endeavors, you may find that it becomes your life blood.

## I promise

Your contract with the client is your promise of what you will deliver. It is during contract negotiations that many architects set themselves up to underdeliver on the promises they make. Most clients have lawyers who argue for stringent clauses. The days of signing an AIA form contract without some revisions are basically over. You should be cautious in what you agree to give the owner under your contract and promise only what you know you can deliver. Remember, you are obligated to deliver what is enumerated in your contract, and you will be judged accordingly. If you agree to conditions that are beyond typical basic services, you may not be able to deliver without incurring increased risk. You should always consult legal counsel when negotiating service agreements. If you do not have an in-house counsel or retained counsel, ask your insurance representative for assistance.

> Only you can make this world
> seem right
> Only you can make the
> darkness bright
>
> —The Platters, 1955

## Only you

Clients want to believe that they made the best decision when they selected their architect. Hopefully, you have convinced your client through past performance or in your recent marketing presentation that you are the best architect for their job. If you feel that you have not, you may need to follow up with some dynamic and compelling exhibitions of excellence. The bottom line is that you must instill in your client the unchallenged belief that they have made the right decision.

## And they're off

Clients want to know that you will jump on the project with a full initiative. When the starting gun is fired, the client expects the design team to begin producing results immediately. It is important to give back tangible results to owners frequently so they will remain calm and satisfied. For example, many architects do not report to their clients between design milestones. Extended periods of time with no communication may be interpreted as inaction. Therefore, it is important that your progress be tangibly reported to the client through drawings, documents, reports, or at least verbal updates to assure them that you are on the track and running.

## Signed, sealed, delivered

For clients to be happy, you must deliver reasonably on time. The best way to improve your chances is to avoid promising unrealistic delivery dates. It is far safer to disappoint the client up front by extending their desired delivery rather than let them down when the results are due and expected. Moreover, some clients are simply not prepared to move as fast as they have projected. In such instances, a more service-oriented approach may go beyond explaining schedules and include services and support to help the project get started.

## Deal or no deal

Clients must believe that you are the best "deal" for the services provided. This does not necessarily mean they are looking for the lowest fee. When the client feels that they are getting real value for their money spent, they will be less inclined to shop around on the next project. Real value includes not only established expertise in a building type or building system, but it also includes an established understanding in how building types and systems relate to the client's business. When clients know they do not have to explain programmatic issues to you at project kick-off, they will more likely feel that you are their best deal.

> Can you see the real me, can you?
>
> —The Who, 1973

## Know the real me

Clients must believe that you know who they really are. Kids' names and birthdays alone are not enough. The more you know about the intricacies of their business, the more likely they will feel that you can serve them in the way that they want. If they feel you know their business intimately, they will be more prone to trust you in providing them with your design services. Time spent gaining knowledge of a client's operations, culture, and business philosophy can be valuable in instilling this level of confidence.

## Beck and call

Being accessible to the client is paramount. We have taken calls from clients as we stood with our family looking over the rim of the Grand Canyon, or as we rode the fantail in search of spectacular blue marlin. You may think it inconvenient to be constantly accessible to your client, but the advantages far outweigh the disadvantages. In addition to providing good service with quick responses, if you are in frequent contact with the owner, you will interact at a personal level that transcends ordinary business and is more meaningful to them. You will also know upfront if a problem is developing. Give them your cell phone number and e-mail address. Clients must feel they have a close working relationship with you if you expect their repeat business. Most clients will not call you at night or on the weekend when they know you are not working. Nonetheless, a short phone call from your client when you are on the golf course or on the boat is a minor sacrifice compared to the benefits gained.

> Strap yourself to a tree with roots. You ain't going nowhere.
> —The Byrds, 1968

## Ain't goin' nowhere

Clients must feel comfortable that you are stable and established in your market. No one would buy a new automobile if the car company may likely not be around next year. The age of a firm reinforces the perception of stability, as do other factors. A stable workforce, repeat business, design awards, a comfortable backlog of work, and a strong industry reputation can support the perception of your business sustainability. The more the owner is aware of these, the better he or she will feel about obtaining your services. Clients are more likely to include you as a regular part of their routine if they believe your company is stable and your future is bright.

## Problem addict

Clients want a comfort level that problems will be reasonably resolved. This can usually be achieved best by demonstration. Responding quickly to problems as soon as they arise can establish your value and dependability. Clients frequently are not as experienced in design and construction and, when problems arise, will appreciate having you available to help, even if the problem belongs to someone else. Although the problem may not be your problem, you can assist them in finding the right person to call. If the problem should escalate to a dispute or litigation, endeavor to remain in the solution loop with your client. It is important to communicate closely with the client during the resolution process. Even if your position is adverse to the client's, remaining in communication and working toward a resolution will demonstrate your good-faith efforts and your concern for the owner's best interest.

## Same ole, same ole

When you are staffing projects for repeat clients, it is important to continue to present them with the same players whenever possible. Encourage your staff to take "ownership" in the project and represent the firm to the client as though it were their own. Clients want to be able to rely on a known and experienced project team. When the client knows in advance and is comfortable with the people who will be on their project, the client will be more likely to give you repeat business. Moreover, working with clients on a continuing basis fosters friendships that transcend the current project; relationships bond and comfort levels stabilize. Although business is still business, a friendly business relationship helps smooth rough times and calm differences. It even makes some of the chaotic process fun. A longtime repeat client once told us, "Life is too short not to work with friends."

## Serious investment

Clients, from time to time, may ask you to do work that you believe is not in your scope of services. Keep in mind that it is as natural for them to ask such things as it is for you to believe they are taking advantage of you. So, before you start threatening punitive additional services requests or fire off a nasty e-mail missile, look at the big picture and think about what is at stake. Are the few hours of service required in writing the meeting notes the contractor was supposed to write or researching an owner's substitution request really the straw that breaks the camel's back? It is likely not. When these nagging little issues come up, refer to the article "Zen and the Art of Construction Administration: How Discipline and Self-Control Can Improve Your Services" in Chapter 3, breathe deeply, and relax. Log the time involved in the nagging little thing under the heading of "Client Investment," and rest easy that you are moving toward becoming an indispensable resource to the client. Look around your office at your valuable employees, new computers, boxes, and papers. Everything you see is supported by the fees you earn that the client pays. Your clients are your prime assets upon which all else in your business depends. Find a way to serve your clients beyond their expectations, and you will also find an easier, happier way to practice.

> Well love is love and not fade away.
>
> —The Rolling Stones, 1964

## Conclusion

Clients are just like you and me. They want the same things that anyone wants who purchases services. Think about the customer service responses that you have experienced. What did it make you think about the company? If the customer service representative blew you off or gave you an unintelligent response, did you feel good? Of course you did not. We want to feel that the services that we purchase are worth the money we spend. Do you go back to the same hair stylist? Why? Apparently you think that she or he knows enough about you personally to take care of your needs. Did you ever notice that the hair stylist remembers your name? What service providers have you been loyal to in the long term? Think about why you have. If you expect your clients to repeat, you must instill in them the same constants that you expect in services provided to you.

There is a firm that recently celebrated a Twenty-Over-Twenty event. It was an occasion where they invited 20 clients who had given them repeat business for more than 20 years to attend a celebration in their honor. What a great accomplishment! But the real gain was having the clients at the celebration meet and mingle with the other 19 attendees. They realized that they were among a group that had been treated very special. They realized that they were in an elite group of clients who had come to the same conclusion about that architecture firm.

So as you are preparing for that client interview and rehearsing your pitch, remember that it is what happens after the interview that really counts. The way that you service the client, if you are successful, is what can grant you repeat status. Remember that repeat business is not merely the goal of maintaining a great relationship with your clients. Repeat business is a reflection that you are accomplishing service excellence in a caring and concerned way. Care and concern for your clients cannot be presented in a marketing meeting. It must be reflected in your attitudes and actions as you provide your professional service. And as you save your PowerPoint and reach for your leavebehinds for tomorrow's marketing presentation, think about that call last week from your old friend John when he hired you to design another one of his projects, and don't forget to be careful out there.

# Smoke, Mirrors, and Snake Oil: Risks in Marketing

Risk management is more often viewed as something we do while delivering professional technical services, and marketing is not always thought of as an area where we should be especially careful. The operative word in this piece is "expectations." Architects, in our zeal to obtain a commission, can innocently raise a client's expectations beyond that which is desirable or possibly even achievable by over promising and using words that convey impossible goals. This piece emphasizes the reality that an adequate measure of risk management must be initiated before the commission is won. Be sure you read this article before you plug in the projector.

> You got to be careful if you don't know where you're going, because you might not get there.
>
> —Yogi Berra

Once there was an illustrated joke where an Egyptian architect was gleefully announcing to his workers that the firm had been awarded the Pharaoh's pyramid contract. The architect was a high-ranking official in his time, and it is well known that high-ranking officials who worked on the pyramids were ultimately sealed in the tomb along with their leader. Although the joke was funny, the thought of an architect entering into a fatalistic contract hits just a little too close to home these days.

Today, we need not worry about losing our life for doing a project, but we should be concerned about losing our livelihood. As we compete for commissions, we may be inclined to embellish our representations in order to present ourselves in the best light. These actions are not intended to mislead, but if we tell our clients that we are the best around, they may expect our work to be better than everyone else's. This expectation exceeds the definition of the standard of care and could come back to haunt us in the event of a claim.

This article will explore the risks associated with marketing and how we unwittingly create expectations that can rise above our capabilities and the prevailing standard of practice. For a general perspective, we will look at AIA Document B431, Architect's Qualification Statement, and the guidance that it gives us in accurately presenting our skills and experiences. The aspects of assembling a project team with other design professionals will be reviewed along with the dangers of "borrowing" the experiences of others to beef up our credentials. Finally, we will examine some aspects of state licensing laws and how they impose limitations on how we can represent ourselves in our practice.

## AIA Document B431–1993, Architect's Qualification Statement

In Article 2, "General Statement of Qualifications," the user is asked to describe the firm's particular qualifications to perform the work on a proposed project. Naturally, we are inclined to present unique qualifications to the greatest extent possible so as to set ourselves apart from the competition. However, the warning is given in the instructions under Section A, General Information, Paragraph 3, Code of Ethics, "All information contained in or attached to the form should be accurate and should not be edited to present a misleading picture of the Architect's experience or capabilities." In short, avoid the smoke and mirrors.

The message is clear that the form is representing that the submitting architect performed the work being presented. Caution must be exercised so that listed work by others is not represented to have been specifically performed by the architect—as Frank Lloyd Wright supposedly did of Louis Sullivan's work in his pursuit of the Larkin Building. The instructions are more explicit in the next paragraph, wherein Canon III of the Code of Ethics and Professional Conduct is referenced, "Under R.3.301, members are enjoined from misleading clients or prospective clients about the potential results of members' services."

One rapidly recognizes that the purpose of AIA Document B431 is to present an honest, accurate representation of the architect's experiences and capabilities. Further, the architect is required to sign the statement certifying that "the information provided in this Architect's Qualification Statement is true and sufficiently complete so as not to be misleading." The architect is required to certify rather than just sign the document in order to eliminate any chance of variation or approximation. To certify, according to *Black's Law Dictionary,* is "to authenticate or vouch for a thing in writing, to attest as being true or as represented." This goes beyond simply assuming a document prepared by others is correct. It indicates that you have complete knowledge of the document's accuracy.

## Been there, done that

The general public appears to believe that being qualified to do a particular project depends upon whether we have previously done a similar project of the same scope or complexity. The modern job market has driven us to the point that many firms have become specialized in specific building types such as health care or retail. However, obtaining the necessary experience for establishing a specialty is much like obtaining your first credit card. In the same way that we once had our parents back us up with their credit standing, architects breaking into a new market sector sometimes seek out experienced firms, consultants, and employees to back up their "experience." Care should be taken, however, that the client is not led to believe that the design work was performed within the architect's office and under the architect's management and direction if it actually was not.

Direct project experience must not be represented if it does not exist. It is sometimes better to take a back seat on a project and give away a good measure of the fee to gain experience in a new project type. If you can get experience on a new project type without losing money, it is not a bad investment for starting up new building type expertise.

Care should also be taken when pursuing work in another state for the first time. All states have specific requirements for providing architecture services, and they vary from state to state. All states require that you be licensed in that state before you can represent yourself as an architect; however, some allow associations and participation in competitions without licensure. Some states require that you give notice to the licensing board of your intent to interview for work and submit proof of your qualifications for obtaining licensure, if you are not licensed there. These technical requirements are often overlooked by practitioners.

Some states do not license architecture firms and require registration with their secretary of state. Consequently, you must exercise caution with the use of your firm's name in business transactions and be sure that you have complied with all licensing requirements. (For more information on individual state licensing statutes, visit the National Council of Architectural Registration Boards Web site and click on "Registration Requirements" for a listing of registration and contact information in the 50 states, the District of Columbia, and the U.S. possessions.) To be completely safe, if you are not currently registered in a state, it is best to call the state board to confirm current registration requirements.

## Every word you write

Perhaps the most common risk incurred in the marketing process is through the wording used in promotional materials. As we sort out our project photographs and compose our illuminating descriptions, we must be careful not to incur risk by representing our capabilities to be beyond the reasonable standard of care.

For example, if we represent our projects as being "of the highest quality," or providing services "of the highest standards," we set ourselves above what can be reasonably measured in comparison to other design professionals. If we promise to design projects of the highest quality, then there are no other projects in existence that are as good, not even our last project. Obviously, this is a standard that cannot be met. It is a great challenge to represent ourselves as being better than our competition without misrepresenting our capabilities or potentially elevating the standard of care in the process.

It is easy to use words with extreme meanings without realizing it. For example, if we should agree to "maximize" or "minimize" the design or our services, we are representing that we will do more than is ordinarily expected or even possible. The word "optimize" carries a level of performance that is beyond all reasonable expectations. It connotes the "optimum" or greatest level of performance. If you are not sure about your wording and representations in your printed material, consult with your professional liability insurance agent or appropriate legal counsel.

A final caution on the risks incurred by printed material relates to renderings. Many clients wish to "see" their project before it is constructed, and with computer graphics technology, producing a rendering of the proposed vision for the project is easier than ever. If there is scope represented in the graphic illustration that exceeds what is in the program documents, there is a chance that the client will be expecting it by the time the project is finished. The same is true for building models. Any medium that influences the client's expectation should be carefully administered.

## Every word you say

We must also be careful in what we say to our prospective clients during presentations. Although your words may not be reflected in your printed material, the presentation may be documented in some other way—from handwritten notes by the interviewers to video records. A well-meant statement that "we will apply our most diligent efforts to enable your achievement of a successful project" creates a promise that you can never fulfill.

At least one state requires that presentations on public projects be video recorded and made an exhibit in the owner-architect agreement. Anything said in the interview can be potentially used to set the expected level of performance. In any case, "real-time" audio and video records dictate that we choose all words carefully and prudently as we extol our greatness. If you have project team members in the interview who do not ordinarily present, it is wise to coach them in advance on the appropriate words to use and avoid.

One should also be cautious when addressing the competition during presentations. Aside from the ethical ramifications, degrading or inappropriately describing other contenders while on public record can easily support allegations of defamation. Take the high road and keep your remarks above board when pursuing a project. The best approach is to represent only you and your firm and do not discuss the competition.

> We promise according to our hopes, and perform according to our fears.
>
> —François duc de la Rochefoucauld

## Over-promised and under-delivered

You must be careful in presenting your credentials, because every word you write and every word you say in marketing your services goes toward setting the client's expectation. If you promise too much and do not deliver, your client will be disappointed. If you promise too little, you may not get the job. Promise a reasonable amount, and provide services that exceed what you have promised, and most of the time you will have a client who is satisfied.

Project schedules can be a particularly challenging subject in marketing, because architects often promise they will meet impossible schedules. It is virtually impossible to know in advance exactly how long a project will take to produce. If you are forced to provide a delivery date, be sure to include reasonable float time to accommodate the unforeseen. Be sure to include a line item after construction has begun for coordination of documents with the contractor's work plan to cover the possibility that drawings will require revision at a later date. This way, you can finish ahead of your float time and look like a hero, or you can meet the time and come out alive. It is safer to lose a job than to agree contractually to a delivery schedule that cannot be achieved.

In addition to promising the "best" or "highest-quality" projects, architects sometimes promise that they can produce work for very low fees, that their documents will be "complete," that their designs are more economical to construct, or even that the client will earn greater revenues because of the special nature of the architect's designs. As a general rule, if you over-promise and under-deliver, you will find that both you and your client will be disappointed. Any way it is measured, disappointment is an inadequate foundation for success.

> Faithfulness and sincerity are the highest things.
>
> —Confucius

## Sincerity and reliability go a long way

Architects go to great lengths to convince clients that they should be awarded a commission. They strategize to present qualifications that are better and more marketable than their competition. These ambitious efforts, if not carefully gauged, can present the impression of professional skills at a level that exceeds the standard of care. At a minimum, they may misrepresent actual experiences and capabilities.

The best approach is to be yourself when trying to convince the client that you can deliver their project. Sincerity and reliability go a long way toward demonstrating how well you can do the job.

Make your contacts and play your cards, but avoid the smoke, mirrors, and snake oil. It takes a while to break into a new market, so be patient and bite off small pieces. A minor role on a project is still a place on the project team. Just remember, one project, and you can claim experience; two projects, and you may claim to have expertise; and after that, there should be nothing to hold you back.

And meanwhile, as you fill out the next B431, be careful out there . . .

# Double-Edged Sword: The Owner's Separate Consultants

This article has awakened many readers to the risk realities of separately contracted design professionals. Architects have become accustomed to holding the prime contract for all the major design disciplines, and we often lose sight of the risks associated with separately contracted designers. With the degree of litigious head-hunting that goes on in today's industry, architects can no longer afford not to pay attention to how other designers of record are administered on their project, especially when it comes to change orders, certificates for payment, and certificates of substantial completion. Although there can be a positive side as well as a negative side to separate consultants, the architect today must pay close attention to who is under contract and how. Affix your registration stamp and sign here, please!

> Never give a sword to a man who can't dance.
>
> —Confucius

Consultants are an integral part of providing design services. Architects by definition do not typically provide "engineering" services such as mechanical, electrical, plumbing, and structural. Nonetheless, we architects are quite accustomed to managing these services and typically include them in our design services agreement with the owner. A typical project will include certifying payments to the contractor and certifying substantial completion.

However, some owners choose to contract directly with the architect's traditional consultants, and in recent years this trend has increased. This approach appears on the surface benign, but if it is administered by the architect in the same manner as if included in the architect's agreement with the owner, the architect can assume increased risks. The scope of these risks can range from assuming responsibility for work outside the architect's contract to violating state licensing statutes.

Many architects do business as usual, oblivious to the risks incurred. After all, it is not a subject that has been examined in depth.

Why is this issue of concern? Owner's separate consultants are a viable and productive option only if it is administered appropriately. It can be quite workable if the proper steps are taken to separate the various design professionals of record. Unfortunately, many architects continue to sign and issue certifications for payment and certificates of substantial completion for work that is not in their contract. In good faith, they process these documents unaware of the potential risks that could threaten.

This article will examine an architect's viewpoint of both options, and you can decide which edge of the sword you prefer to use on your projects. Be cautioned that this sword can cut both ways.

## Looks OK from here

The pen is mightier than the sword, and considerably easier to write with.

—Marty Feldman

Architects who have done battle in claims involving disciplines other than architecture can appreciate the benefit of not having those disciplines under their contract. When consultants are contracted directly with the owner, claims for deficiencies in the consultant's services cannot rightfully be made through the architect for those alleged misdeeds.

In addition, should the consultant fail to provide services in an acceptable manner, the architect can potentially criticize them without shooting oneself in the foot. Alternatively, when these services are provided through the architect in the prime owner-architect agreement, the architect is as responsible for the consultant's work as if personally performing it, and criticism in this case could be perceived as self directed.

Although the separated contract approach appears beneficial, one downside can be that the architect has no leverage over the consultants to compel them to perform, since the consultant is not being paid by the architect. This criticism usually includes the reasoning that the consultant is primarily loyal to the owner and not the architect or other team members.

## Cautions

Caution is the eldest child of wisdom.

—Victor Hugo

When the architect holds the prime agreement for the complete building design, she or he is the Architect of Record, and in this capacity the architect usually issues drawings, signs change orders, processes RFIs, and certifies contractor payments. When the prime consultants contract directly with the owner, each consultant becomes the design professional of record for his or her portion of the work, and state licensing statutes may require the consultants to administer these documents individually and under their signature. Complications can and often do arise for the architect when the documents are not processed and administered separately by the separate consultants.

When the design disciplines are contracted under one owner-architect agreement, construction documents are typically administered under one design professional's overall responsibility. If this approach is taken when design disciplines are contracted separately, the signer can accrue additional risk for the work they did not design. In short, if you issue another designer's documents within your documents, if you sign change orders for their work, if you receive and process their RFIs, and only one certificate for payment or one certificate for substantial completion is issued that includes their work, you may be viewed by others as assuming, or you may actually be accepting liability for their work as if you contracted for it.

In this instance, it is wise to consider which edge of the sword is cutting whom? One must use care in these contracted scenarios. Accommodations should be made to keep the documentation of the work of others separate from your contracted work and the representations and certifications you provide.

For example, if you package and transmit documents prepared by the other designers of record with your signed and sealed documents, you should have your documentation clearly indicate the separation of all parties' services and responsibilities. It is wise not to include the other designer in your title block if your seal and signature is also included in the title block. By all means you should not affix your seal on their drawings without a clear qualification for why you have done so. If you issue their documents to the contractor, it is wise to include an explanatory notation that you have included the other designer's documents in your package or transmittal for convenience only.

If a change order is required for another designer's portion of the work, they should issue it under their signature. Change orders for each design contract should be identified so they can be differentiated within the project records. Although the architect may agree to be the "design manager" on a project, care must be taken to avoid endorsing or authenticating change orders involving design or engineering that is not within the architect's contract, construction documents, or realm of responsibility.

Prefixes such as "A" for the architect and "SE" for the structural engineer, or "MEP" for the mechanical, electrical, and plumbing engineer can be used to tell documents apart in a change order, RFI, or shop drawing log. The objective is to have the tracking documents reflect a clear and undisputable delineation of design responsibility between each contracted designer of record. Complicated, isn't it?

Similar issues arise in reporting job site observations. If you report on the work placed in accordance with construction documents that you did not prepare, beyond simple coordination with your own design scope, other parties may opine that you are accepting a portion of the design responsibility for that work. Field observation reports are covered further in "Visible Means: Site Visits and Construction Observation" in Chapter 5.

A more complex and challenging issue is the contractor's application for payment. How do you identify your portion of the work certified when there is only one schedule of values and one amount certified? Have you signed such a document? For example, have you ever certified a payment application that included site work designed by a separately contracted civil engineer? If you have you are not alone. Many architects have taken these actions in good faith, failing to recognize that the owner's separate consultant should rightfully bear the responsibility for certifying work performed on the basis of designs and documents that the separate consultant prepared.

The most desirable approach is to have separate application and certificate for payment forms for each contracted designer's portion of the work.

However, the contractor will likely want to use only one application and certificate for payment since it is less complicated and easier for the contractor to administer. After all, the contractor typically has only one contract with the owner.

If one application and certificate for payment must be used, the next most desirable option is to separate the disciplines in the schedule of values and include for each a certification signature line and separate amount certified line for each separate consultant on the front page. One contractor added separate columns in the schedule of values indicating his assessment of which design professional's contract applied to the line item.

If these approaches are not achievable, the next option is to maintain one schedule of values with multiple certification signature lines on the front page. Include a corresponding note stating that each signing professional is certifying only the amounts applicable to the work related to their contracted portion of the project. As a last resort, if your certifying signature is the only one on the payment certificate, you should qualify the certification with a notation indicating that other work is contained within the application for payment, and you are certifying only the work under your contract. However, we consider this to be marginal documentation and it should be utilized only if all other efforts fail.

Finally, to aid in clarification, care must be taken to address only the work under your design contract when certifying substantial completion. You can accomplish this by qualifying your certification with a reference to your contract. It is also advisable to suggest that the owner obtain certificates of substantial completion from the other designers of record for their contracted work. Certificates of substantial completion are covered further in "Substantial Completion, Where Art Thou? A Challenging and Elusive Milestone" in Chapter 5.

## En garde

> When choosing between two evils, I always like to try the one I've never tried before.
>
> —Mae West

These variances from the normal way of administering construction, although necessary for proper documentation, will likely encounter pushback if not established at the onset of the project. Your chances of achieving widespread cooperation will be greater if you broach these sensitive issues up front. The best occasion is when the owner first informs you that the contracts will be separate.

You should be prepared to explain the administrative complexities and why you (and your insurance carrier!) frown on your certifying work that you did not design and are not responsible for. You will not be in danger of over explaining the complexities of this issue to the owner. If you need assistance, have your attorney or insurance agent help explain the issue.

Another opportunity to establish the desired format for all documentation is in the preconstruction conference. The more you address the subject and discuss the issues, the more likely it is that you will achieve your documentation goals.

A good idea is to prepare general conditions, supplemental conditions, and bid documents to reflect the necessary special requirements for administering the project. Everyone should be aware up front that separating the design contracts is no less complicated than separating the trade construction contracts. It can be done, but not without extra effort and planning. The contractor should be given an opportunity to account for any additional administrative work in their bid or negotiation.

Alternatively, if the owner desires to simply hire you to report on the work of others, and certify pay applications and the certificate of substantial completion in the stead of other separate consultants, then you may have additional research to do and tough questions to ask. Will these activities be covered by your professional liability insurance policy? Are you prepared, or even qualified, to replace the eyes, ears, and judgment of the other consultants? If you do so, will you be engaged in the unlicensed practice of engineering in your state? There are other responsibilities that you likely cannot provide without practicing engineering, such as checking engineering shop drawings, responding to some engineering-related RFIs or revising the signed and sealed drawings of other separate consultants.

The issues involved can carry serious risk implications, and they must be approached and administered with great caution. It is easy and natural for the architect to do business as usual, processing the documents as if they were in one owner-architect contract. Risks can be managed if your project involves owner's separate consultant contracts, but there is no simple solution.

## The last word

> Forewarned, forearmed; to be prepared is half the victory.
>
> —Miguel de Cervantes

One last place to address the complexities of separate prime designers of record, but not the least place, is in the owner-architect agreement. While your scope of services will generally be addressed in your agreement with the owner, most AIA agreements also contain language along the following lines:

> Terms in this Agreement shall have the same meaning as those in the edition of AIA Document A201, General Conditions of the Contract for Construction, current as of the date of this Agreement.

A201-2007, General Conditions of the Contract for Construction, defines "Work" as follows, with similar language in A201-1997:

> THE WORK—The term "Work" means the construction and services required by the Contract Documents, whether completed or partially completed, and includes all other labor, materials, equipment and services provided or to be provided by the Contractor to fulfill the Contractor's obligations. The Work may constitute the whole or a part of the Project.

Relative to separate prime consultants this relationship becomes problematic in clauses found in AIA 201-2007 such as:

> The Architect, will visit the site at intervals appropriate to the stage of construction, or as otherwise agreed with the Owner, to become generally familiar with the progress and quality of the portion of the Work completed, and to determine in general if the Work observed is being performed in a manner indicating that the Work, when fully completed, will be in accordance with the Contract Documents.

The architect, under the separate consultant scenario, would be well served to include a clarification to the A201 definition to the effect that the "Work" as it applies to the owner-architect agreement and the architect's services includes only the work you have designed, and does not include work designed by other designers of record. Again, your attorney can help you with the specific language.

## Conclusion

> Our swords shall play the orators for us.
>
> —Christopher Marlowe

Separately contracted design consultants are a growing trend in the industry. While it appears benign and it is in some ways perceived as beneficial, the advantages do not come without a price. The important message here is that the owner and the contractor should be made aware of the complexities up front to facilitate success in proper administration and to allocate the responsibilities and the risks appropriately.

Many people do not fully understand the implications of professional registration for architects and engineers. States do not require owners to be registered to be owners, and although some states require contractors to be registered, their requirements relate more to minimum competency than to practice requirements. But all states require architects and engineers to be registered in order to meet certain standards of practice, and each one has strict requirements for issuing, signing and sealing, changing, and certifying the work of another design professional.

Architects are licensed to practice architecture. Engineers are licensed to practice engineering. Although many states recognize these as allied professions where there is likely to be some overlap in professional services, generally they are viewed as separate but complementary disciplines. Checking engineering shop drawings, certifying engineering designs or work performed from engineering designs, or changing drawings prepared by engineers (as in responding to an RFI that effectively changes a design) may be deemed to violate the state licensing statutes and constitute the practice of engineering.

Owners and contractors are not going to study and be familiar with your licensing requirements. It is incumbent upon you to prepare them for the implications and documentation requirements of each method of project delivery. An architect is no longer the silent, learned design professional, with cape and flat brimmed hat, going about his or her duties in reverent separation. Our practice now requires decisive interaction and discussion if we expect clients and contractors to understand our risks and cooperate with us.

You may encounter push back as you negotiate these separate consultant issues because owners may not fully understand the risks involved. Nonetheless, if the issues are properly addressed and administered, having separate prime owner-designer agreements can and often does result in well designed and executed projects.

So as you gather your files and prepare for that meeting with the owner to discuss project contract structure, be prepared to discuss candidly all the issues involved with the project delivery approach they propose. Explain that each approach usually has advantages and disadvantages; two edges that may cut both ways. Use whatever time it takes to help them understand the risks and the rewards of each; and along the way, please remember to be careful out there.

# The Power of One: The Effective Owner-Architect-Contractor Team

This type of subject is sometimes difficult to write about in that it may be dismissed by some as corny *kum ba yah*. Our primary objective in this article is to point out the benefits and efficiencies of getting along and being a team. We can easily remember the projects that went well were the ones where everyone got along. We try to stay away from group hugs and campfire singing and stick to what works and what makes sense. Alternatively, the way some participants in our industry treat architects, there may be some benefit in group hugs and campfire singing, especially with s'mores.

> Each of us holds the key
> It's inside of you and me
> Each of us holds the key
> To the power of one
>
> —Donna Summer

Ah, remember the project that went so well? You know, the one where the contractor didn't send so many RFIs and the owner was quick about making decisions. It was one of those projects where everyone could almost relax. No surprise attacks. No hidden agendas. What a project! You have to wonder what made things go so well.

It appeared to be just another project like the rest of them. Oh, yeah, we had problems, but they were all solved quickly, and there were no claims afterward. The contractor laid out their work in spite of our original conflicting dimensions. As soon as everyone found a problem, the designers and contractor jumped in and revised their work without any delays or additional charges, and the contractor even gave us their corrected layout dimensions to check against our drawings. And we certainly didn't mind helping the contractor when they installed that pier in the wrong location. It didn't take much time for our structural engineer to come up with a solution that would transfer the loads. Anyway, by then we would have done about anything to help those guys. After all, they had done so much to help us.

It was as if a higher power eschewed strife and wanted us to succeed. Why was this project so different from the rest? Absent was the overt criticism normally present among the parties. Gone was the anticipated weekly berating in the owner-architect-contractor meetings when architects normally are publicly castigated for alleged late submittals or RFI responses. The atmosphere was one of cooperation and teamwork; owner, architect, and contractor working with a common purpose toward a common goal.

This article will explore those project experiences that have few problems even among many challenges. We will examine the project team and the correlation of how beneficial interaction affects the ultimate outcome. We will examine how the team working together produces a special power, the power of one initiative by multiple players to achieve success.

## The game

> In war, you win or lose, live or die—and the difference is just an eyelash.
>
> —General Douglas MacArthur

Modern design and construction is by its own makeup a game of competition and confrontation. Just like football or baseball, each team strives to outdo the other while preserving its own interests. Unfortunately, these gaming strategies usually yield some amount of conflict, and conflict stifles productive construction team interaction. In sports there must be two teams in order to compete, but on the job site it is more effective if there is only one.

When was the last time that you worked with a contractor who was genuinely interested in your success on the project? Moreover, when was the last time that you were genuinely interested in the contractor's success on the project? Projects these days often have players with opposing agendas, reflecting a polarity spawned by decades of legal jousting and advantage seeking. Yet in the midst of such wrangling, now and then a project goes smoothly with few disputes or claims, and it is viewed as rewarding to those who participated.

Projects that go really well seem to be fewer these days. When one does come along, maybe it is because a contractor wants to impress you to get future work. Maybe you want to impress the owner or contractor with your teamwork skills. Maybe it is an owner who just wants to enjoy the design and construction experience. And just maybe, it could be because the architect successfully demonstrated to the contractor that he or she is there to play their part in delivering the project and assisting those in need.

Unfortunately the game doesn't go smoothly all of the time. Many owners want the architect to be a terminator who breaks the contractor's back if things are not exactly right. Some contractors are convinced that the architect is trying to put them out of business, or that all architects want to make contractors responsible for design mistakes. The adversarial nature of many architect-contractor relationships does not promote teamwork or peace and love. Many projects are positioned so that the architect's priority is looking for work that is wrong rather than assisting the team in producing work that is right.

We have a tendency to assume that the other players are out to take advantage and everything they do is in their own best interest. It is no different than knights jousting on the field. If someone is to win, then someone must be defeated. If you've been to a youth soccer game or attended a professional sporting event recently, you have seen firsthand that modern society tends to give lip service, but no real credence, to the idea that everyone can be a winner.

## Analyze this

Let's take a closer look at projects that went well. Perhaps we can learn something about improving our chances of success by asking some questions.

Did you have a good relationship with the contractor and/or the subcontractors? Had you both done a successful project together before this one? This is frequently the case. When we have a good experience with a builder, we are more likely to feel optimistic on subsequent projects with them and try harder to make things work out. When architects have a long-term relationship with a builder, we often help them market new work, even when we aren't the architect. When we have a long-term relationship that is built on trust, we tend to be as concerned with their success almost as much as with our own.

Did you have a good experience with the owner? Was the owner responsive in his or her required decisions, and did he or she understand the importance of contingencies and allowances? Did you stay in close contact with him or her and try to answer their questions as they arose? Did the owner understand your human imperfections, or did he or she constantly remind you that they "bought a complete set of plans"? Those "complete set of plans" guys tend to make the project more difficult and erode chances for success, and they tend to ask you to pay money or forfeit fees at the end of the project. Have you had opportunities to work for owners who show loyalty to your firm in response to your commitment and hard work?

These factors just may be a contributor to the success of your "exceptional" projects. The key to success just may be inside you and me; the key to the power of one.

A meaningful case study is a large sports facility that was aggressively fast tracked under a very restrictive budget. Although the project was very successful, it did not run particularly smoothly. Sports facilities are notorious for conflicts and claims. Meetings on this project were intense and often confrontational. Yet almost everyone involved considered each other a friend. Project difficulties, though often dealt with under very tense conditions, were resolved not with accusation and domination, but based on what was possible within each person's constraints. Success was judged based on a strong sense of accomplishment and fulfillment, not on whether one person won and another lost. When the last piece of framework was hoisted into place, the signature of everyone who had worked on the project was written in gold ink on the steel beam. When the last piece of granite was set in the main concourse, more than a thousand names of a very successful project team were engraved on its face. No one got sued. Everyone got tickets to circuses, rodeos, and games.

What made this project successful? How and why did it survive these arduous challenges? How did it escape the fate that often befalls public sports facilities? We took a look and here's what we found:

- The architect and contractor had worked together before and had developed a long, successful relationship.
- Everyone on the design and construction team was interested in maintaining a good relationship with the owners.
- The subcontractors recognized the contractor and the architect as a source of future work.
- The project team was made up of seasoned professionals who had experienced tough projects in the past.
- The project was the centerpiece of the community, and everyone was grateful to be a part of the project team.
- The owners had a vision of success in their minds and looked hard for the things their architect and builders did to help fulfill their vision.
- Everyone upheld the success of the project as a priority, they respected each other, and they worked toward that end.

Many of these ingredients have existed on projects that were unsuccessful. We believe that a significant reason for success is the last one listed. Without a mutual desire for success, all of the other factors will not work. The power of one is dependent upon all participants seeking a common unity. Our goal is and always has been the same: provide quality services, make money, and deliver projects that meet their intended purpose. It is the recognition that we share this common goal and a respect for each other's pursuit that makes success possible.

## The real world

> Reality is merely an illusion, albeit a very persistent one.
> —Albert Einstein

This brings us to the basic realities that affect how people do business. When these are acknowledged in our actions and behavior as we interact on a project, our working relationships often benefit. We should pause to consider these factors and how they can be applied to the way we work. They include the following.

**The object of doing work is to make a profit.** Unprofitable projects seldom run smoothly, but when everyone is meeting their budget goals, relationships and interaction are improved. Financial impact should be considered in all activities. Owners who don't want to pay the contractor a fair fee are not acting in their own best interest, as unprofitable projects are prone for trouble. Negotiating all of the profit out of consultant and contractor pricing merely increases the chance of confrontation and strife. Alternatively, relationships benefit from parties who look for fair returns and not windfalls. Bouncing from client to client in search of the highest profits is not an activity that will support long-term relationships.

**People want their projects to succeed.** Although you may be involved in natural conflict with other team players, their primary objective is the same as yours. They want the project to be successful and the client to be satisfied. With these common goals, it should not be difficult to find common ground. Alternatively, the contractor that wages an intensive RFI attack, just in case they need added protection from the owner or architect, is not seeking oneness.

**Delivering a successful project will get you good references and help bring future work.** We all depend on references to help us gain new clients, and we strive to maintain an acceptable list of satisfied customers. We cannot deliver a project solo; we must rely on others to help us do it. Sometimes helping others helps us.

**If you commit random acts of kindness to others, sometimes they will reciprocate in kind.** There was a project where the owner was also the contractor. The owner had gained a reputation for beating up on architects. This owner always considered the architect to be a low priority and suffered allegations of uncoordinated drawings, errors and omissions, and the like on the architect so that a portion of fees paid the architect could be recovered at project completion. On one project this owner/contractor mislocated 17 drilled piers. The architecture firm, which also provided the structural engineering, designed pier cap modifications to correct the problem and did not charge the owner/contractor. From that time forward, the project ran without conflict. The architect also made some mistakes, but the contractor made the necessary corrections, and there were no lingering disputes. The owner/contractor did not make claims for a return of a portion of the architect's fees and applauded the extra effort to salvage the mislocated foundations. Although this will not happen on every project, demonstrations of assistance and support in daily activities can instill similar behavior on the other side. But, lest you be overconfident of fallible memories, please see the article "To Document or Not to Document: Basic Documentation Requirements" in Chapter 1.

**Combative behavior to others, they will usually reciprocate in kind.** How many times has the thought, "I'll show that son-of-a-gun!" crossed your mind? If it did, it was likely your reaction to someone treating you in a less-than-desirable manner. The human reaction to mistreatment is to mistreat in return, given the opportunity. Likewise, if you mistreat, you will likely experience similar behavior. Life itself is a great mirror. Always endeavor to treat others the way you want to be treated. If they don't treat you well in return, that is a reflection of their values, not of yours.

## Life is short

> Rather would I have the love songs of romantic ages, rather Don Juan and Madame Venus, rather an elopement by ladder and rope on a moonlight night, followed by the father's curse, mother's moans, and the moral comments of neighbors, than correctness and propriety measured by yardsticks.
>
> —Emma Goldman

Given these facts of life, how do we achieve this level of harmony, mutual respect, and productivity within the team? Is it possible in today's risk-averse yet risk-filled industry to assemble dependable teams that can be anything other than confrontational and filled with conflict? In most design and construction projects today, risk is apportioned much like a pyramid. Owners take the greatest financial risk because they own the completed project and they reap the greatest rewards. The contractors take the next greatest risk with responsibility for the cost of construction, and their rewards are proportionate. The designers take the least risk with the least rewards, taking primary responsibility for the cost of design, although responsibility for some construction cost is possible.

The owner provides the construction documents to the contractor, and in so doing, may impliedly warrant under the Spearin Doctrine that the plans and specifications are reasonably free from defects. On the premise of Spearin, some contractors launch an assault on the architect's documents and design services from the very onset of the project in an effort to build a defense against potential owner claims, or to build an offense in support of claims for additional costs of construction. Many contractors have come to consider this preemptive action necessary to protect themselves in today's claims-prone environment. Since there is no perfect set of plans, the opportunities contractors have to claim negligence by the designer are legendary. Thus, a search for errors and omissions will inevitably succeed. If this sounds fatalistic, well . . . it is, because it is true.

This is where prior experience, an established relationship, a hard-earned reputation, mutual trust and respect, and significant knowledge about realistic outcomes are important. Unfortunately, life isn't perfect enough for all of these circumstances to exist on every project. However, if just a few of them exist, that may be enough. It depends on your willingness to communicate effectively and to be trusting.

## Conclusion

When that really good job comes along, we always are in awe of why it happened in the first place. We think about what was different, and we wish that we could bottle it up and save it for the next project. Compared to all the troubled projects, we see it as a shining star that makes our work as an architect worthwhile. Projects such as this one prove that the process can work.

Remember the facts of life and guide yourself by them. We address the merits of the cool and collected approach in the article "Zen and the Art of

Construction Administration" in Chapter 3. Remember that the friendly and helpful approach will be received more gracefully than ringing the doorbell with a hammer. On the other hand, if it isn't meant to happen, then so be it; you don't have to stand idly and be punched in the nose.

Yet success and fulfillment are important ambitions . . . stay after them. Don't give up trying to foster a team that acts as one. This is a human desire that exists in almost everyone. Every professional wants to work on a project that flows smoothly and is gratifying. Almost everyone has the same aspirations and goals.

So as you prepare your preconstruction conference agenda and think about how you will attempt to be the catalyst for bringing occasionally adversarial players together as a cohesive and effective team, don't forget to be careful out there.

# Chapter 3

## Power and Proficiency

## Project Manager or Risk Manager?
## The Architect's Dual Role

T his article addresses the demands of the new-dimension architect. Passive, "just do the job" behavior is not always enough in our litigious environment these days. Today the architect must manage how they do things as much as what they do. But at the same time they must be transparent to the owner and not let protective behavior overshadow effective services. It becomes a sort of ambidextrous project management. Juggling, anyone?

> I would give my right arm to be ambidextrous.
>
> —Jay Leno

When the topic of risk management comes up in discussions among project managers and senior project leaders, comments such as "Is this really necessary?" and "I don't have time for this!" are common. Risk management is frequently looked upon as an external activity that must be imposed upon our services. Seasoned practitioners have learned that this is not only necessary but vital to our practice. However, risk management applications in services need not be disruptive or different from the way we normally do our work.

You may ask, "What if I don't work that way?" Although a valid question, the risk management component of an effective project manager can be so integral to the way services are provided that it is transparent to the client, the contractor, and even coworkers. Understanding and incorporating effective risk management ideas and techniques into daily activities can be seamless and feel so normal that it may alleviate the paranoia many often experience.

### Remember the past

Electric typewriters have disappeared from our workplace. Remember the first time that you read or composed a letter using a computer monitor? The inability to see the full document was almost claustrophobic. For many, being unable to hold the document in their hands was unpleasant and left a great void. Today, we think nothing of composing and sending digital communications without holding a piece of paper or licking an envelope.

Less than 10 years ago, e-mail was not the rule, and a computer on every desk was not a reality. How did this change happen so fast? More importantly, why did it happen?

It happened because our business was compelled by technology to move in that direction.

We must think of risk management in the same way: It is driven by more than just technology, but it is also not to be denied, for we must embrace this change or face adverse consequences. The good news is that risk management can be like the digital world. It can be incorporated into our practice seamlessly and become an invisible aspect of our services. Although many think of project management and risk management as two different activities, this article will explore how they can be integrated such that an effective project manager is also an effective risk manager.

## Project and risk management defined

The answer to the question "What is project management?" could fill volumes and take years to answer and understand fully. However, for the purposes of this article, we'll use a short version:

> Project management is the act of overseeing and guiding a project. It may include different duties for different managers and different projects. Project management involves employee, client, consultant, and contractor relationships and effective communication. Project management includes the act of creating and overseeing the delivery of plans, budgets, and schedules.

Likewise, the scope of risk management in our practice seems to grow increasingly. The description below explains why risk management can be incorporated into traditional project management activities:

> Risk management involves activities, as opposed to the duties involved in project management, which can occur while project management is taking place. Risk management is the process by which risks are recognized, understood, evaluated, and managed. It includes activities ranging from avoiding high-risk ventures to candidly explaining decisions to clients so as to enable and obtain their informed consent.

An effective project manager who develops risk management as an integral component of project management is rarely viewed as a "risk manager," but is more often seen as a client advocate and a good leader.

## What do project and risk managers do?

Some firms employ a person who is outwardly described as a "risk manager." This person may be a lawyer or an architect and usually is involved with negotiating contracts as well as managing claims and litigation. This type of risk manager tends to be employed by larger firms that have the resources and wish to pursue vigilant and explicit risk management. Most architecture firms are not large enough and do not have the resources to employ a full-time risk manager.

However, architecture firms have a recognizable need for project managers. In the course of their jobs, these project managers fulfill the need to lead, communicate, and plan effectively. Project managers therefore become the legionnaires on the front lines who have the primary opportunity to assess risks, be aware of pitfalls, and inform clients of potential adverse outcomes.

> Real valor consists not in being insensible to danger, but in being prompt to confront and disarm it.
>
> —Sir Walter Scott

## Project manager attitudes and behavior

The effectiveness of project managers is largely determined by how they approach a project and how they behave. In addition to administering project services responsibilities, project managers must learn what clients like and do not like in order to incorporate effective risk management into their management duties. They must learn to discuss the things that clients do not like about architects' services as well as the pleasant experiences. Errors and omissions must be addressed with clients in their true context as common, anticipated occurrences, so that the client's expectation will be realistic. Because architects represent many of the client's interests during the design process, clients typically expect them to be aware of and anticipate in advance what may go wrong.

Common project issues that clients do not like include:

- Exceeded budget expectations
- Cost overruns
- Unapproved installed work
- Non-performing buildings (e.g., leaking roofs)
- Operational and maintenance challenges
- Errors and omissions mistakes

Common project manager behavioral characteristics that clients do not like are:

- Being late for meetings
- Failing to follow through; not doing what was promised
- Being unprepared
- Forgetting assignments
- Confrontation
- Arrogance
- Inadequate responses
- Uninformed answers; responses without research

On the other hand, the more a client likes how the project manager approaches the job and how he or she behaves, the less likely that contentious issues and subsequent claims will arise. Project management traits that clients typically appreciate are:

- Use of understandable lay terms in conversations and correspondence
- Well-planned and well-executed project meetings
- Prompt and informative meeting reports
- Prompt written responses to questions, especially when mistakes are involved
- Constant availability by phone and email

## Those difficult discussions

In "The Importance of Risk Management" in Chapter 1, we note that the only way to completely avoid risk is to close your office and go home. The practice of architecture inherently includes risk. When risks are encountered, the best policy is to address threatening issues quickly and directly. Examples include an onerous contract clause or condition proposed during negotiations or a value engineering proposal or substitution request from which the architect has experienced poor results in the past. There is a tendency today, because e-mail is so direct, to sit down immediately and compose a "missile" response in an effort to prevent or rebut the issue. It is advisable, however, first to do the research, prepare the response and explanation supported by the facts, and arrange a meeting or a telephone call with the involved parties. You may eventually decide to send the missile, but it will be more effective after you have made contact and thoroughly explained your position.

An area of practice where architects frequently feel pushed around, which can be the source of trouble on a project, is value analysis, also known as value engineering. The proposing party, usually the client or contractor, typically has a vested interest in implementing a reduction in quality. The client may perceive that they are saving money while maintaining an acceptable level of quality, or the contractor may be earning all or a part of the money that is "saved." Nevertheless, in spite of the perceived benefits, the client or the contractor is often unwilling to accept the responsibility for any negative outcome associated with the change.

### Example

An architect specifies a window system with integral water-management capabilities for a three-story brick veneer building. The contractor has proposed to substitute a standard storefront system that does not internally manage infiltrated water and does not direct the water to the exterior, thus serving only as a rain barrier. The change has been proposed as a savings in cost, and the proposal has been accepted by the client. In this scenario, one of two results can be achieved, depending on the decision of the project manager. The two options are:

- The architect knows the project is in need of budget management and acquiesces and accepts the substitution. The architect reviews and approves the shop drawings for the alternative barrier system. If the system leaks, the architect will likely be viewed as the culprit, and the client could have a valid claim that the architect failed to inform initially that the barrier system was a risky reduction in quality.

- An alternative outcome, involving the concept of "informed consent," could be the architect advising the client as follows: "It has been our experience that the substituted storefront, which is a rain barrier system in this instance, cannot manage the rainwater that will penetrate the brick veneer. Our concern, should you accept the proposed quality reduction, is that the rain barrier window will possibly allow water to leak into and damage the building interior because the storefront system does not direct the water to the outside of the building." In this alternative, the client becomes an informed party when making the decision.

It is likely the client will not be happy with the architect's position and recommendation. However, in this instance, a frustrated client is a better alternative than a leaking and damaged building and the claims that often follow.

Other difficult discussions with clients involve being candid about making mistakes. Architects generally find it very difficult to discuss the fact that mistakes are a common reality. We have addressed the growing tendency among some clients and contractors to believe that perfection is a reasonably expected standard of care for architects. Such a standard is unachievable, and the architect will never be able to perform to this expectation. Although written reference works and laws may address this issue, there can be no substitute for a face-to-face conversation about the reality of making mistakes. You should assist your client in understanding that a few mistakes are to be expected, and that they should include a contingency fund in the budget to pay for these inevitable costs.

If the client is angered by this truth and is inflexible in anticipating and accommodating mistakes on the project, you should consider one of two tough risk management options:

- Decline the project commission
- Anticipate paying for mistakes out of your own pocket

## Absolutes

The tendency of the client to think that no mistakes will be made on a project is perpetuated by the use of "absolute" language by architects. This is addressed in "Smoke, Mirrors, and Snake Oil: Risks in Marketing" in Chapter 2. Absolute language plays a dramatic role in influencing expectations on a project. Examples of absolute language include "100% Construction Documents Set" and "Final Project Schedule." These examples convey that nothing is missing or wrong in the contract documents and that the project schedule will not require or undergo changes. Absolute language can set a standard, either legal or perceived, that is impossible to achieve. The quality of project management is enhanced and risks are better managed when absolute language is removed from the lexicon of the project manager's documents and services.

Unfortunately, absolute language can be included in the architect's work without the architect realizing it. For example, when issuing the schematic design package, if it is labeled, "Final Schematic Design Set," the connotation is that the set is complete, is fully accurate, and contains no variations or information lost in translation. A more appropriate and accurate label would be "Issued for Review and Approval," which does not indicate an absolute or complete document.

The same risk exists in the wording of field observation reports. If the architect reports that "the drywall is complete," the representation has been made that there are no remaining completion or correction items. The architect is only required in AIA Document B101-2007, in Article 3.6.2.1, ". . . to determine, in general, if the Work *observed* is being performed in a manner indicating that the Work, ***when fully completed***, will be in accordance with the Contract Documents" (emphasis added). Please note that the word "observed" does not appear in AIA Document B141-1997, Part 2.

The architect does not determine if the project is fully completed until notified as such by the contractor at the end of the project. (Refer to Article 9.10.1, General Conditions of the Contract for Construction.) Therefore, at this point in the project, it is more appropriate to state, "The drywall appears to be complete," so as not to represent an essentially unknown built condition.

## The client's advocate

The single most effective risk management activity for a project manager is that of being the client's advocate. The architect's position in representing the client, in Article 4.2.1 of the General Conditions of the Contract for Construction, requires the architect to "be an Owner's representative during construction." If the client perceives that the architect is their representative, the less likely the chance is that they will be combative on services issues. Although the architect must "not show partiality to either" the client or the contractor (as required in General Conditions Article 4.2.12), the more the architect can demonstrate that he or she is aware of the client's interests, the less likely there will be disputes and negative confrontations.

Do this by putting yourself in the client's shoes and trying your best to understand the client's point of view. Clients who perceive through your actions that you are representing them and the needs of their project present a lesser risk than clients who think otherwise.

> Some people feel the rain. Others just get wet.
>
> —Bob Dylan, 1965

## Conclusion

Project management is changing. It is no longer a matter of designing the project and producing documents the way we have always done and passively administering construction. Effective project management now includes risk management. Today, architects must play an active role in delivering the project within their contractual and professional limitations.

Risk management is now a required part of the way we think and act in managing projects. It can be incorporated into our routine work habits seamlessly, and, if it is effectively applied, clients will view it as simply good management. If effectively undertaken, those difficult discussions will likely be viewed as just taking care of business. In turn, client expectations may be more realistic and disputes potentially less prevalent.

The architect must manage risks and manage the project to increase the chances of success, and this evolutionary change eventually will be a distant memory. Much like the old typewriter in the corner of the print room, some day you may stumble across an old meeting report or a piece of correspondence with wording that causes you to stop and ask yourself, "Did I really once work that way?"

Today, there need not be a difference between a risk manager and a project manager. The actions required to be effective are one and the same.

Meanwhile, if you are about to send that "missile," we'll leave you with a final thought: Be careful out there.

# Master and Commander, Part 1: The Architect's Authority

Practitioners sometimes get confused as to the authority they have on a project, and such confusion can lead to increased risk. This article addresses the types of authority the architect possesses and the importance of knowing when and how to use them. You must agree that Captain Jack Aubrey provides a fitting analogy for the architect who must know when and how to use authority in delivering professional services. Aye, mate?

The authority of the architect when providing services can be an issue with diverse viewpoints. Owners may look on the architect's authority as being very limited or perhaps nonexistent, or they may expect the architect to control all of the design and construction activities. Contractors may struggle with the architect's "document interpretations" and consider themselves to be responsible for final design configurations, or they may look to the architect to confirm all design interpretations. Architects may struggle with a desire to be the master builder with control and leadership over the entire project delivery process.

Indeed, some architects feel intense ownership of their projects and demand strict adherence to their design requirements. Much like Russell Crowe's character Captain "Lucky" Jack Aubrey in Patrick O'Brian's *Master and Commander,* they seek complete control of project activities, their crew, and all whom they encounter.

The reality is that the architect's authority is typically determined by two external sources. Certain powers are conveyed by our service contracts, and others are compelled by the standard of care consistent with the practice of architecture. Although our duties can be influenced by owners' and contractors' opinions and expectations, the base line of our obligations and authority is typically well established at the onset.

Execution of the architect's authority falls into three categories: making decisions, giving recommendations (shared responsibility with owners and/or contractors), and leaving the responsibility entirely to others. The architect is typically in command of the outcome on a few occasions related to the former category—when making definitive decisions—yet can only attempt to influence the outcome on the many other occasions when sharing responsibility and giving recommendations. In those instances when the responsibility is entirely up to others, it is probably best to leave well enough alone, because, as any risk manager will tell you, no good deed goes unpunished.

This article—in two parts—will examine some of the primary areas of the architect's authority relative to decisions and recommendations. It will address when it is appropriate to act as master and commander and take control, and in Part 2, when it is appropriate to leave decisions to those who hold that contractual responsibility, This is an all-important issue of the professional standard of care, which is what defines professional responsibility, as well as how the perception of others can influence required actions.

## The architect's basis of authority—common authority

The architect's authority is typically derived from essentially two external sources: the services agreement and the professional standard of care.

> It's leadership they want . . . strength . . . find that within yourself, and you will earn their respect.
>
> —Captain Jack Aubrey

A factor governing the level of services that the architect must provide in a contract is the professional standard of care. The standard of care is typically defined by state law and varies from jurisdiction to jurisdiction. A general description can be found in the Glossary of *The Architect's Handbook of Professional Practice*, 14th edition:

> Standard of care: usually defined as what a reasonably prudent architect, in the same community at the same time, facing the same or similar circumstances would do.

However, this standard, and sometimes the law, cannot be strictly applied in the judgment of professional performance. A qualified architect, serving as an expert witness, must address the performance of an "accused" practicing architect regarding conformance to the standard of care. Simply stated, an architect typically is required to decide, advise, and/or recommend in a prudent manner consistent with other architects engaged in a similar practice.

## The architect's basis of authority—contracted authority

> Quick is the word, and sharp is the action.
> —Captain Jack Aubrey

Many of the architect's duties and responsibilities on a project are established in the owner-architect agreement. They can range from a brief study to complete basic services required for the design and construction of a building. In any case, the architect is contracted to act and provide services to the extent set out in the agreement with the client.

In AIA Document B101-2007, Standard Form of Agreement Between Owner and Architect, the architect's decision-making powers are noticeably limited. The same is true in the previous edition, AIA Document B141-1997.

Aside from designing the project and preparing documents to be used for construction, there is no specific mention of what the architect is to do for the owner until B101-2007, Article 3.6, Construction Phase Services, paragraph 3.6.1.2, wherein it states:

> The Architect shall advise and consult with the Owner during the Construction Phase Services. The Architect shall have authority to act on behalf of the Owner only to the extent provided in this Agreement.

Similar language is found in A201-2007, Article 4.2 and in A201-1997, Article 2.6.

## The architect's basis of authority—exclusive authority

> Much depends on your accuracy, make your shot count!
> —Captain Jack Aubrey

Chief among the architect's exclusive authority is probably aesthetic design. On most projects, the architect is generally looked upon as the party involved who is most qualified to address matters of aesthetic intent. Many owners choose to either delete this from the AIA documents or share the authority with the architect. However, the owner-architect agreements, rather than assign this responsibility in the form of absolute authority up front in the architect's scope of services, instead authorize the architect to decide aesthetic issues if related to a claim or dispute.

This is addressed with similar wording in AIA B101-2007, in Article 3.6.2.4, and B141-1997, in Article 2.6.1.9, and in AIA B103-2007, in Article 3.6.2.4: as well as in A201-2007, Section 4.2.13

> The Architect's decisions on matters relating to aesthetic effect will be final if consistent with the intent expressed in the Contract Documents.

Regardless of the strict tenor of this language, and aside from the fact that an architect is usually asked to at least give an opinion, in reality, matters of aesthetic intent are rarely decided by the architect as an absolute commander. Even when this authority is conferred, issues such as schedule and cost often cause the architect to arrive at a decision heavily influenced through collaboration with the owner, contractor, and other parties.

**Initial Decision Maker.** Typically the architect has had sole authority to render decisions on claims. However, AIA Document A201-2007, General Conditions of the Contract for Construction, Section 15.2, identifies the "Initial Decision Maker" as the person identified in the agreement with the authority to render initial decisions on claims. Prior to the 2007 document revisions the architect performed this duty.

In the 2007 documents, the architect is the Initial Decision Maker by default unless the owner and contractor designate another person to serve in that capacity. While some may view this change as an abdication of authority by the architect, many think that losing such authority also decreases risk.

**Certification of contractor payments.** An exclusive duty of the architect that typically survives the owner-architect contract negotiation is the architect's authority to certify the contractor's applications for payment. This certification is required for the owner to make payment to the contractor. Although the architect's certification is based on "the best of the Architect's knowledge, information, and belief," it is nevertheless an area of risk that the architect should not take lightly. This certification need not be based on detailed inspections but it is necessary to show diligence in gathering the information upon which the opinions certified are based.

**Substantial completion.** The date or dates of substantial completion are yet another certification that the architect is typically required to provide. Substantial completion is defined in AIA Document G704-2000, Certificate of Substantial Completion:

> Substantial Completion is the stage in the progress of the Work when the Work or designated portion is sufficiently complete in accordance with the Contract Documents so that the Owner can occupy or utilize the Work for its intended use.

This certification has significant legal and financial implications because it:

- Determines if the contractor has met its contract obligation
- Triggers payment of the contract balance to the contractor
- Sets the time limit for the contractor to complete or correct the work
- Sets out the responsibilities for security, maintenance, heat, utilities, damage to the work, and insurance
- Initiates the start of warranties for completed work
- Determines the start of legal statutes in most states

Although the architect typically has sole authority for determining this date, pressures are frequently brought to bear by the owner and contractor, for proprietary reasons, to influence the date. Therefore, the issuance of this document, like all other architect certifications, should not be taken lightly, and the information on which it is based should be diligently gathered and documented.

As a caution, AIA Document G704-2000 indicates that the warranties for the work indicated on the punch list "will be the date of issuance of the final Certificate for Payment or the date of final payment," unless otherwise agreed to in writing. To avoid confusion, it is suggested that you line out one of these milestones when you issue the certification. Also, the date of issuance and the date of substantial completion are the same on this form. Since these two activities seldom, if ever, occur on the same day, it is suggested that you add above the architect's signature line, "The date of Substantial Completion is____." The "date of issuance" on the signature line will remain as the issue date.

**Final completion.** The act of determining the date of final completion is also left to the architect. However, in this instance, no certificate is issued for a very specific reason. If the architect were to certify final completion of the project, this act could be viewed as a representation that the architect had determined that the work was 100 percent complete and in 100 percent conformance with the contract documents, a responsibility that is rightfully left solely to the contractor who put the work in place and warrants the work to be in compliance with the contract documents. To avoid such a representation, the architect administers final completion as stipulated in Article 9.10.1 of AIA documents A201-2007 and A201-1997:

> Upon receipt of the Contractor's written notice that the Work is ready for final inspection and acceptance and upon receipt of a final Application for Payment, the Architect will promptly make such inspection and, when the Architect finds the Work acceptable under the Contract Documents and the Contract fully performed, the Architect will promptly issue a final Certificate for Payment . . .

The final certificate for payment essentially becomes the document that establishes the date of the contractor's completion of the work. The AIA documents do not include a certificate of final completion, and the architect is cautioned not to issue such a document. If this action is requested by the owner, consult your insurance agent and your legal counsel.

**Performance of the owner and contractor.** Both the owner-architect agreements and the general conditions empower and obligate the architect to render decisions regarding the performance of the owner and the contractor under the contract. The architect is required to be impartial when rendering such decisions, and generally should not be found liable for these decisions as long as they are rendered in good faith. B101-2007, Article 3.6.2.3, states:

> The Architect shall interpret and decide matters concerning performance. . .on written request of either the Owner or Contractor.

A201-2007, Article 4.2.12, and B101-2007, Article 3.6.2.4, and A201-1997, Article 4.2.12, with similar language state:

> . . . the Architect will endeavor to secure faithful performance by both Owner and Contractor, will not show partiality to either and will not be liable for results of interpretations or decisions rendered in good faith.

## The architect's absence of authority

> It would serve no purpose for the men to see this weakness in me, even this most human of weaknesses.
>
> —Captain Jack Aubrey

There are circumstances and practices within the construction process wherein the architect has, or should have, no authority. This occurs when issues involve work or actions totally within the contractual responsibility of other parties. Examples include means and methods of construction, an agreement to accept defective or nonconforming work, or a decision to stop the work.

**Means, methods, and safety precautions.** Means and methods of construction are the tools that are required of the contractor to execute its unique plan for procuring and placing the work. The architect should not have, and is not contractually granted, the authority to decide the means and methods of construction.

AIA Document B101-2007, Article 3.6.1.2, states:

> The Architect shall not have control over, charge of, or responsibility for, the construction means, methods, techniques, sequences or procedures, or for safety precautions and programs in connection with the Work . . .

The 1997 AIA owner-architect agreements contained similar language.

The contractor's plan and responsibilities for procuring and placing the work is addressed in the article "Drawing the Line" in Chapter 4.

**Construction schedule.** The architect is not responsible for preparing or managing the construction schedule, as is stated in A201-2007, Article 3.10, and A201-1997, with similar language:

> The Contractor . . . shall prepare and submit for the Owner's and Architect's information a Contractor's construction schedule for the Work.

The architect may review and make use of the information contained in the construction schedule, but the architect is not responsible for preparing, approving, or confirming use of the schedule. The architect is also not responsible for planning the procurement and placement of the work to accommodate the contractor's schedule, all of which fall within the contractor's work plan.

**Acceptance of nonconforming work.** The architect cannot accept non-conforming work. The architect may or may not present recommendations or opinions about nonconforming work, but only the owner has the contracted right to accept nonconforming work.

**Stopping the work.** Only the contractor and the owner can stop the work process. The architect has no authority to stop the work, and there is no reference to stopping the work in the AIA contracts or general conditions.

## Commanding vs. consulting

> Run out the guns, run up the colours!
>
> —Captain Jack Aubrey

While the architect is typically empowered to make many decisions, these privileges stop far short of placing the architect in overriding command of a project. Captain Aubrey is not alive and well when it comes to practical behavior by the average architect. The architect's primary "authority," save for a few specific exceptions, is an intangible one of leadership toward compromise. Even in the few circumstances where the architect is the only party empowered to act, consideration of the opinions and desires of others is often an important and unavoidable priority.

For the most part, when "decisions" are required, the architect is not necessarily the "commander" but rather the "consultant." A consultant advises and recommends but seldom actually "decides." However, the architect is given the authority to reject nonconforming work in the AIA documents.

Owners who do not have expertise in design and construction may enter into a project with expectations of the architect's performance that unrealistically exceed what an architect actually is or should be empowered to do. It is in this circumstance that it is most important for the architect to know the difference between commanding and consulting. Enlightening the owner of the differences between the two can make the difference between a successful experience and a failure. Helping the owner to make the decisions that they rightfully should make, or providing them with information or advice they may need to arrive at their decisions, is simply good project management.

# Master and Commander, Part 2

Execution of the architect's authority falls into three categories: making decisions, giving recommendations (shared responsibility with owners and/or contractors), and leaving the responsibility entirely to others. This article—in two parts—examines some of the primary areas of the architect's authority relative to decisions and recommendations. Part 1 addressed when it is appropriate to act as master and commander and take control, and when it is appropriate to leave decisions to those who hold that contractual responsibility. Now, in Part 2, we will tackle when to act as consultant and only give recommendations. This is an all-important issue of the professional standard of care, which is what defines professional responsibility, as well as how the perception of others can influence required actions.

> We must survive this day, we must get about it gentlemen!
>
> —Captain Jack Aubrey

## Shared with the owner

The architect shares a key element of the design process with the owner.

**Design phase completion.** Although the architect has some authority for monitoring and maintaining the aesthetic design during construction, that authority is not absolute and is very limited in earlier phases. During both the schematic-design and design-development phases of the architect's services, the architect is not entitled to proceed to the next phase until the owner has approved the designs proposed by the architect. B101-2007, in several locations states:

> ...the Architect shall prepare...documents for the Owner's approval...

And:

> Based on the Owner's approval...and on the Owner's authorization of (Schematic Design or Design Development Documents) ... and any adjustments ... authorized by the Owner in the program, schedule or construction budget ...

This language makes it clear that the owner is to play a major role in deciding the design of the project, albeit normally based upon the recommendations and proposed designs prepared by the architect.

## Shared with the contractor

**Submittal schedule.** In accordance with A201-2007, Section 3.10.2, and A201-1997, with similar language, the contractor is required to submit a Submittal schedule for the architect's approval. The contractor is representing that this is the sequence and timing in which it intends to submit its submittals, but the architect must determine if that proposed process is consistent with reasonable operations. For example, if the wood doors, hollow metal frames, and hardware are not submitted concurrently, you may have to wait until you have all three to conduct an effective review. With maximum review time requirements often included in your services agreement, this wait could cause a failure to meet those requirements, and it could result in a claim.

**Submittal review.** Embedded in the process of most modern construction projects is the mistaken belief that only the architect is responsible for submittal review. As we explain in Chapter 4, "Drawing the Line," nothing could be further from the truth. The architect's role in submittal review is decisively subordinate to the role of the contractor and should commence only after the contractor has completed a thorough review of the submittals. Thus, the architect shares the responsibility and authority for submittal review with the contractor. This shared responsibility is made abundantly clear by A201–2007, Article 3.12.4, which states:

> Shop Drawings, Product Data, Samples and similar submittals are not Contract Documents. Their purpose is to demonstrate **the way by which the contractor proposes to conform** to the information given and the design concept expressed in the Contract Documents . . .

A201-1997, Article 3.12.6, contains similar language:

In other words, shop drawings, product data, samples, and similar submittals are the manifestation of the contractor's plan for what building systems and materials it proposes to procure, and how it proposes to incorporate those systems and materials into the work.

A201–2007, Article 3.12.6, and A201-1997, with similar language further clarify the contractor's responsibility for *reviewing and approving* submittals:

> By **submitting** Shop Drawings, Product Data, Samples and similar submittals, **the Contractor represents** to the Owner and Architect that the Contractor has (1) reviewed and approved them, (2) determined and verified materials, field measurements and field construction criteria related thereto, or will do so and (3) checked and coordinated the information contained within such submittals with the requirements of the Work and of the Contract Documents. (Note that the 1997 documents required the contractor to stamp and sign each submittal.)

As a caution, if you work with a contractor who consistently submits unmarked and thus clearly unchecked submittals, then you may consider placing the owner on notice that the contractor does not appear to be honoring its obligation to review, coordinate, and approve submittals. Telltale signs are submittals with only the contractor's approval stamp and signature and no other marks or comments. This could be true especially if you are encountering a large number of apparent discrepancies in the submittals.

**Rejection of nonconforming work.** An important requirement of the architect during the construction phase is the determination of work conformance to the contract documents and the subsequent rejection of nonconforming work of which the architect becomes aware. Likewise, the contractor, whose contract with the owner requires strict conformance to the contract documents, is accordingly required to reject any work that does not conform.

It follows that the contractor has a duty to determine, during its detailed review and coordination of submittals and its inspection of the work, if conformance is being met and to reject any proposed work that does not conform to the contract documents. An issue apparently misunderstood in many contractor submittals is that the architect may rightfully assume that the contractor's submittals represent proposed work that the contractor has determined will conform to the design concept expressed in the contract documents.

## Shared with the owner and contractor

**Project quality.** Although the architect is required in A201-2007, Article 4.2.2, and A201-1997, with similar language, to determine:

> . . . in general if the Work observed is being performed in a manner indicating that the Work, when fully completed, will be in accordance with the Contract Documents.

In so doing, the architect must determine "in general" if the quality of the work falls to a level that would prevent it from conforming to the contract documents. Although the owner may decide to accept a quality that does not conform to the documents, the owner has the privilege of accepting what the architect may determine to be "owner-accepted nonconforming work."

The contractor, on the other hand, has a duty and guarantees to provide quality work. In A201-2007, Article 3.5, Warranty, and A201-1997, with similar language:

> The Contractor warrants to the Owner and Architect that materials and equipment furnished under the Contract will be of good quality and new . . . **and will be free from defects . . .**

The words "of good quality" are a contracted assurance that the work will be of a quality that does not contain defects or deficiencies not inherent in the materials and systems purchased and installed in the work.

The bottom line is that, although the architect reports nonconforming work to the owner, the contractor may produce poor-quality work that the owner may choose to accept for cost benefit reasons or to expedite the project. If this should happen, the architect should first determine if the work meets the intent of the contract documents and, if not, qualify it in the certificate of substantial completion as "owner-accepted nonconforming work."

One final caution about changes in the work is necessary. In an effort to move the project along and be a team player, architects sometimes agree to a field modification or a "work around" proposed by a contractor. They agree that the work should proceed accordingly. Caution must be taken that the change, although minor, does not ultimately affect the contract sum or time, for, if it does, the architect will have exceeded or may appear to have exceeded, his or her authority. For this reason, even minor changes should be well documented, and all such documentation should contain the caveat that "the contractor shall not proceed with this work if it results in a change in contract sum or time unless first approved by the owner." Both the Architect's Supplemental Instruction (ASI) and the Request for Information (RFI) documents contain this provision.

**Changes in the work.** The scope of the contractor's work is expressed in the contract documents, and A201–2007, and A201-1997 states in Article 1.1.1 that the scope can only be changed with:

> . . .(1) a written amendment to the Contract signed by both parties, (2) a Change Order, (3) a Construction Change Directive or (4) a written order for a minor change in the Work issued by the Architect.

The architect can order minor changes in the work that do not affect the contract sum or time as allowed in A201-2007, Article 7.4, with similar language in A201-1997:

> The Architect has authority to order minor changes in the Work not involving an adjustment in Contract Sum or extension of the Contract Time and not inconsistent with the intent of the Contract Documents.

This can be accomplished through AIA Document G710-1992, Architect's Supplemental Instructions. In this case, the architect can change details and design configurations as long as the contract sum and time is not affected. This is somewhat idealistic because these days contractors tend to claim additional cost and/or time on RFIs and ASIs with most changes.

Generally, when change orders are executed, the owner decides ultimate approval, but the architect indicates approval as well. The architect's approval is to indicate knowledge and acceptance of the change. The architect's signature does not determine if the change is to be approved, but the architect has the authority to reject the change by not signing the change order document. Such an action would be taken if the change appears not to be valid. When this situation occurs and pressures are brought to bear, some architects have a tendency to acquiesce and sign the document. This can lead to problems later if the owner should decide that the change was caused by an error or omission in the architect's documents or if they subsequently come to believe that the change order pricing was excessive.

As a final note, to clarify the architect's authority in approving changes, the importance of managing scope changes is addressed in the AIA 2004 Code of Ethics and Professional Conduct, wherein it is stated:

> Rule 3.103: Members shall not materially alter the scope or objectives of a project without the client's consent.

The architect's authority notwithstanding, it is worthy of note that the owner also has authority to make changes without the consent or acknowledgement of the architect.

## Conclusion

> Discipline will count just as much as courage. True discipline goes to the board!
>
> —Captain Jack Aubrey

Captain "Lucky" Jack Aubrey was a person of conviction. He knew his rights and his duties to the king, but he knew his limitations as well. He sailed the HMS *Surprise* successfully and to the benefit of his country by knowing and acting on those parameters. Captain Aubrey wasn't "Lucky" at all. He was a sailor's sailor, a master tactician, courageous, and brutally efficient with both cannon and sword.

Within our contracted services, we are sometimes master and commander, but we are also sometimes a consultant who will only advise and recommend. We will only be able to tell the difference between the two and act appropriately if we know our documents and our duties.

The activities over which we do have authority carry high risks. Owners depend on us to determine work conformance, certify payments, and determine project completion. Contractors strive to conform to the design concept as they develop their Plan for the Work. They depend on our judicious and timely actions, but we must know our power and our limits of authority. We must be aware of when we are master and commander and when we are merely a consultant. The ability to differentiate between the two, as Captain Aubrey might attest, will influence the success of our efforts.

Meanwhile, as you approach your projects and call your crew to quarters, and as you set sail on your next endeavor, we will kindly remind you to be careful, because the *Surprise* may be out there.

# Top Gun: Targeting and Resolving Problematic Issues

We believe that targeting and resolving problematic issues is perhaps the single most important aspect of effective project management. We all have problems, and we have only so many hours in the day to resolve them. We have learned from and taught many good project managers, and we have observed that truly great managers who rise above their peers are ones who identify, engage, and solve problems quickly, and on the first pass. The best project managers tend to be a little paranoid, because they are always on the lookout for the problems that will likely arise. That's a roger, team leader, bogeys at twelve o'clock.

Summary: Anyone established in project management has at some time encountered a problem that seemingly would not go away. After multiple meetings, discussions, and attempted resolutions, the problem crept back into the project meeting and back onto the action items list, consuming valuable time and causing uncomfortable feelings to linger. This problem apparently had not been "closed" in the initial resolution attempt. A vital accomplishment of project management is solving a problem only one time. The ability to pursue and close out a problem so that it does not arise again allows the project manager to move on to the next issue with reliance that past resolutions will not be revisited. Like the fighter pilot, who must hone skills for neutralizing enemy aggressors in dogfights to allow the primary mission to succeed, the project manager must learn to identify, lock on, and resolve problem issues on the first pass so that the business of project management and contract administration can continue with efficiency and effectiveness.

Solving problems is a skill that is not always easily achieved, but when it is mastered, the manager moves to a higher level. In this article, we will explore the challenges of problem resolution in project management and the tendency for issues to reappear when they have been inadequately processed. Suggestions will be offered for identifying problems early, taking effective steps for achieving resolution, closing out the conflict once and for all, and moving on to the next challenge.

The movie *Top Gun* is an excellent example of the importance of neutralizing problems on the first attempt. As Tom Cruise's character, Lt. Pete Mitchell, struggles with the challenges of overcoming the enemy in a dogfight, we are reminded that the same parameters can determine our success and survival on a project. A manager who can perfect skills at problem resolution can increase productivity and effectiveness and become a "Top Gun" in his or her project management and construction administration efforts.

> Roger, that's your bogey.
>
> —Ship's Radio Officer

## Zeroing in on problems

To solve a problem, you must first be able to identify it. Like a fighter pilot with an RIO, or Radio Intercept Officer, who looks ahead with electronics to detect bogeys, or threatening aircraft, the project manager can also look ahead to detect problems at the time they first arise. Effective job monitoring requires proactive involvement. Conducting and/or attending project meetings, remaining in the communications flow, and remaining in touch with project issues can be effective in staying on top of the action. It is time-consuming to be in the e-mail path of project communications, but it will give you a "heads up" on problematic issues as they arise.

Frequent contact with the owner and contractor is also advisable for staying on top of the issues. When an owner is troubled or unhappy, or a contractor is faced with a problem they cannot or will not resolve, you should be the first one to know it so that you can take appropriate action.

For example:

- Attend construction meetings and pay careful attention to the contractor's expressed concerns about cost, schedule, or your construction documents.

- Read construction meeting minutes carefully if you are not preparing them. Follow up on any problem areas reported.
- In concert with the construction meetings, ask the contractor if he or she has any areas of concern.
- Call the owner regularly, no less frequently than every two weeks during construction. Ask explicitly if the owner has any concerns.

## Know your bogeys

Issues we consider "problems" can take many forms. Likewise, problems can be caused by any of the parties involved in the design and construction of a project. A problem usually affects cost or time, and resolution often requires the input of more than one party. Examples of "bogeys," or problems requiring resolution, include the following.

**Bogey 1.** The contractor has submitted RFI no. 123 as follows: The window frames for the floor-to-floor penthouse windows have arrived on site and are 4 inches too short to fit in the floor-to-floor opening. The windows were fabricated to the architect's dimension markups on the returned and approved shop drawings. Please advise how to resolve this conflict.

**Bogey 2.** The area of the warehouse roof north of building expansion joint no. 3 has no roof drains or overflow drains. The roof expansion joint cover prevents drainage to the roof drains south of the joint. Please advise how to resolve this conflict.

**Bogey 3.** The foundation subcontractor has located all of the piers in the classroom wing 1 foot-4 inches too far to the north. Is it acceptable for the columns bearing on these piers to be installed off-center?

With these examples, some of which may require complex answers and corresponding research, as a context, we will look at ways to target and intercept problems while a project is under construction.

> Ice, that bogey is behind you, I'm maneuvering for a shot!
> —Fighter Pilot "Maverick" (Tom Cruise)

## Engage your targets

When a problem arises, it usually will not resolve itself and just go away. For a project manager to become an effective leader in problem solving, the tendency to ignore problems when they first arise must be overcome. We've written many times that "Bad news does not get better with age." The project manager or construction administrator must therefore learn to treat emerging problem issues with a sense of neutrality, harboring no fear about how the problem may affect him or her, or the firm. Like the fighter pilot, reluctance in engaging problems is not a viable option for the project manager. The primary objective is to move in and understand the problem in all respects to help facilitate a solution.

## Who is the target?

A tendency fundamental to the human experience is to ponder who is at fault before buying into the process of solving a problem. Consequently, many managers adopt a wait-and-see attitude about problems, looking to find fault before getting involved, lest some other party mistake active involvement as an expression of responsibility. Indeed, in the construction business today, it seems that any issue that arises on a job site tends to be automatically logged as the fault of the architect. Causes listed in open items logs and change order requests are often noted as "Drawing Error," "Non-constructible Design," or "Lack of Coordination." Regardless of whose fault a problem issue may be, a rapid and fearless response by the architect will not lessen one's position if a fight subsequently ensues. Moreover, it will demonstrate that the architect is not only service oriented but has the owner's interests at heart.

> Ten minutes? . . . This thing will be over in two minutes; get on it!
>
> —Flight Operations Officer, "Stinger"

## Act quickly

When a problem arises, the efficiency of resolution is directly proportionate to the speed of your reaction. Usually, the faster you respond to the issue, the more easily it can be resolved. To respond quickly, you and your attitude must be ready and you must know the day-to-day issues as stated above. Like the dogfight maneuvers taught at the Navy's Fighter Weapons School, Top Gun, it may be helpful to have a plan of action established with your project team to take the necessary steps for mitigation and resolution. It is common for owners to be confused and not understand conflicting issues as they arise. Quick action to assist in understanding the scope and impact of a problem can put clients at ease and facilitate a less complicated resolution. Be aware, however, that you should have your research well advanced and have as much relevant information as possible at hand when you report on the status. Misinformation and misunderstanding can do more harm than good and make a small problem into a larger one.

> If I reversed on a hard cross, I could immediately go to guns on him.
>
> —Maverick

## Have a "go-to" plan of action

A quick-response plan should contain complete information for problem resolution. Typical steps in the problem resolution process could include:

- Advising your project team that a problem issue has arisen
- Contacting the contractor and requesting all available information
- Gathering data (visit the site if appropriate)
- Notifying the owner with an update as soon as you have evaluated the problem

- Documenting conditions present at the site, requesting electronic images
- Making a preliminary estimate of project impact (design, cost, schedule)
- Performing appropriate research
- Making a preliminary determination of resolution options
- Obtaining pricing from GC, if appropriate
- Convening a conference call or meeting to review and decide actions
- Obtaining appropriate owner decisions
- Documenting decisions
- Helping facilitate implementation of the desired action (drawings, specs, site visits).

As the fighter pilot makes a "hop" into potentially threatening territory while tracking on their computer screens and heads-up displays, likewise the project manager must be attuned to project problems and be ready to respond with a plan of action capable of neutralizing the problems.

> It takes a lot more than just fancy flying.
> —Russian MiG Expert, "Charlie" (Kelly McGillis)

## Make your actions count

When problems arise, they are seldom anticipated, especially in the contractor's schedule. Many problems can cause more damage in delay than in cost of replacement or remediation. Accordingly, it is important that all actions taken be as appropriate and efficient as possible to minimize time and effort.

For example, when a problem arises, identify all of the relevant parties and include them in communications. The omission of a critical team member can cause delay and the need to repeat actions or resend information. Also, make sure that you have as much information as possible to begin your review of potential remedial actions. An erroneous assumption or incomplete data can stall out well-intended efforts. Resolutions discussed among the parties typically involve conference calls or meetings, and you should be certain that your research and information gathering is as complete as time and circumstances allow before the assembly is convened. Unanswered questions and incomplete data can end the discussions without conclusion and require subsequent discussions to be scheduled.

> There are no points for second place.
> —Instructor Pilot, "Viper" (Tom Skerritt)

## Knock it out the first time

As in a dogfight at 10,000 feet with limited rockets and response measures, for the project manager the essence of success is the ability to knock out the bogey on the first pass. In order to accomplish this, there are several conditions that must be in place. These conditions include:

- All relevant parties must be involved.
- All participants must desire resolution.
- Each representative must have decision-making authority.
- Unified team action must be taken.

Anything less can result in another visit to the meeting table and a protracted dispute interval. If an involved party is not a part of the resolution, all damages may not be recovered, or worse, the issue could be challenged in a separate dispute or claim later on.

> I'm moving in. I've got the shot.
>
> —Maverick

## Take decisive action

There may be occasions when involved parties do not elect to act on a resolution. This is more likely to occur when a participant fears they may have to bear some or all of the cost. In these instances it may be necessary to force a resolution by taking decisive action. If the issue involves nonconforming work, it may be necessary to withhold certification of payment for the affected work or even reject it as allowed in AIA Document A201, General Conditions of the Contract for Construction. If the contractor refuses to correct or complete the work, it may be appropriate to recommend that the owner pursue correction of the work with other forces. Nonetheless, the old adage that "a good solution today is better than a perfect solution tomorrow" generally applies when construction is in full swing, significant money is being spent on construction operations each day, and general conditions expenses are accumulating.

Frequently an owner will refuse to acknowledge responsibility for betterment costs involved in resolving problem issues. Betterment, although a fairly simple concept, is broadly misunderstood in the industry. Many owners do not understand that they are not entitled to free work or materials, although an error or omission may have been committed. We address errors and omissions and betterment in "A Loss Cause" and "A Loss Cause Too" in Chapter 4. These articles may be helpful in explaining these realities to your client.

An overall strategy should be to take the necessary action to minimize negative impact on the project. Ideally, all parties will recognize the value of a quick resolution, and they should be willing to participate in timely mitigation activities. If it appears that progress may be stalling because of some participant's fear of costs or fault, it may be time to start asking what it will take to get the resolution in motion. To address the owner's concerns, it may require asking the question, "What will it take to make you comfortable with the solution—or, to make you feel whole?" For the contractor, it may involve discussions on the merits of avoiding protracted disputes that instill lingering negative memories.

> Son, your ego is writing checks that your body can't cash.
>
> —Stinger

## Don't let your mouth overload your assets

It is important to remember that problems often involve every player in some way. One should be cautious not to assume that everyone is wrong except you, or conversely to assume, as some architects feel compelled, that everyone is right except you. A part of your research should include introspection and a critical review of your own involvement. It is better to know your vulnerabilities and your strengths up front rather than to gain awareness after the bullets have passed through your fuselage. Unlike in the movie, there is no ejection seat to extract you from the fray and parachute you safely to the ground. Though you must not automatically make such an assumption, should you turn out to be the bogey in the fight, you must evaluate your position and take appropriate remedial action. You must decide what the value of the encounter is worth. A repeat client can have greater influence on your decision to fight or give in. But as we have cautioned in the past, don't forget that an admission of wrongdoing can negatively affect your insurance coverage.

Problem resolution actions should conform to the requirements of your professional liability insurance policy. This may be a good time to call in support from your wing man (your insurance agent) and an approved panel counsel. They can guide you appropriately in actions involving admissions of fault or settlement and damage contribution.

The above notwithstanding, there is always the overriding issue of the future client relationship being more valuable than the immediate penalty, whether the penalty is fair or not. Right, wrong, or noble, conciliation may be the logical path. Conversely, if the premium is too great, staying with the dogfight to the finish may be your only viable option.

> You need to be doing it better and cleaner than the other guy.
>
> —Stinger

## Document the resolution

Problem resolution cannot be effectively substantiated without adequate documentation, and it is better to have too much than too little. We note in "To Document or Not to Document" in Chapter 1 that we know of no record of a claim being caused by too much documentation.

Should you contribute money or services to the resolution of the problem, there is a good chance that your insurance provider will request a release and indemnity for the portion of the work that has been corrected. Even if the magnitude of the issue is relatively minor, a release signed by the owner instills a greater level of respect in them for your actions taken in resolving the issue. Your insurance agent and/or attorney can assist you in creating a release and indemnity document.

> It's just a walk in the park.
>
> —Maverick

## Close, and move on

The desired bottom line for problem resolution is to close out the issue once and for all on the first pass. Unless the fighter pilot sees black smoke and parachutes or the red engine glow of the bogey "bugging out," he or she is a candidate for a return encounter. A Top Gun is a project manager or a construction administrator who gathers the information, does the research, brings the concerned parties together, makes an informed decision, and helps facilitate a decisive resolution to the issue once and for all.

The problem-resolution process is an integral part of the construction phase, and although a manager may solve one issue, it is reasonable to expect that another may soon follow. Problems that linger take away valuable time for resolving subsequent challenges, and, accordingly, the ability to close on problems and move on to future challenges cannot be overemphasized.

## Resolution requires affirmation

A necessary ingredient for resolution is that all participants must desire that the issue be finalized and put away. Should you approach an issue where one or more of the opposing participants do not wish to reach a resolution, efforts for settlement will likely be futile. Accordingly, it is necessary to be sure that all participants are empowered to make approved decisions for set-tlement when pursuing resolution.

The bottom line is that if one or more of your opposing parties do not wish to resolve the issue at hand, the chance of resolution is diminished. In fact, if only one of the participating parties refuses to pursue a solution, the effort is condemned to failure. All engaged players must exhibit a desire to put the issue away, once and for all. Absent total buy-in from all involved, you may be destined to take your dogfight to a greater battle at the media-tion table or in the courtroom.

> Mustang, this is Voodoo 3, remaining MiGs are bugging out.
> —Radio Intercept Officer, "Merlin" (Tim Robbins)

## Be humble; be aware

The ability to effectively target, zero in, and close on a problem is a manage-ment proficiency that places the manager in an elite position. It is a skill set that is necessary for becoming the best of the best in proactive project management, a Top Gun. However, to achieve success, you must cultivate a neutral but fearless attitude, develop a plan of action, and make your actions count. You must be cautioned, however, that egotism and feelings of per-fection have no place in the process. Humility and self-awareness can be beneficial in helping others to relate and be aware of your position. The primary objective is to identify the issue, take decisive action, and resolve it on the first pass.

The final resolution should be well documented so that the record will be clear and memories consistent. When priorities differ, memories can deviate as well. When all has been resolved and recorded, the manager is free to move ahead and engage the next challenge. There is no more effective skill in project management than that of the proficient problem solver.

So as you check your e-mail and note the urgent message from the contractor advising you of the beam/ductwork conflict, and the owner's e-mail expressing concern over lighting costs exceeding allowances, while you are notifying your project team and initiating your quick-response plan, remember . . . be careful out there.

# Zen and the Art of Construction Administration, Part 1: How Discipline and Self-Control Can Improve Your Services

When we set out to write about construction administration, we wanted to address risk management issues during construction from the most advantageous viewpoint. Although there are many risk management tools and processes that can be applied during the construction phase, it really makes no difference how good your management skills and techniques are unless you know how to engage and deliver with them. Keying from fond memories of the 1970s *Kung Fu* TV series, we address risk management as if we are David Carradine on a Zen journey through the job site. Don't step on that nail, Grasshopper!

> We do not learn by experience, but by our capacity for experience.
> —Gautama Buddha, born 563 BC

Architects tend to approach construction administration with wariness and trepidation. Financial success for this phase of work is often challenging, and, at this point in the project, creative thoughts equate to money spent rather than fulfillment of design expressions. To make matters worse, almost all claims against design professionals arise during the construction phase, although the genesis of the claim may have occurred at a much earlier time.

As a result, many architects have come to view the construction phase as a time-consuming and unrewarding negotiated service. Many prefer to practice passive construction contract administration and act only when requested to do so. In fact, not too many years ago, insurance providers recommended that the designer omit this phase of services from their contract entirely, presuming that no interaction with the builders would present the architect as a smaller target and thus be the safer recourse. This proved to be a bad idea because it did nothing to reduce claims. Moreover, it denied the architect the opportunity to make informative clarifications that could possibly reduce or avoid the claim altogether.

However, since our exposure to claims is greatest during this phase of work, there is no feasible alternative other than to confront construction administration rather than avoid it. If we want a fair chance at managing our risks, we must be involved proactively during construction phase activities to mitigate problematic issues that arise and develop an acceptable comfort level for work conformance and fulfill our contractual requirements. A reluctant spirit has no place in our construction administration mindset as problems and conflicts typically do not get better with age.

However, the construction phase can indeed be an unpleasant experience when our documents or services are being challenged and our mistakes publicized. It is easy to assume a defensive position with a "we versus they" attitude. Before we know it, we have subscribed to a bunker mentality where we make efforts to protect ourselves with documentation while we take shots at the perceived offenders, and the paper war begins.

Confrontation is required in situations where we must defend ourselves and rebut accusations, but we must be mindful that such confrontation need not be hostile or overly consuming. Valuable time and energy can be wasted in defensive documentation and trading accusations and insults.

It will be more beneficial if we discipline ourselves to approach construction administration with a peaceful attitude, somewhat like the followers of the Zen school. Much can be accomplished if we remain calm, study and develop responses to the threatening dangers, and become intuitive in our risk management actions and behavior. Zen, which originated in India and predates Buddhism, is a discipline for attaining awareness through meditation.

We can increase our effectiveness by developing a self-discipline reminiscent of David Carradine's character, Kwai Chang Caine, in the 1970s TV series, *Kung Fu*, by coolly maintaining our emotions, carefully thinking things out, and acting with calm deliberation only after a reasonable recourse has been determined. Although it is a martial art, the highest level that can be reached in Shaolin Kung Fu is Zen.

This article is a lot about construction contract administration (CCA) attitudes and a little about the admirable discipline of Zen. CCA is a broad topic that could fill many volumes, but these observations will be limited to the effectiveness that can be developed through our approach to CCA, along with embracing it as the professional service that it is. In the mix of these topics, we will address and offer suggestions for more effective management and loss prevention while examining ways to assess calmly and seek control of threatening circumstances, all the while striving to maintain our sanity as well as our sanctity.

## Why me?

> Accept the anxieties and difficulties of this life.
>
> —Zen Master Kyong Ho

There is a tendency by some architects to ask, why me? CCA is not emphasized in many architecture schools. Anyway, the contractors are the ones who are supposed to know how to build the building. We didn't spend all that time in school to wear work boots and act like contractors; we studied to be architects!

It is true that the technical aspects of our practice are not as celebrated in architecture school as is design. Frank Lloyd Wright and Ayn Rand's character Howard Roark in *The Fountainhead* exude the image of what many think an architect is supposed to be. Technical skills simply do not hold the glamour of an artiste creating iconic designs. But the reality is that architects are judged in the courts more on technical ability, and claims against architects are primarily aimed at their products of service, their technical documents, or their actions. Since almost all claims arise during the construction phase and are usually focused on the documents, architects must embrace and interact with this part of the work.

To understand fully why architects need to practice proactive construction administration, a review of AIA Document A201-2007 and A201-1997, General Conditions of the Contract for Construction, may help. Architects are required in Section 4.2.2 to visit the site and:

> . . . determine in general if the Work observed is being performed in a manner indicating that the Work, when fully completed, will be in accordance with the Contract Documents.

Additionally, Section 4.2.9, states:

> The Architect will conduct inspections to determine the date or dates of Substantial Completion and the date of final completion . . .

CCA activities essentially become governed by the desired final result, as will be certified by the architect in AIA document G704-2000, Certificate of Substantial Completion. This certificate is a document that carries significant legal implications. The gravity of this inspection and certification is evidenced by the lead-off language in the certificate:

> The Work performed under this Contract has been reviewed and found, to the Architect's best knowledge, information and belief, to be substantially complete.

The certificate then goes on to require that the architect attach a list of any incomplete or defective work, along with a cost estimate to correct the incomplete or defective work. Though often overlooked as a prior accord, this list should include any owner-accepted nonconforming work.

The certificate of substantial completion represents that you, in your capacity as the architect, have fulfilled your contractual responsibilities for determining substantial work conformance. If you certify substantial completion when it is not, or if you fail to qualify and list owner-accepted nonconforming work or any known defective work on the certificate, you could have problems down the road.

The question is sometimes argued as to whether architects should be responsible for defective work of which they are not aware. This topic is best discussed in the context of the standard of care to which the architect should have conformed. The standard of care may be evaluated by how difficult the information would have been to obtain.

## For example

Improperly installed brick ledge flashing is allowing water to leak into the second floor of a building, damaging the second floor and the floor below. Brick ledge flashing is typically concealed work, and some defective work could have been covered without having been directly observed by the architect. If the leaks are widespread, and the installation of the defective flashing occurred in a time frame spanning multiple visits to the site by the architect and was visible without using specialized climbing equipment, a claimant may argue that the architect had ample opportunity to observe the defective work and determine that it would present a future problem. On the other hand, if the leaks have occurred in a single area, the architect may represent that the condition is an isolated latent defect that they should not reasonably have been expected to observe and be aware of.

*The Architect's Handbook of Professional Practice*, 14th edition, contains a chapter entitled "Project Closeouts," which addresses important activities related to substantial completion. It includes a project closeout checklist and emphasizes the need to list any nonconforming work as an exception to the certification. All projects incorporate some measure of nonconforming work, and unless significant conditions are noted, the certificate could be looked upon as a representation that nothing significant is wrong.

To enable the architect to fulfill the conformance determination, the architect is empowered by the owner-architect agreements to perform certain duties and responsibilities. For example, AIA Document B101-2007, Standard Form of Agreement Between Owner and Architect, includes:

> — § 3.6.2.1 ... shall keep the Owner reasonably informed about the progress and quality of the portion of the Work completed, and report to the Owner (1) known deviations from the Contract Documents ...
> — § 3.6.2.2 ... has the authority to reject Work that does not conform to the Contract Documents.
> — § 3.6.6.1 ... conduct inspections to determine the date or dates of Substantial Completion and the date of final completion ...

Some of these contractual requirements cannot be effectively executed from the architect's office. Even with today's Web cams, tablet PCs, and PDAs, the architect will go to the job site at appropriate intervals and observe the work in progress. If you decide to forgo visiting the site and observing the work, and stay in your office, then you will be unable to know if the project, in general, is in accordance with the contract documents or when it is substantially complete, and you may be blamed for problems that you could have resolved or avoided had you physically been there.

## Why you?

> Catch not the shadow and lose the substance.
>
> —Korean proverb

Some architects may desire to just hire someone to do CCA or perhaps assign it to a team member who is not as busy, even a junior staffer. If you are the architect with responsibility for the project, it is likely that if anything really serious comes up, it will make its way to your desk anyway.

There are some very legitimate reasons why it should be you or an adequately qualified other person performing construction administration. If you are senior enough to have signed the documents, it could be your license on the line. If you are high enough up in the company, it could be your money on the line. If you were involved with the creation of the design, it could be your reputation on the line. In today's market, it likely will not work out if we do as Frank Lloyd Wright suggested and advise the client to plant vines if there is a mistake with the building. Today, if there is a serious problem, you and your insurance policy will surely be invited to the dance.

## Proactive involvement

> Technical knowledge is not enough. One must transcend techniques so that the art becomes an artless art, growing out of the unconscious.
>
> —Daisetsu Suzuki

So dust off that hard hat and check to be sure that you have your steel-toed boots, your protective goggles, and your orange safety vest. Women should be mindful that most construction sites prohibit skirts and heels, so do be safety conscious and follow the contractor's OSHA safety requirements. You may also want to grab a tape recorder, a steel measuring tape, a flashlight, and a mirror for observing hard-to-get-to places.

You should be ready now to set up and administer the construction phase of your project. To brush up on required construction phase activities, take a look at *The Emerging Professional's Companion,* Chapter 12, "Construction Phase, Office," and Chapter 13, "Construction Phase, Site" at www.epcompanion.org. This reference material was jointly published by the AIA and NCARB to prepare interns for the Architect Registration Exam. It is also provided as a resource for in-house training of architectural services.

## Preparation

> The less effort, the faster and more powerful you will be.
>
> —Bruce Lee

It is necessary to be prepared to be effective. The following suggestions will assist you in organizing and maintaining your management effort to your best advantage. Documentation, communication, and responsive actions are dependent upon an organized, efficient CCA process.

**Use AIA documents.** AIA documents have been in existence for more than 100 years and represent the standard of practice in our profession and industry. They have been written with the specific goal of balancing the interests of all the parties and have been tested in the courts. An AIA form is available for all typically required activities during the construction phase.

**Organize your contract documents.** Get your contract documents in order. Print out a paper copy of the version of the drawings and specifications that have been issued to the contractor. Maintain a record set of document publications in your office to use for tracking changes and contract modifications. Remember, the contractor also must maintain a set on the job site, but you should keep a control copy in your office for your own records.

**Keep a journal.** During this complicated phase of work, many contemporaneous activities and actions occur. If you keep a journal with you as you go about your activities, you can record critical information immediately rather than relying on your memory at a later time. Maintaining a journal has been recommended by AIA documents for many years. *The Handbook of Architectural Practice,* published in 1920, the first edition of what is now *The Architect's Handbook of Professional Practice,* extensively addressed the use of a journal.

**Establish a filing protocol.** If your firm does not have a filing protocol, there is a suggested format in *The Architect's Handbook of Professional Practice,* 14th edition, in the chapter entitled, "Information Management." You should have an organized method for filing all project-related correspondence, both paper and electronic.

**Establish project procedures.** Project procedures during the construction phase are addressed in AIA Document A201-2007, General Conditions of the Contract for Construction. This information is amplified in Division 01 of MASTERSPEC. Review these documents thoroughly and discuss specific requirements in the preconstruction conference.

**Schedule project meetings, site visits, and key conferences.** It helps to publish a site visit schedule and go to the site on the same day of the week at the same time. The project team will adapt more easily and will usually be more responsive. You can always drop in unannounced, or by special invitation if you feel it necessary, but stick to the schedule for meetings and conferences if practicable.

# Zen and the Art of Construction Administration, Part 2

> In activity there should be calmness, and in calmness there should be activity.
>
> —Daisetsu Suzuki

If your preparation has been thorough, you can more effectively go about your administrative tasks. The actions that you take during the construction phase can greatly affect your level of risk and determine if the project will go smoothly. Here are some guidelines.

**Conduct conferences and project meetings.** The most significant planning event of the construction phase is the preconstruction conference. A suggested agenda is provided in *The Architect's Handbook of Professional Practice,* 14th edition, in the chapter, "Construction Phase Services." Send the agenda out in advance and conduct the meeting. The detailed meeting notes that are published from the meeting can serve as a "procedures manual" for the project. Conduct scheduled project meetings during the course of construction. Regular, structured meetings can facilitate the efficient exchange of communication and required documents.

**Contractor deliverables.** Enforce the submittal of contractor-provided documents and information as required in the contract documents. These items are addressed in the article "Drawing the Line: Why the Architect's Documents Cannot Be Used for Construction" in Chapter 4, and they are essential for the Contractor's Work Plan. They include the following items normally required by the contract documents:

- An acceptable submittal schedule
- Specified submittals—no more, no less
- Preinstallation conferences
- Coordination drawings
- Clarification sketches
- Mockups
- Contractor marked-up drawings
- Stored material backup on payment applications
- Construction schedule and updates

**Effective documentation.** The actions that you take on a project during construction may not help you if they are not adequately documented. Oral communications aren't worth the paper they're written on, and people sometimes suffer from selective amnesia when it is convenient. We have previously stated that we are not aware of any lawsuit that was ever successfully prosecuted against an architect for having prepared too much documentation. Documentation activities can include:

- Field observation reports
- Project meeting reports
- Document control log entries
- Written memoranda
- Entries in your journal
- Written response to any accusatory correspondence
- Transmittal letters with outgoing documents
- Received stamps on incoming documents
- Architect-generated RFIs sent to the contractor and tracked

Some architects may be unfamiliar with the process of the architect sending an RFI to the contractor. The RFI is a method of documenting a request for an answer to a question or for information. AIA form G728-2004, Request for Information, is available for this purpose. The architect can use RFIs to document a request for information such as the submittal schedule, meeting notes from preinstallation conferences, or submittals that are past due according to the submittal schedule.

**Maintain good relationships.** The way in which the architect and contractor interact during construction can be affected by the type of contract, previous work together, the owner's behavior, the contractor's business priorities, or the architect's attitude. But regardless of the issues, it is always advantageous to maintain an amicable relationship.

If the contract is hard bid, there is a greater likelihood that the contractor will more intensively scrutinize your document content than if it is a negotiated cost-plus contract. If you subcontract to the contractor in a contractor-led design-build scenario, your requirements for evaluating work conformance may be reduced, or may not be required.

The owner's behavior can greatly affect the way that the team interacts. One-time owners less familiar with the construction process sometimes introduce friction into the team relationship because their expectations are not realistic. Developers, on the other hand, who build repeatedly, have a greater understanding of the sometimes bumpy process, and their expectations are usually more reasonable.

The construction phase involves pressures induced by time and money, and administering the construction contract while maintaining your composure can be challenging. Always maintain a professional attitude. Try to look at problem issues from both sides. A calm approach when dealing with tense situations is advantageous.

When tense situations arise, you should endeavor to minimize emotions to the greatest extent possible. It has been suggested that when in a heated exchange where your counterpart is yelling or speaking loudly, you should respond in a low voice, forcing him or her to lower his or her voice to hear you. Effective project management goes well beyond merely conforming to the contract and meeting deadlines. Problems can be solved and decisions made much more easily and in less time when the project team interacts with respect and civility.

## Being there

> Put off for one day and 10 days will pass.
>
> —Korean proverb

The essence of proactive construction contract administration is being there. This involves being available to the owner and contractor, responding quickly to any issue or need, constantly communicating with team members, and running at the problems that arise. Remember that during construction, the owner's money is usually being spent at a high burn rate, and time spent addressing problems can affect the rate. Regardless of how good your design is or how pretty your drawings are, the owner will likely remember more about her or his unpleasant experiences during construction. We have always said that construction administration is the service that leaves the "last taste in the owner's mouth," and the positive effect that CA can have on repeat work and giving favorable references to future clients is simple math.

A good way to be available these days is to give out your cell phone number and carry a wireless communications device. If your clients know they can readily reach you at any time, you have established a link with them on a very personal level. If there is a problem on the project, you need to know about it as early as possible.

Most clients spend the construction phase worrying about time and money. It follows that if you do not want them to think that you are costing them money, you should respond as quickly as you reasonably can to all critical issues. It's a good idea to establish a protocol at the office so that, if you are unavailable, someone can cover for you and respond rapidly and appropriately. A quick-response program also includes the timely issuance of reports and other important project documents.

Constant communications means exactly that. Just because there are no emergencies is no reason not to touch base regularly. You may not have to worry about frequent communications with the contractor, because they will likely be calling you, but you should make a point to stay in close touch with the client. Remember that last taste?

If it is taking an extended amount of time to research a problem and develop a response, an occasional message to the client reporting your progress will put them at ease and demonstrate that you are working on the problem. Clients usually assume that no communications means inactivity and inaction.

## Problem seeking

> You must take care not to make mistakes. But when they happen, learn from them. Use your mistakes as a springboard into new areas of discovery; accidents can hold the key to innovation.
>
> —P. T. Sudo

Effective problem solving should go beyond the reactive resolution of problems as they arise. It should include a constant scrutiny of the contract documents and the work as it is being constructed. This should be a mindset more than a planned activity. It could involve such things as a follow-up visit to check on a problem issue to determine if all is going well, or a phone call to the contractor after a sensitive RFI has been answered to be sure that the response is understood.

It is helpful to develop habits that complement and support your problem-seeking activities. If you carry a recording device with you on the job site, you can give yourself prompts on site conditions and details to recheck when you get back to your office. You could add "potential challenges" to your regular project meeting agenda to invite early detection of problematic issues. Contractors who prepare an effective Plan for the Work, as required by their contract, will usually pinpoint challenges and complications well in advance.

Another preventive activity is to cross-check your projects. When there are multiple projects in an office, a problem in the documents encountered on one project may be systemic to the internal document development process. Some firms have construction administration departments where the CAs can compare notes and openly discuss issues. Firms that are not departmentalized can hold scheduled meetings to discuss document performance issues. The article "Your Grandfather's Working Drawings" in Chapter 6 addresses the inherent challenges in adapting CAD library details to fit unique project conditions.

Remember, time is money during the construction phase, and problems, if detected early enough, can often be resolved before related construction work is put in place. The problem-seeking mindset allows for more opportunities to discover and resolve issues within a more efficient time frame.

## Conclusion

> Zen is not some kind of excitement, but concentration on our usual everyday routine.
>
> —Shunryu Suzuki

Most young architects enter the job market generally unprepared for construction phase services, and most firms struggle with providing appropriate construction services with the goal of financially breaking even. Add to this challenge the task of avoiding a claim after the project is completed.

Let's face it: Construction administration is neither easy nor glamorous. We display photographs and renderings of our projects around our office to impress our clients, but we do not display change orders and field observation reports. The media will sometimes credit the building designer, but they don't seem as interested in the architect of record. It is not common to see a major box office star playing the part of a construction administrator, adorned with tape measure, mirror, and boots. Paul Newman's architect character Doug Roberts, in the movie *The Towering Inferno,* was represented to have weak construction administration skills as he discovered design and construction defects in the building during the fire.

Yet we must provide adequate services during construction if we wish to avoid claims, and we want the owner to have fond memories of our overall performance. We must stay on top of the game if we expect to survive the value analysis and substitution process and develop a reasonable comfort level for work conformance. We cannot afford to be passive and let things fall as they may.

The best recourse is to run at and embrace construction administration instead of avoiding it. The better we become at it, the more successful we will be in our practice. We must keep our eyes open and proactively administer construction phase services. Availability, quick responses, good documentation, and informed decisions will hopefully leave a good taste in the owner's mouth, thus bringing good references and repeat business.

Yet construction administration need not be tenuous and stressful. It is best to be calm and approach each challenge with cool professionalism. The young Caine in *Kung Fu* warned, "If one's words are not better than silence, one should keep silent." And don't point out blame too quickly, lest you find yourself staring at your own index finger. Attempt to develop an intuitive approach to issues and conditions, remaining sensitive to potential problems and the concerns of others. Don't be overly defensive, as it will cloud your understanding of and ability to resolve problems.

So now, Grasshopper, put on your hard hat, protective goggles, work boots, and safety vest, and as you go about your construction administration duties, remember, be careful out there.

# Chapter 4

## Essentials

## A Loss Cause: Drawing Discrepancies and Ensuing Damages

This is the first risk management article that we coauthored. We felt a pressing need to help architects not only understand the issue of errors and omissions but also understand how to talk to their clients about it. First published in *Texas Architect* magazine, the article broaches a number of topics that we address in more detail in other articles. Inherent discrepancies in drawings, impact damages versus betterment, and when drawing discrepancies should be compensable are among the topics addressed.

There is a growing tendency among owners and contractors to believe that all discrepancies, errors, and omissions committed by a design professional are actionable offenses. This belief persists whether or not the owner or contractor is actually damaged. Increasingly, owners and contractors pursue payment from the designer for project costs including added scope, or betterment, with the belief that the documents produced should be pristine and contain no discrepancies of any kind. The reality is that construction documents typically contain errors and omissions, and the missing and corrective information is developed during the construction process. This reality is emphasized in *The Architect's Handbook of Professional Practice*, 14th edition wherein it states, "The construction documents are not intended to be a complete set of instructions on how to construct a building."

Nevertheless, claims for errors and omissions are on the rise, and loss payouts are reaching new levels. Designers are being held responsible for a level of performance in their documents that is not only a higher standard than that required by AIA contracts but is a level that cannot be achieved under any reasonable definition of ordinary standard of care. There is no industry standard as to what constitutes a "complete" drawing because the content of construction drawings is substantially infused with subjectivity and professional judgment. Consequently, it is impossible to provide the "complete" drawings that many owners and contractors mistakenly expect. Unfortunately, completeness is a seemingly finite, but in reality a very subjective and unachievable concept in the realm of design and construction.

Drawings that are not quantitatively complete can be, and in fact are, used to construct buildings because they are sufficient for that purpose.

This article will examine errors and omissions in construction documents and the belief by many that the design professional is always and solely responsible. This overview is intended to enable a better understanding of the naturally occurring discrepancies that are considered by many to be avoidable errors and omissions.

## The design concept

While the documents attempt to set out in detail the requirements for construction, the many variables imposed on the original documents lead to variations that often render a completed project that contains measurable differences. It is the design professional's job to determine that the work is in substantial conformance with the documents.

So how does the design professional accomplish this? When construction tolerances render conditions that differ from the drawings, manufacturers' proprietary requirements creep into the picture, and local trade customs cause variations in assembly, it becomes obvious that a design professional's documents cannot be used in strict measurement when determining conformance of the work in place. This examination of drawing discrepancies should make clear the widely misunderstood conceptual nature of construction drawings. In reality the design professional can only evaluate the work in place as an "interpretation" of the design concept expressed in the documents and not as a physical illustration of the design concept.

## Construction drawings and contractor submittals

The process of converting the conceptual building design to a completed project is not achieved solely through the preparation of construction documents by the design professional. There is no way for the designer to know in advance of the contractor's buyout which product or building system will be available at the best price. Also, there is no way to determine precisely how the product will interface with adjacent products or systems. That is why the subcontractor prepares shop drawings that specifically detail dimensions and illustrate conditions of precise physical conformance. This process typically fleshes out conceptual variations in the designer's drawings that may not, or possibly could not, have been previously determined. Thus, the shop drawing must be expected to have some level of variance from the designer's drawings. These inherent variances, or discrepancies, are often considered avoidable, and they are often judged by owners to be errors and omissions, when in reality they are merely a product of the process.

### Inherent discrepancies

Harmless discrepancies are inherent in architectural documents. Architectural documents are not intended to be a complete depiction of a real building project. They are intended to be a sufficient description of the project to allow builders to plan their construction and prepare the shop drawings as they manage and construct the project.

An example of a harmless discrepancy commonly built into a project is the use of fractions to describe dimensions. It is common to have a certain overall length that must be divided into three equal parts and to need a dimension that must describe each of the three parts. Convention in construction generally demands that dimensions be presented in units of a multiple of 1/8 inches; thus, convention makes it impossible to accurately describe a length that cannot be divided by 3 in even units of 1/8 inches. For example, when you divide 100 inches into 3 parts, it results in 33.3334 inches, which can closely (but not exactly) be described by a dimension of 33 3/8 inches. The result is a technical dimensional error of .0417 inch. In this case the designer has built an inherent error into the drawing. But has anyone been damaged by this action? Is not the error unavoidable and thus fully in compliance with a reasonable standard of care?

Another example involves partitions on a 1/8-inch scale floor plan drawn a set scale dimension of 5 inches apart. Actual partition construction is depicted in a partition schedule, and the partition types have many different actual dimensions. Thus, the plan might show a nominal 5-inch partition width at a 1/8-inch scale, while the larger-scale partition-type drawing reveals the actual width of the partition to be 6 1/8 inches, thus creating a graphic drawing error of 1 1/8 inch. The purpose of the floor plan is to locate the partition, and the purpose of the partition schedule is to describe the partition. As long as the designer's given dimensions numerically add up to the required dimensional location and clearances, regardless of whether the plan is drawn to scale or not, the information provided is adequate. The problem with drawing scale arises when the design professional allows the contractor to use her or his CAD files to prepare shop drawings. When the contractor begins to take measurement picks using CAD software, apparent discrepancies arise because not all building elements are drawn to scale. Most architects and contractors generally acknowledge that drawings are not now, and never have been, reliably drawn to scale. However, once again, the designer has introduced an inherent, although insignificant, error into the drawing. Again, has anyone been damaged?

It is reasonable to expect contractors to ask questions about the implications of such inherent errors when they identify them and cannot work out their own interpretation or solution to a perceived conflict. However, it is not reasonable to expect that any party would be damaged by such conditions. Yet it is obvious that anyone looking for such technical errors as examples of negligence will find many opportunities for pursuit.

## Discovery impact in the construction process

The magnitude of impact expense associated with document discrepancies is greatly affected by when the variation is discovered. The following three examples will demonstrate this varying magnitude.

The first example concerns a drilled foundation pier that was inadvertently omitted from the foundation plan. Prior to drilling the foundations, the contractor submits an RFI informing the architect that a pier has been omitted from the northwest corner of a stair and asks for direction. The architect and structural engineer review the design and inform the contractor that the pier indeed has been overlooked and must be added. The contractor informs the owner that additional costs will be incurred. Since the mistake was addressed before construction activities had begun, there are no impact costs, and the owner is not entitled to recover the additional construction costs from the design professional, in the absence of extraordinary contract language to the contrary. The controlling issue is that the missing pier is in fact a requirement of the design, and if it had been originally shown on the drawings, the owner would have paid for it in the original scope.

The second example involves the same design condition. In this instance the contractor does not discover the missing pier until much later in the project after all the other piers have been drilled and forming of the grade beam has begun in the area of the stair. In this instance the designer's omission of the pier causes a delay in the forming of the grade beam and will require the pier driller to remobilize for drilling one more pier. The costs for buying the additional pier out of sequence and for delaying the subcontractor forming the grade beam are considered to be impact or consequential costs. In this instance, the owner is entitled to recover these costs, but not the cost of the additional pier, since it would have been included in the original project cost had it been shown on the drawings.

Owners and contractors often mistakenly believe the absence of the pier on the drawings constitutes an actionable omission wherein the design professional should reimburse the full cost of the added work. In reality, as a general rule, only those costs incurred over and above the essential scope of construction may be rightfully recovered.

The third example involves the same condition, but this time the missing pier is not discovered until after construction of the stair above the grade beam has been completed. This omission results in the structural failure of the grade beam. In this circumstance the first cost of the pier pales in comparison to the catastrophic impact expense incurred through delay and the removal and replacement of the grade beam and stair above.

These three examples illustrate the varying magnitude of damages depending upon when the problem is discovered. They underscore the importance of early detection and timely responses.

## The clarification process

Most inherent discrepancies in architectural documents are minor and do not require correction of the drawings or specifications when they are "discovered." Other discrepancies can be more serious and may require correction through the formal change process that is specifically addressed in AIA professional service contracts. These minor discrepancies may need no formal corrective action, other than answering AIA Document G728, Request for Information (RFI), or at most clarification through AIA Document G710, Architect's Supplemental Instruction (ASI). The existence and use of RFIs and ASIs anticipate these minor changes, and they support the conceptual nature of the designer's documents.

## Impact damages due to errors and omissions

There are occasions where damages from design drawing errors and omissions can result when there is no added scope. The damages can occur only after the construction is in place, and they can involve conditions such as areas of the project that do not conform to code. For example, it could be an inadequate door offset or an insufficient toilet room size. The solution is to relocate portions of the project to effect compliance, which will result in the same scope but only in a different location. The Americans with Disabilities Act has brought this type of problem to the forefront in recent years. This type of change represents impact expense or damages because no new scope has been added. The damages are the cost for demolition, the cost for building the portion of the project a second time, and possibly increased costs for delay. In these instances the design professional should expect to be held accountable for such damages if she or he should have known of the requirement when preparing the documents.

If a discrepancy should require more extensive corrective action, such as revising the drawings and specifications, the change process addressed in Article 7 of the AIA Document A201: General Conditions of the Contract for Construction, would be followed. AIA Document G709-2001: Work Changes Proposal Request, would be issued to the contractor, and upon acceptance of the quoted costs, AIA Document G701-2001: Change Order would be prepared. These documents clearly anticipate that changes will likely occur on a project. Since errors and omissions occur on virtually all projects, the owner and contractor should recognize that anticipated changes due to errors and omissions are a natural part of the change process.

## When should a discrepancy be compensable?

We have examined how a discrepancy can occur in the documents but impose no damages. This type of problem generally does not warrant compensation, as no party was injured. So when does an error or omission rise to the level of compensable damages? When a nondamaging error or omission is discovered, the owner should expect the design professional to provide all necessary design services for corrective action at no cost. They should expect quick action and an acceptable solution with all necessary documentation. Although many owners and contractors tend to believe that any error is a compensable cause of action against the design professional, governing laws typically mandate that recovery can only be made against actual damages that arise from the architect's negligent acts.

## Betterment

The cost of betterment (also known as added value or added scope) is almost always the responsibility of the owner. ("Betterment" is defined in *Black's Law Dictionary* as, "an improvement put upon a property which enhances its value more than mere replacement, maintenance or repairs.") Since both impact expense and betterment are often involved in an issue, the design professional is frequently viewed as the cause of the problem and thus inappropriately deemed responsible for all associated costs. If a portion of the costs involves work that would have been necessary to construct the project regardless of whether the mistake had been made, this work, or betterment, enriches the owner and should be her or his responsibility. Owners agonize when discrepancies are encountered late in the project, and they feel that the designer should be responsible because no money remains to cover the costs. This is no justification for damages, and it emphasizes the importance of realistic contingencies.

When should an owner expect to be paid for "first costs" associated with their building? If an owner decides that she or he does not like white painted gypsum drywall in their newly completed home and directs the design professional to design a wood paneled wall to replace it, is the owner justified in expecting the designer to pay for the new paneling? Certainly in this example there are some impact costs for taping, bedding, and painting the wall. However, the change is being made only because the owner changed their mind about the type of finish they desired and previously directed. In this case, 100 percent of the cost of the change is the responsibility of the owner. On the other hand, if the architect had presented finish designs for approval early in the project and then neglected to detail and specify the wood paneling as was selected by the owner, the owner would be entitled to recover the costs of the unneeded taping, bedding, and painting. But again, as a general rule, the designer would not be responsible for the cost of the new wood paneling because it is betterment.

A common misunderstanding about betterment involves the cost of "putting things right." Damages to an owner caused by an error or omission must be calculated not based upon the cost of replacement of the work affected by the error, but based upon the original cost of the erroneous work plus the impact cost of installing the new replacement work.

This is clearly illustrated in the case of an owner who hires an architect to design a house. The owner instructs the architect to specify gold-plated faucets in all lavatories. When the project is completed, the owner discovers that pewter faucets of the same design as the gold faucets have been installed instead, and he demands that the architect pay for replacement of the faucets. The gold faucets are priced at $1,000 each at the plumbing showroom. The pewter faucets cost $200 each and cannot be returned to the vendor. The plumber informs the owner and architect that the replacement cost is $75 for each faucet. What is the actual amount that the owner has been damaged for each faucet?

In this case, the total damages to the owner for each faucet is $275 ($200 for the original unusable faucet plus the $75 labor charge). The owner must rightfully pay for the $1,000 gold faucet. An unfortunate misunderstanding in many disputes is that owners often believe the damages should be either $1,075 or $1,275, both of which represent unjust enrichment.

## Impact damages

In the absence of specific contract language to the contrary, when considering damages, the owner should not expect to recover the first time cost of building the project. The owner should only expect to recover costs that are incurred as a consequence of mistakes made by design professionals and that add no value to the project. Many owners mistakenly believe that if a design professional leaves something out of the construction documents, the item becomes an "omission," and the designer therefore should pay for the full cost of adding the item into the project. Under this scenario the owner would become unjustly enriched by the designer's mistake. (The unjust enrichment doctrine is addressed in *Black's Law Dictionary* as, "General principle that one person should not be permitted unjustly to enrich himself at expense of another, but should be required to make restitution of or for property or benefits received, retained or appropriated, where it is just and equitable that such restitution be made.") Therefore, the owner should realistically expect to recover only the additional costs that are expended to add the item at the later date.

## Summary

Errors and omissions will always exist due to the conceptual nature of the construction documents and the variables involved with the construction process. Tolerances, product options, and variations in trade installations will yield a completed project that can never be fully anticipated by the design professional and expressed in their documents. Drafting techniques and computer technology contain inherent variances that cannot be accurately resolved in illustrated dimensions. As a general rule, the cost of betterment, or added scope, will always be the responsibility of the building owner because only they will be enriched by it.

Design professionals should not be expected to provide perfect and flawless services or construction documents. Realistically, owners should expect and budget for a reasonable number of mistakes. Commercial developers, building managers, and owners who are savvy to these realities utilize allowances and contingencies to effectively manage this process. That is, the design professional's drawings are conceptual, and not a "complete set of instructions on how to construct a building." Finally, neither the law nor the ordinary and reasonable standard of care places the burden of perfect performance of professional services on a design professional. Therefore, some level of imperfection must be expected. Though aggravating and seemingly unfair, owners must budget and pay for a reasonable amount of errors and omissions when they undertake a project.

---

This article is reprinted with permission from the May/June 2004 edition of *Texas Architect.*

# A Loss Cause Too: Betterment

This article continues the discussion on "betterment" that was raised in the previous "A Loss Cause" article. Widely misunderstood by many, and intentionally misinterpreted by some, the betterment issue is one that architects will do well to explain to clients to help them better understand that owner-architect agreements are not performance based, the architect's standard of care does not require them to guarantee the cost of construction, and the owner must pay for their entire building at least one time. As simple as that concept sounds, many owners, when they file claims, insist that the architect owes them money for things the owner hasn't yet paid for. Let's see a show of hands: How many of you have ever had an owner ask you to pay them some money? Can you say "ka-ching"?

We addressed the concept of betterment, or added value, in the previous article. Central to the confusion and general lack of understanding of the concept of betterment is if and by how much owners are damaged when an architect, engineer, or contractor makes a mistake on a project. Secondarily, there is a general lack of understanding that some errors and omissions are to be expected, and thus some amount of damage caused by them is also to be expected. At the risk of jumping in the shark tank once again, we will address the issues surrounding betterment in more detail in this article.

As with most of our work, this article contains references to court pleadings, allegations by plaintiffs, and citations from AIA documents and publications, as well as *Black's Law Dictionary* and *Roget's Thesaurus*. We have been criticized for citing these sources instead of strictly following court rulings. However, this material has repeatedly proved to be helpful in settlement of arguments, and since 97 percent of lawsuits settle out of court, according to Legal Reform Now, case law, although meaningful and relevant, is not always the most useful tool in the architect's dispute resolution efforts, essentially because most architects are not lawyers, and most lawyers are not architects.

We encourage you to consult your lawyer, but also to study all material sources that will assist you in understanding your options in explaining complex subjects to your clients as you attempt to resolve disputes. This article is written with the intention that it can be presented to your clients, other business associates, and even your lawyer for the purpose of explaining betterment from the viewpoint of an architect. Hopefully, it will assist you in avoiding disputes regarding betterment in the future.

## Unjust enrichment

The matter of unjust enrichment lies at the foundation of most issues surrounding betterment in the context of building construction. *Black's Law Dictionary* addresses unjust enrichment as the: "General principle that one person should not be permitted unjustly to enrich himself at expense of another, but should be required to make restitution of or for property or benefits received . . ."

In civil disagreements, laws provide an organizational structure designed to help the parties in dispute reach a just and equitable resolution. If an architect providing professional services is negligent and damages another party, and an agreement as to restitution of the damage cannot be reached through an alternative method of dispute resolution, then the laws of the land will help the parties reach a resolution. It is not the intent of the law that any party be unjustly enriched by the outcome of a lawsuit. The fundamental intent of the law is that a party bringing a lawsuit be restored to the same position they would have been in if no damage had occurred.

Betterment can be a complex issue in a damage claim when one is considering both the measure of damage and the measure of improvement upon the property. The measure of improvement must be viewed as betterment, and the damages caused by the expense of correcting the mistake, or impact expenses, are the measure of restitution. Nonetheless, when owners are confronted with repair and betterment costs, they frequently do not differentiate between them and often feel the design professional is responsible for both. This attitude grows more likely if much time passes before the mistake is discovered.

There can be circumstances, imposed by contract, where an architect may be liable for all costs over a certain amount, including betterment. This can occur when an architect agrees to guarantee the total cost of construction. Although it is rare in architecture today, architects should be very careful when signing contracts with wording that constitutes a guarantee of construction cost or budgets, and they should never consider such clauses without the advice of an attorney.

## Betterment

*Black's Law Dictionary* describes betterment as:

> An improvement of a . . . building that goes beyond repair or restoration.

Examples of betterment include:

> Five light fixtures have been designed over a dining room table. The owner decides, after construction commences, to add a sixth fixture to accommodate a longer table recently purchased. All expenses related to adding the fixture are betterment.

> In another example, no light fixture has been shown in an entry closet. During construction, the owner decides to add a light fixture in the entry closet. All expenses related to adding the fixture are betterment.

> And, in another example, as a project nears completion, the owner decides to add a storage room in the attic of a new home, above the two-car garage. All expense related to adding the storage room is betterment.

All of these examples involve changes that the owner decided to make after the design was completed and construction had commenced. Nonetheless, owners sometimes make claims against architects for the cost of changes that they decide to make because of something that the architect, ostensibly, should have known. Such changes, made at the sole discretion of the owner, will always be betterment.

## The standard of care: mistakes

Architects are human like everyone else and make mistakes. Accordingly, the standard of care for the practice of architecture is not perfection or perfect performance. Logically, if perfection is not the standard, a certain measure of imperfection becomes the standard. Although architectural services must be sufficient in providing designs, documents, and services, those services and products of service cannot reasonably be expected to be perfect.

When a mistake does occur, conformance to the standard of care will be determined by whether or not another architect might have made the same or similar mistake given the same facts and circumstances. It follows that the standard of care will not be that there was no chance for a mistake at all.

By any measure of expectation for the performance of an architect, there must be some level of expectation of mistakes. Logically, this is true for any professional in any discipline, be it engineering, construction, or law. Given the fact that most mistakes cost money to correct, contingencies should be provided within the budget to cover the cost of mistakes that are reasonably expected to occur.

## Is betterment involved in errors and omissions?

Betterment is involved in the majority of errors and omissions claims when an architect has made a mistake in the construction documents or has omitted or left something out of the documents that is required to build the building.

In the first "A Loss Cause" article in this chapter, we cited an example of betterment that effectively describes the fundamental balance between value added to the project and the impact damages caused by remediation:

> An owner . . . hires an architect to design a house. The owner instructs the architect to specify gold-plated faucets in all lavatories. When the project is completed, the owner discovers that pewter faucets of the same design as the gold faucets have been installed instead, and he demands that the architect pay for replacement of the faucets. The gold faucets are priced at $1,000 each at the plumbing showroom. The pewter faucet costs $200 each, and cannot be returned to the vendor. The plumber informs the owner and architect that the replacement cost is $75 for each faucet. What is the actual amount that the owner has been damaged for each faucet?
>
> In this case, the total damages to the owner for each faucet is $275 ($200 for the original unusable faucet plus the $75 labor charge. The owner must rightfully pay for the $1,000 gold faucet.

This example succinctly clarifies the reality that the full measure of appropriate restitution includes only the cost of the original defective design, plus the remediation costs, and not the total cost of the remediation.

An unfortunate misunderstanding in many claims made against architects is that owners believe the damages in this example should be either $1,075, or $1,275, both of which represent unjust enrichment to the owner.

## Damages when betterment is involved

If all or a portion of the cost for a particular claim issue involves work or scope that would have been necessary to construct the project regardless of whether the alleged error or omission had occurred, this work, or betterment, enriches the owner and is the owner's obligation. Further, when remedial work is required, whether it be reconstructive or simply added scope, the solution to the problem arising from an error or omission must be reasonable in the context of the original project design conditions. For example, if the project was designed and constructed under a very restrictive budget and extensive "value engineering," the resolution of a damage claim must include restitution consistent with the cost restrictions originally guiding the actions of the project team. A "gold-plated" or "Cadillac" resolution would be inappropriate and would likely represent unjust enrichment.

Expert consultants often confuse their own preferences with the standard of care. What an expert employed by the plaintiff would have preferred to do is not the standard of care. There is frequently, if not always, more than one way to arrange information on a drawing, represent a design, or detail a complex assembly. Different professionals do things differently and yet arrive at similarly sufficient and satisfactory results. The standard of care is not defined through determining that an architect could have done something differently, but through determining if the way the design professional did something was not objectively sufficient.

Unfortunately, when a lawsuit is filed, many experts hired by the plaintiff are not motivated to find a reasonably priced solution for a client who believes they have been damaged. These plaintiffs are upset about the damage, and they want to be made whole in every respect. The plaintiff's expert is more likely to lean toward a solution that is guaranteed not only to fix the problem but also to make sure the plaintiff is happy with the "fix." The experts select better systems and better-quality materials for the remediation than the owner paid for or had the ability to pay for originally. It is common in such circumstances to find that these "fixes" often include betterment, and they are implemented on the belief that the architect is going to make the owner whole in every respect and is going to pay for the full cost of the fix. In such circumstances, the plaintiff's experts may try to camouflage betterment within the argument that the full cost was required for "remediation" of the damage.

The spectrum of damages impacting the architect can range from no damage costs, as in the case where the entire resolution of the claim is betterment, to all costs incurred, as in the case where the resolution results in no improvement to the property or added value to the owner. We will look at examples of each of these conditions later in the article.

## Damages when betterment is not involved

There can be cases where the architect has made a mistake and no betterment is involved in resolving the mistake. If the resolution of the mistake involves only remediation of the condition and does not result in increased value, the entire cost may be compensable repair damages. Consider the following example:

An owner has constructed a high-rise office building. In the men's restrooms, the urinals have been designed with alcoves that are separated by drywall partitions that have been clad with ceramic tile. After the owner occupied the building, the local code official denies tenant construction permits because the urinal alcoves are too deep for their width and thus do not comply with the ADA Standards for Accessible Design, which had been made a part of the local code. The solution to the problem is to demolish the alcoves and make them shallower so that the width of the alcove complies with ADAAG. In this example, there was no improvement beyond restoration, and thus the entire cost of the solution represents impact expense attributable to the architect.

## Why the owner is responsible for betterment

Many owners struggle with the fact that they must pay for all or a portion of someone else's mistake. The reason is very simple. The architect's contract is not based on perfect or complete performance. As with all professional services, the measure of the standard of care is whether the services provided were sufficient with respect to a reasonable standard of professional care. There are conditions in the general contractor's contract that require them to provide "complete" or fully functional systems and assemblies, but the architect is not ordinarily bound to such conditions. The architect is not responsible for the work or a "complete" scope. Completeness in professional services is almost always subjective and not objective. While the architect tries to provide complete drawings and specifications, the human factor will always prevent this from occurring in an absolute sense.

The architect's drawings and specifications are not a product, and the obligation for completeness does not exist such as when you purchase an automobile. You have the right to expect the vehicle to be complete in every way, and if it is not, you exercise the automaker's "warranty" to be made whole. Any part that is missing or defective must be provided or replaced. Under general legal principles, the architect provides no warranty regarding the drawings and specifications. These are only the architect's instruments of service, the adequacy of which is judged by the standard of care previously discussed, and they will always require some measure of interpretation and clarification when they are used for construction.

That is why the owner must pay for added scope and the architect and the contractor do not. Consider the following example that might occur in everyday life:

A landscape company sells flowering plants installed by the flat. A homeowner orders seasonal flowers for his flower beds at his house. The landscape company estimates 10 flats to do the job. When installation begins, it is discovered that 10 flats are not enough, and 2 more flats are required to fill out the beds. The landscape company sold 10 flats and they are only responsible for installing 10 flats. The homeowner will have to pay for installation of 2 more flats if he wants the flower beds filled.

It is puzzling that so many owners struggle with betterment, a condition where additional scope or product is required, when dealing with design and construction and the cost of their buildings.

## What plaintiffs often claim

Unfortunately, when claims are made against architects, the claims seldom recognize appropriate value for betterment. Commonly in a plaintiff's pleadings, a simple listing of proposed change orders, change order requests, or change orders is presented as the measure of damage that the plaintiff wants to be reimbursed for. In other words, "I spent the money, so you pay me back." In almost all cases, even a cursory review reflects that most or all of the claim issues involve tangible additions to the building, or betterment. Consider the following example:

The owner has built an office building with a meeting area and a lobby constructed in a portion of the basement. The original intent was to pour the basement wall in architectural concrete and leave the concrete exposed in the lobby. The architect failed to specify architectural concrete, and the plaintiff was not happy with the structural-grade concrete finish. The architect proposed a remedial solution of coating the basement wall with plaster with a "Venetian" finish, at a cost of $25/sf. The owner asked for designs for cladding the walls with burled maple paneling. The owner selected the paneling at a cost of $60/sf and demanded that the architect pay the entire cost.

In this example, the owner rejected the reasonable resolution, a resolution that would have put him in as nearly the same position as he should have originally been, and instead selected a resolution that could never have been anticipated based on the original design environment. The more expensive wood paneling is betterment to the extent that the actual damage to the owner was approximated by the $25/sf cost of the proposed Venetian finished plaster, a similar grade of finish. The owner would be unjustly enriched if the architect were required to pay the full $60/sf cost of the wood paneling.

## Too much betterment

Plaintiffs also often claim that the additional costs related to errors and omissions got out of control and deprived them of the opportunity to manage their budgets. In such cases, the plaintiff's experts are likely to opine that there was "too much betterment," so the architect should pay for some or all of it. Plaintiffs may attempt to justify their gains due to betterment within the argument they would not have proceeded with the project if they had known in advance what the final cost would be.

This "too much betterment" allegation disregards the reality that the owner is the sole beneficiary to the added value to the project. Requiring the architect to pay for the full scope of betterment represents unjust enrichment and is not a fair measure of damage. In reality, people who invest their money in the scope of buildings, as these owners request the architect to do, retain some degree of ownership.

Claims such as this can be especially problematic on fast-track and negotiated GMP projects where there is no fixed construction cost and construction has proceeded before the construction documents are completed. (For a more complete discussion, refer to "Managing Fast-Track Projects," by Simpson and Atkins, in *The Architect's Handbook of Professional Practice*, 14th edition).

## The timing of discovery

Although beyond the scope of this article, the stage of project progression can dramatically impact the measure of compensable repair damages involved in a mistake. For example, if a mistake is discovered during the bidding and negotiation phase, the mistake will involve a solution that is entirely on paper, and probably will have minimal, if any, impact expenses. On the other hand, if the construction is complete and the project is about to be occupied, the amount of impact expenses may greatly outweigh the amount of betterment.

## Observing the standard of care

This article is not intended to convey the idea that all parties involved in an architectural project should carry a calculator and constantly keep score on each other in the mistake game. Nonetheless, "score" in today's construction industry always relates to money. It is reasonable, although perhaps not in concert with the strict measure of the law in the liability and damage relationship, that the architect should not have to pay the owner for every part, piece, and parcel of impact expenses related to errors and omissions. Mistakes, or errors and omissions, are always going to occur, and owners should wisely establish budgets that include contingencies to cover the cost of a reasonable measure of human mistakes.

As a caution, architects should also pay heed that excessive impact expenses related to errors and omissions they make may well exceed a reasonable standard of care and thus give rise to a reasonable expectation by an owner that the architect should reimburse those excessive expenses.

## Conclusion

The issue of betterment ranges from obvious black and white to chaotic conditions of great complexity. When time, inconvenience, and unforeseen expenses enter the argument, the emotion and intensity usually increases. Nonetheless, the overriding issue is that the legal system was not intended to allow a party in a dispute to become unjustly enriched.

Solutions to errors and omissions may contain no betterment and consist entirely of impact expenses, they may totally consist of betterment, or, more commonly, they may be made up of both. In any case, when such disputes arise, the better the parties are informed, the more likely an equitable settlement can be reached. While most courts do not hold designers accountable for the cost of betterment, since almost all cases settle out of court, a clear understanding among the parties can help facilitate a quicker resolution. Don't forget to be careful out there.

# Absolute or Absolution? Observations, Inspections, and the Contractor's Warranty

This article chronicles the unfortunate evolution of industry expectations of the architect's site observations from that of objectively reporting what is observed to being the total quality control filter for the contractor's shortcomings. In spite of copious wording to the contrary in the AIA documents, owners and contractors seek to have the architect responsible for any and all discrepancies while holding perfection as the expected outcome. Should the architect be absolutely responsible for the contractor's finished work, or should the architect be rightfully absolved of the responsibilities of others? Read on, but be prepared to breathe deeply and count to 10 from time to time.

Building construction requires many workers and many trades. The contractors and subcontractors must coordinate and interface their work and plan how all the separate parts and pieces will fit together. A contractor coordinates the subcontractors and develops a work plan for delivering a completed project that conforms to the architect's design.

Because the contractor is solely responsible for conformance of work with the contract documents, they must continuously inspect the work as it goes in place to determine that subsequent work can be placed over it, documenting minor variations for the owner's information.

The architect observes the work at certain times during the construction phase, but on a much less frequent basis and for different purposes than the contractor. Architects are charged only with being generally familiar with the work and reporting the general progress and quality of the work, as completed, to the owner. The standard of care is that the architect should be responsible for discovering and reporting nonconforming work of which he or she becomes aware, yet the profession has been affected by a trend that indicates an attitude of a much higher standard among owners and contractors. Many such claimants have asserted that the architect has a responsibility similar to that of the contractor and should discover any and all defects. These expectations can become so distorted that owners and contractors in some instances essentially have asserted that the architect should be a warrantor of all work placed by the contractor. This has increased the risks associated with the architect's construction phase services, particularly the requirements for observing and inspecting the work.

Courts have ruled that architects failed to detect the contractor's defective work, holding that they have a duty to endeavor to guard the owner against all nonconforming work on the project, although much of that work is installed when the architect is not present.

This article will explore the issue of work conformance and the responsibility for finding and preventing defective work. It will examine who is contractually and physically responsible for work conformance, as well as the continuing attempts by plaintiffs' lawyers to hold the architect accountable for this obligation.

## The contractor's obligation

First, we will examine the contractor's obligation under the contract. In AIA Document A201-2007 and A201-1997, General Conditions of the Contract for Construction:

> 3.1.2 The Contractor shall perform the Work in accordance with the Contract Documents.

This requirement is straightforward and absolute. There are no qualifications or overriding conditions that can alter or relieve this obligation. In fact, A201 states:

> 3.1.3 The Contractor shall not be relieved of obligations to perform the Work in accordance with the Contract Documents either by activities or duties of the Architect . . . or by tests, inspections or approvals required or performed by persons or entities other than the Contractor.

In addition, A201 requires continuous inspection of work already in place, by the contractor:

> 3.3.3 The Contractor shall be responsible for inspection of portions of Work already performed to determine that such portions are in proper condition to receive subsequent Work.

The bottom line is that the contractor controls the work, the contractor is required to inspect the work for conformance, and the contractor contractually warrants the work to be free from defects. This responsibility is absolute, and it is not superseded by the architect's observations, inspections, or approvals.

## The architect's standard of reasonable care

*The Architect's Handbook of Professional Practice*, 14th edition, generally addresses the "standard of reasonable care" as follows:

> The architect is required to do what a reasonably prudent architect would do in the same community, in the same time frame, given the same or similar facts and circumstances.

*The Architect's Handbook of Professional Practice* also addresses matters that relate to the level of perfection that must be achieved in performing architectural services:

> **The Architect's Legal Responsibility:** The law does not require perfection in meeting a client's expectations from an architect. As with any complicated human endeavor in which success depends on exercise of reasoned judgment and skill, the law recognizes that perfection in architecture is practically impossible to achieve.
>
> ... **Accordingly, the law does not look to architects to guarantee, warrant, or otherwise ensure the results of their efforts ...**

and:

> **Expectations of project participants** ... Many clients do not understand that architects are neither able nor required to perform perfectly. Such clients have high expectations for their projects and want their design professionals to provide guarantees ...
>
> ... not understanding that **architects, like lawyers and doctors, provide their clients with services, not products.** These individuals may also fail to realize that professional judgment is required at each step. Architects need to remind these project participants that buildings, unlike automobiles, cannot be pretested. Despite the effort, care, and conscientiousness of the architect, the process of taking a project from drawing to reality has a lot of unknowns.

The architect should be responsible for discovering and reporting defective work of which it becomes aware. However, expectations in the industry have risen above this level of duty, and today court pleadings are filled with allegations of absolute responsibility on the part of the architect.

## De facto approval of defective work?

When the quality or conformance of the work is questioned, the assertion is often made that the architect "approved," "allowed," or "permitted" the contractor's defective work by certifying an application for payment, signing a change order, or certifying substantial completion. Although the owner can accept nonconforming work if they so choose, there is no provision contained within the AIA documents that allows the architect to accept work that is not in conformance with the contract documents. Moreover, in A201, the architect is empowered to reject nonconforming work:

> 4.2.6 The Architect has authority to reject Work that does not conform to the Contract Documents.

In addition, A201 clearly states that the architect's certification of a payment application does not represent approval of the work:

> 9.6.6 A Certificate for Payment . . . shall not constitute acceptance of Work not in accordance with the Contract Documents.

This avenue of making claims overlooks several other important aspects of the provisions of the AIA documents, all of which are intended to prohibit the architect from accepting nonconforming work rather than place a finite obligation on the architect to detect nonconforming work.

A201-2007 addresses defective work placed by the Contractor:

> 3.5 The Contractor warrants to the Owner **and Architect** that . . . **the Work will conform to the requirements of the Contract Documents and will be free from defects . . .**

A201-1997, Article 3.5.1, contains similar language.

Here, the contractor provides an expressed warranty to both the owner and the architect that there will be no defective work on the project. Unfortunately, the contractor's warranty to the architect, should the architect experience a loss caused by the contractor's defective or nonconforming work, may be of little value if the contractor is bankrupt or no longer in business. Moreover, the architect not only does not provide such a warranty concerning the quality of the work, the architect has no responsibility for the contractor's performance, as indicated in A201.

> 4.2.3 The Architect will not be responsible for the Contractor's failure to perform the Work in accordance with the requirements of the Contract Documents. The Architect will not have control over or charge of and will not be responsible for acts or omissions of the Contractor, Subcontractors, or their agents or employees, or any other persons or entities performing portions of the Work.

So how is it that many have come to believe that the architect's obligation to discover defects on a project is similar to, or even greater than, the contractor's guarantee that there will be none? Perhaps some derive this erroneous notion from the architect's authority to reject nonconforming work of which the architect becomes aware as stated above in A201, and in AIA Document B101-2007:

> 3.6.2.2 The Architect has the authority to reject Work that does not conform to the Contract Documents.

There is absolutely no obligation conferred in this paragraph to detect nonconforming work, only authority to reject it if discovered.

## Claiming in style

Claims against architects are often styled to try to take advantage of a particular state law or to put the design professional in as unflattering position as possible. The following examples are styled after actual claims filed against design professionals, and they are typical of what a design professional may expect if an owner unhappy with the quality of the work claims the architect should pay all or a portion of the cost of remedying nonconforming work. In all of these examples, the contract documents include the standard AIA contract language cited in this article, found in B101 and A201. In addition, in all of these examples the owner is claiming damages by the architect in the full amount of the cost of remedying the nonconforming work placed by the contractor and covered by the contractor's warranty.

**Catch me if you can.** The plaintiff's lawyers claimed as follows, admitting that the contractor did the work badly, but only because the architect did not catch them:

> The roof drains are not installed properly; scuppers are not installed properly; gaps in the flashings exist; pitch pans on the roof are not fully filled . . . The architect failed to document and report defective work.

In addition, this one also reflects a belief in the awesome power of the architect to "allow" the contractor to perform badly:

> The contractor performed work well below acceptable industry standards, provided and installed inferior materials, failed to perform required testing . . . failed to adequately supervise work of the subcontractors. The architects failed to provide acceptable contract administration services by permitting substandard work and poor workmanship . . .

**The director.** Plaintiffs' lawyers also are fond of claiming that the architect should have been directing the work, as in this example:

> Failure to properly perform construction administration responsibilities. Architect was responsible for poor sequencing among the various trades.

This claim was filed, although A201 clearly states in Section 3.3 that directing and coordinating the work of the subcontractors—and construction sequences—are the contractor's responsibility.

You bought the farm. Another favorite avenue of plaintiffs' lawyers for making claims against architects involves certifications for payment by the architect:

> The contractor executed substandard and nonconforming work . . . by certifying the contractor's Applications for Payment that included costs for nonconforming work, the Architect failed in his duties during the Contract Administration phase and failed in his responsibility to the owner.

**Adult supervision.** The assertion that the architect has a stronger duty than the contractor to supervise the work is evidenced by the following claim. This disingenuous allegation is so prevalent in lawsuits against architects these days that it could be viewed as generic:

At the time that contractor's defective work was performed, Architect was supervising the work at the site. Additionally, the work was performed while Architect was in charge of the work. This evidence creates a genuine issue as to whether Architect violated its contractual duty to "guard the Owner against defects and deficiencies in the Work."

**Most expertly, if you please.** Not only do plaintiffs' lawyers make claims not supported by the AIA documents or the standard of care, such claims are also made by plaintiffs' experts. The following style of an "opinion" submitted by an "expert" is also so prevalent that it could be considered generic as well:

> ... most, if not all, of the issues noted are the result of poor workmanship and nonconforming work performed by the contractor. These problems were exacerbated by the Architect's failure to observe nonconforming work, notify the owner, and require that the work be redone.

Once again, the claim acknowledges that the primary issue is poor workmanship and nonconforming work, but asserts that the architect should pay for the cost of remedying the problems because the architect did not catch the contractor's poor performance.

None of these examples survives scrutiny when compared with the architect's responsibilities as defined by the AIA documents, with a reasonable standard of care, or with any reasonable interpretation of who should be responsible for nonconforming work. It is physically impossible for an architect to witness and have knowledge of every component placed within a building. There is simply no reasonable or logical way to conclude, "Sure, the contractor built it wrong, but it's your fault because you let him do it."

## The architect "shall endeavor to guard"

Plaintiffs' lawyers often attempt to use a clause in B141-1997 to place the architect in the role of policing the contractor. The architect's obligation is as follows:

> 2.6.2.1 The Architect, as a representative of the Owner, shall . . . **endeavor** to guard the Owner against defects and deficiencies in the Work . . .

*Merriam-Webster Dictionary* defines "endeavor" as:

> to attempt (as the fulfillment of an obligation) by exertion of effort . . .

The definition of endeavor is "to attempt to do," "to try to do"—but there is neither absolute obligation nor overriding cause for the architect "to do," such as there is with the contractor's obligation to inspect continuously those portions of the work that are to receive subsequent work.

Rightfully, these clauses related to endeavoring to guard the owner against the contractor's defective work must be balanced against the limited nature of the review of the work the architect is required to do when the architect visits the project site. This is addressed in B141 with almost identical wording in A201:

> 2.6.2.1 The Architect . . . shall visit the site . . . (1) to become **generally** familiar with and to keep the Owner informed about the progress and quality of the portion of the Work completed . . . (3) to determine **in general** if the Work is being performed in a manner indicating that the Work, when fully completed, will be in accordance with the Contract Documents. However, **the Architect shall not be required to make exhaustive or continuous on-site inspections** to check the quality or quantity of the Work.

*Merriam-Webster Dictionary* defines "generally" as:

> in disregard of specific instances and with regard to an overall picture.

Thus, although the architect has authority to reject any nonconforming work that is apparent, the architect does not have a duty to discover all defective work. In fact, the expectation that an architect could discover all defective work on a project is unrealistic due to the architect's limited presence on the site. Even when the architect provides a full-time on-site project representative on larger projects, the representative's obligation in this regard is limited compared to the contractor. Architects do have a duty to endeavor to guard the owner against defective work, but this obligation is restricted by the limited duty to become *generally familiar* with the work.

The AIA documents and the standard of care are clear that the contractor's obligation and responsibility to install competent and conforming work are not overridden by placing a stronger responsibility on the architect to "catch" him if he does not. In the absence of a specific contract requirement, the architect is not an insurer, ensurer, guarantor, or warrantor of the contractor's performance. No architect possessed of sanity would agree to such a provision in a contract, and it is not the intent of the AIA documents or the standard of care to place such a responsibility on the architect.

The language, "endeavor to guard," has been removed from the 2007 AIA document revisions. However, it is anticipated that plaintiff's tendency to claim that the architect is responsible for finding all of the contractor's mistakes will continue unabated.

## Performance and payment bond

Some owners undoubtedly desire that faithful performance of all parties involved in designing and constructing their projects be covered by some form of insurance. One such avenue is a performance and payment bond. Under ordinary circumstances, the owner has the right to require that the contractor ensure its performance by requiring a Performance and Payment Bond as described in A201-2007 and A201-1997:

> 11.4.1 The Owner shall have the right to require the Contractor to furnish bonds covering faithful performance of the Contract and payment of obligations arising thereunder as stipulated in bidding requirements or specifically required in the Contract Documents on the date of execution of the Contract.

In traditional project delivery, there is no such requirement in the AIA documents or in industry practice for the architect to provide a bond covering the contractor's faithful performance, and we are not aware of an instance where an architect has provided such assurance through either a contract or a bond.

If owners want a financial guarantee of the contractor's faithful performance, that protection should rightfully be purchased through the contractor and not pursued indirectly through the architect's professional liability insurance policy.

## Absolute power

The contractor has well-defined responsibilities and obligations to *ensure* that the work does conform to the requirements of the contract documents, including supervising the work and providing a "warranty" to the owner and the architect, as cited in the paragraphs above. The primary reason that the contractor makes a warranty to the architect is that the architect can never be in the position of observing all of the work of the contractor, subcontractors, and other parties performing the work. It would literally require an army of architects continuously present on the site to see all of the work at every stage of the work. Professional service of that sort would certainly be considered *exhaustive or continuous on-site inspections,* if not direction and supervision.

*Merriam-Webster Dictionary* defines "supervision" as:

> the action, process, or occupation of supervising; especially: a critical watching and directing (as of activities or a course of action)

The architect does not supervise or direct the contractor or the work. The responsibility for supervising and directing the work rests solely with the contractor. A201-2007 and A201-1997 are very explicit about these responsibilities:

> 3.3.1 The Contractor shall supervise and direct the Work using the Contractor's best skill and attention. The Contractor shall be solely responsible for, and have control over, construction means, methods, techniques, sequences and procedures and for coordinating all portions of the Work under the Contract . . .

And:

> 3.3.2 The Contractor shall be responsible to the Owner for acts and omissions of the Contractor's employees, Subcontractors and their agents and employees, and other persons or entities performing portions of the Work for, or on behalf of, the Contractor or any of its Subcontractors.

In addition, we have already seen that 3.3.3 requires the contractor to continuously inspect the work in progress.

## Affirmation

The issue of observing the work and detecting and reporting deficiencies is fraught with risks, as we have enthusiastically put forth. However, all of the above notwithstanding, an architect can be found responsible for failing to "endeavor to guard" as in the example where site visits and observations are made, and defective work readily available to be observed is not cited or reported. Challenging inequities does not absolve the architect from performing in accordance with a reasonable standard of care. While the architect should not be required or expected to warrant the contractor's work, the architect's contracted duties during the construction phase should be taken seriously and performed appropriately.

## Absolution

AIA Document A201 clearly states that the contractor is solely responsible for the work. The contractor controls every aspect of the work. This control includes final decisions about which materials and product vendors will be used. They determine how the work is to be installed and how the work installation is to be divided and coordinated between subcontractors. Moreover, perhaps the contractor's most important responsibility is the obligation to make sure the work conforms to the contract documents. The contractor provides an express warranty to both the owner and the architect that the work will be in conformance with the design concept expressed in the contract documents.

The architect interprets the contract drawings and reviews the contractor's submittals, coordination drawings, and clarification sketches, which anticipate the finished project, for conformance with the design concept. The architect observes the work to form general opinions about progress and quality and reports the status to the owner. At no time does the architect approve the work in its totality. There is no reasonable way that the architect can see each piece of material as it goes into the project. Only the contractor is in a position to provide that service. Substantial completion is "substantial" but not "total." Final completion is the correction of known, but not necessarily all, items that require correction or completion.

The architect's certification of the contractor's applications for payment is based on the general progress of the observed work and the contractor's notarized certification that the application is accurate and consistent with the work progress.

The architect and the owner must rely on the contractor's written guarantee that the work is in conformance. According to A201, this obligation withstands all actions of the architect, including observations, inspections, submittal approvals, and payment certifications. This absolute power of the contractor to control and be responsible for the work is never shared, assigned, or assumed by any other party.

By contrast, architects have no authority over subcontractors. They have no power over construction, and they have no obligation or duty to warrant that the contractor's work is free from defects and deficiencies or is in strict conformance to the contract documents. The architect's obligation is to endeavor to guard the owner against defects and deficiencies in the work and means nothing more. The premise that "guarding the owner" includes detailed knowledge of every building component is not only unachievable; it runs counter to the contractor's "sole responsibility" and the warranty that backs it up.

Administering the construction contract provides valuable services to the owner, and it increases the chances of preserving the design concept. It also gives the architect a chance to address errors and omissions, hopefully, before the work is installed. However, observing and inspecting the work absolutely brings risks that may not result in absolution, and we must be mindful of the claims owners, their lawyers, and contractors sometimes make regarding the ways they believe the architect should be an insurer, supervisor, director, and guarantor of the contractor's work.

And as you go along the way, watch where you step, keep a lookout overhead, and be sure to be careful out there.

---

This article is excerpted with permission from the May/June 2006 edition of *Texas Architect.*

# The Good, the Bad, and the Ugly: Challenges and Risks of Nonconforming Work

This article shook the ground a little when it rolled out, and well it should have. Although architects do not control and cannot cause nonconforming work, they are often in the path of the bullet when it occurs; and it occurs on virtually every project. If the architect does not adequately document significant nonconforming work, there is a chance of elevated risk. Not enough is being said about this often treacherous subject, so we thought we would lob one out there to stir things up a little. Hey, that's not like the drawings! Tear it out!

> Your discovery of the contradiction caused me the greatest surprise and, I would almost say, consternation . . .
>
> —Gottlob Frege

Summary: Work conformance is an important measure of a successful project because it fulfills contracted obligations. Yet when buildings are constructed, there is always some amount of nonconforming work—always. The variances may be minor. Hopefully, they are. But they are always there. Architects may not be aware of all of the discrepancies, and that is why we certify "substantial" completion rather than "final" completion, and why certifications for payment are limited to our knowledge, information, and belief. We do not and cannot know precisely how all of the work has been put together because we do not manage construction, and we do not observe each and every act by every worker every day.

Architects are hired to design projects, and contractors are hired to construct projects. The architect's activities during the construction phase are focused on observing the work in progress, reporting defective and nonconforming work that is observed, certifying amounts owing to the contractor, and ultimately determining substantial and final completion of the project.

These activities carry with them some amount of risk, on which we have made many observations. We address general construction contract administration responsibilities in "Visible Means: Site Visits and Construction Observation" in Chapter 5.

When the variances are minor, there is little to be concerned about, but when the variances are more substantial, issues can arise. This article is about the prevalence of nonconforming work in all projects, its causes, and the options available for dealing with it. Nonconforming work is often accepted by the owner, but the architect seldom escapes if the differing condition adversely affects the work. We will offer some suggestions for improving risks through documentation, and we will explore the options available when the owner and architect disagree on acceptance. We will also take a look at claims made by contractors in attempts to shift responsibility for conformance to the architect.

> Faultless to a fault.
>
> —Robert Browning

## Thou shalt

We will begin by reviewing the contractual obligations of the parties. The sole responsibility for making sure the work conforms to the contract documents lies with the contractor. AIA Documents A201-2007 and A201-1997, General Conditions of the Contract for Construction, explicitly state this requirement with similar language. In Section 3.1.2, "The Contractor shall perform the Work in accordance with the Contract Documents." In Section 3.5, "The Contractor warrants to the Owner and Architect . . . that the Work will conform to the requirements of the Contract Documents . . ."

Importantly, the implementation of compliance is entirely the contractor's responsibility, in accordance with Section 3.3.1: "The Contractor shall be solely responsible for and have control over construction means, methods, techniques, sequences and procedures and for coordinating all portions of the Work under the Contract . . ."

To further confirm that the contractor has met their obligation to provide work that conforms to the contract, the contractor may be obligated to certify before a notary—for instance in AIA Document G702, Application and Certificate for Payment—". . . the Work covered by this Application for Payment has been completed in accordance with the Contract Documents."

Further, in A201-2007, Section 12.2.1: "The Contractor shall promptly correct Work rejected by the Architect or failing to conform to the requirements of the Contract Documents . . . Costs of correcting such rejected Work . . . shall be at the Contractor's expense."

Also, in Section 12.2.3: "The Contractor shall remove from the site portions of the Work that are not in accordance with the requirements of the Contract Documents and are neither corrected by the Contractor nor accepted by the Owner."

Under the AIA Contract Document framework, the architect has no explicit obligation to make the work conform to the contract documents. Instead, the architect is required to have general knowledge of work conformance and report the status to the owner. In A201, Section 4.2.2: "The Architect . . . will visit the site . . . to determine in general if the Work observed is being performed in a manner indicating that the Work, when fully completed, will be in accordance with the Contract Documents."

Further, in Section 4.2.3: "The Architect will not be responsible for the Contractor's failure to perform the Work in accordance with the requirements of the Contract Documents." Based on this provision, the architect has no responsibility whatsoever to make the work conform or for work that does not conform.

Likewise, the owner also has no obligation to make the work conform to the contract documents. The owner can, however, get someone else to make the work conform if the contractor does not. In A201-2007, Section 2.4: "If the Contractor . . . neglects to carry out the Work in accordance with the Contract Documents . . . the Owner may . . . correct such deficiencies. . ."

The owner also has the option to accept work that does not conform to the contract documents. In A201-2007, Section 12.3: "If the Owner prefers to accept Work that is not in accordance with the requirements of the Contract Documents, the Owner may do so instead of requiring its removal and correction, in which case the Contract sum will be reduced as appropriate and equitable. Such adjustment shall be effected whether or not final payment has been made." This clause recognizes that the owner loses value when the work does not conform, and it requires the contractor to give money to the owner to compensate, even if the project has been completed and final payment has been made.

Finally, lest there be any remaining confusion about the responsibility to provide Work that conforms to the contract documents, A201, Section 3.1.3 settles the issue: "The Contractor shall not be relieved of obligations to perform the Work in accordance with the Contract Documents either by activities or duties of the Architect in the Architect's administration of the

Contract, or by tests, inspections or approvals required or performed by persons or entities other than the Contractor."

## Cause and conditions

People mistake their limitations for high standards.

—Jean Toomer

Since, under the AIA Contract Documents framework, only the contractor is solely responsible for the work and its conformance, only the contractor can cause nonconforming work. Although the contract requires conformance and the contractor typically wants the work to conform, there is always some amount of work on a project that does not conform. Ideally, the errant conditions are minor and are caused by the inexact nature of the construction process. Such conditions need not be cited by the architect unless they are both detrimental and obvious or have a material adverse impact on the project.

For example, if a room is a smidgeon smaller than designed, and its use is not adversely affected, it need not be documented. However, if the contents of the room will not fit or its use is otherwise adversely affected, it should be cited as nonconforming, and the owner should choose whether or not to accept it.

Some conditions that can cause nonconforming work include mistakes in building layout, contractor substitutions, contractor preference, coordination errors, installation errors, and manufacturer variances. (See the concept of conceptually equal but nominally different in the next article in this chapter, "Drawing the Line.")

Hopefully, mistakes in building layout are inconsequential and do not require documentation. However, significant differences may require a variance from the local governing authority. Manufacturer variances can cause a revision in building layout. MASTERSPEC, Section 017000, Execution Requirements, Article3.2, Preparation, requires the contractor to take field measurements and verify space requirements and dimensions of items shown diagrammatically on the drawings to determine if a change in the documents is required to make things fit appropriately.

Both contractor substitutions and nonconforming work can only be accepted by the owner. In A201-2007, Section 3.4.2, "... the Contractor may make substitutions only with the consent of the Owner, after evaluation by the Architect and in accordance with a Change Order or Construction Change Directive." Unauthorized substitutions can be, and by definition are, viewed as nonconforming work. Substitutions can be as challenging as nonconforming work, and they are worthy of a separate article.

There are typically instances of installation errors that do not materially affect the use of the project. While these conditions may be significant enough to be documented, if the building use and appearance are not adversely affected, they are usually accepted. Many installation errors and other forms of nonconforming work that are not obvious go without notice or documentation.

There may be conditions where the contractor inadvertently constructs or prefers to construct the project in a way that is different from the contract documents. In such cases, if the contractor is aware of the deviation, he or she is obligated to ask the architect if the variation is acceptable. Since the architect is only on site occasionally, there may be conditions that are constructed in variance to the documents that are known only by the contractor and never known by the architect. This may be acceptable as long as such conditions do not adversely affect the completed project.

## Options for nonconforming work

> Not every absence of good is an evil.
>
> —Thomas Aquinas

When nonconforming work is discovered, the architect must first determine if it adversely affects the building use or appearance. If it is found to be unacceptable to the architect, unless the owner wishes to accept it, it must be removed and replaced with work that conforms. Should such removal and replacement affect the completion schedule, or perhaps the cost of the work, the work is often accepted by the owner under pressure so as to preserve the completion date or protect the budget.

Nonconforming work can create conditions that unfairly compromise the building design. Should this occur, a deduction in project cost commensurate with the compromise should be levied against the contractor. Clearly an opinion about cost adjustments may create adversity, and the best course is to discuss any nonconforming work and potential cost or schedule adjustments regularly in project meetings. Unfortunately, many owners and architects view discussing nonconforming work as "airing dirty laundry"; they consider it an adversarial discussion and are reluctant to keep the topic as a regular part of the site meeting agenda.

If the architect finds the nonconforming condition to be acceptable, a recommendation for acceptance is made to the owner. If the owner accepts the variance, the architect may or may not choose to change the documents to reflect the varying condition. The architect may instead wish to recommend that the contractor document the change in the contractor's as-built records. In any event, the owner's acceptance of nonconforming work must be documented in writing.

## Owner-accepted nonconforming work

> You have many choices. You can choose forgiveness over revenge, joy over despair. You can choose action over apathy.
>
> —Stephanie Marston

Only the owner has the authority under the construction contract to accept nonconforming work. In A201-2007, Section 12.3: "If the Owner prefers to accept Work which is not in accordance with the requirements of the

Contract Documents, the Owner may do so instead of requiring its removal and correction."

When this occurs, the contract documents are often changed to reflect the varying condition. When the documents are changed to conform to the nonconforming condition, the design becomes that of the architect as if it had been included in the original documents. This arises from state licensing statutes that require supervisory control over document content along with the professional obligations associated with signing and sealing contract documents.

However, because of the reasons stated above, the architect has no obligation to change the documents to match the nonconforming work. The architect's obligation to meet the professional standard of care overrides the contractor's mistakes and the owner's preferences. The architect's ability to practice may be on the line for the errant condition, and only the architect can make the judgment call on changing the contract documents.

When such challenges arise, the architect should help the owner understand the practice ramifications associated with acceptance of the error. Since the owner can freely accept nonconforming work (except when nonconformance results in a building code violation or dangerous condition), there should be no adverse effect on the built project if the documents remain unchanged, and the errant condition is simply documented by the architect to be "owner-accepted nonconforming work."

## Side effects

> Logical consequences are the scarecrows of fools and the beacons of wise men.
>
> —Thomas Henry Huxley

Some architects propound that there is no danger when the architect recommends acceptance of nonconforming work when it does not meet the architect's professional standards. They posit that a "qualification" in the change order declaring innocence and absolution is sufficient to protect the architect's practice. These actions may suffice if you know of the variation, it complies with codes and standards, it complies with the standard of care, and the owner is unlikely to reject its acceptance at some point in the future.

Those who have been in practice for a while may recall the aftermath of the savings and loan debacle of the 1980s. Many architects were not cognizant of the nonconforming work on their projects, and they signed pristine certificates of substantial completion for work that contained elements that did not conform.

These acts went unpunished until the real estate market collapsed and all those inadequately collateralized projects experienced foreclosure. The assuming lenders immediately hired consultants to do "due diligence" reviews of the completed work. The errant conditions were noted, and lawsuits were filed for the discovered "nonconforming" work that was not documented by the architect.

As the lawsuits played out, architects were asked in deposition why they certified substantial completion with no qualifications when there were so many nonconforming conditions present. Many architects were then asked to make the owners whole for the cost of restoring the project to design conformance.

We aren't proposing that owners are justified in making such claims, especially given our record of examining the limited nature of the architect's presence on the typical construction site. We only wish to point out that the risks associated with these owner-made claims remain a threat.

## Contractor claims

If I can catch him once upon the hip,
I will feed fat the ancient grudge I bear him.

—William Shakespeare

While most contractors uphold and make good their responsibility for nonconforming work, there are some who join in the claim game when nonconforming work is discovered. The first position often taken by the offending contractor is that they built the project per "plans and specs," and that any nonconforming work is therefore the architect's fault. The second argument they use for their defense is likely to be something along the lines of: "The architect was on the site regularly, and he did not tell me I was building it wrong."

The following examples are taken from actual claims filed by contractors against architects, and you could encounter them on a project that has serious disputes involving nonconforming work:

- The architect had the authority to require the contractor to correct the nonconforming work and failed to do so. . .
- The architect approved the contractor's work when it decided not to require the contractor to make obvious corrections. . .
- The architect did not withhold payment for nonconforming work, so the contractor was entitled to believe the work was approved. . .
- If the way the contractor was installing the work was not acceptable, the architect should have required alternate means and methods and sequences.

These positions seek to avoid the direct responsibility for defective and nonconforming work, and fly in the face of the AIA Contract Documents and the traditional relationship between architects and contractors. It should be the goal of all parties to build a well-crafted project and bear appropriate responsibilities. It is unfortunate that some contractors and their legal experts take this approach, because it reflects an emerging belief that contractors are not responsible for their own contracted actions.

## Trail's end

Some trails are happy ones,
Others are blue.
It's the way you ride the trail that counts.

—Dale Evans Rogers

In the event you encounter nonconforming work, whether you as the architect discover it or the contractor reveals it, it is beneficial to track the deviation to its conclusion. It may be sufficient to mention the deficiency only once and document that the owner and contractor were made aware. However, the best risk management approach is to discuss it at project meetings, note it in field observation reports, and list it on an attachment to the certificate of substantial completion. You may wish to annotate it on payment certificates, especially if deductions are made, since the contractor is required to remove and replace it, and payment at that time would not be appropriate. By keeping nonconforming work issues in the field of vision of all participants, you improve chances of avoiding future allegations that you did not keep the owner, and even the contractor, informed about the deviation.

The options for reaching a conclusion are to have the contractor tear out the nonconforming work and replace it with work that conforms, or accept the deviation and move on. The architect can attempt to be helpful by offering opinions, but only the owner can make the final choice.

## Conclusion

> Anyone will be unhappy until he recognizes his true calling.
>
> —Unknown

The full scope of the defective and nonconforming work discussion is far too great to cover in this short article. Other in-depth discussions on the subject could delve into nonconforming work caused by supervision, inspection oversights, or submittals and shop drawings. The topics of contractors' selection of unqualified subcontractors or lesser-quality materials are also worthwhile examples.

Although the AIA Contract Documents endeavor to establish specific responsibility for nonconforming work, and they clearly draw the conclusion that only the contractor can cause it, the fact remains that the architect will always be dragged into the fray if a project is beleaguered by extensive nonconforming work. The most effective risk management approach for an architect is to try reasonably to find nonconforming work. The next best risk management approach, when nonconforming work is discovered, is to discuss it at regular meetings and keep the subject open until the issue is resolved.

When you do encounter nonconforming work, you should expect that you may be blamed for causing it. That seems to be the game these days. You should face the heat, and bring along your dog-eared and faded owner-architect agreement and A201 in your briefcase so you can cite terms and conditions.

It is unfortunate that so many risk circumstances arise from the architect's construction administration efforts. This is largely because the other stakeholders—owners and contractor, subcontractors and vendors—do not have a clear understanding of what architects can and are supposed to do. So, as you sit at the picnic table in your backyard and ponder the greenhouse you'd like to build, think about what you can do to help others better understand the architect's duties, and be careful out there.

# Drawing the Line: Why the Architect's Documents Cannot Be Used for Construction

Although this article is about existing documents and industry practices, it was much like ringing the doorbell with a hammer. It highlights the reality that the architect's drawings do not tell the complete story required for finished construction and that the contractor also must provide services and produce documents to assist in the process. Praise and criticism were both at their highest levels, ranging from cries of "must be required reading" by many to accusations of architects becoming "glorified draftspeople." Seldom has an aspect of the profession been discussed at such a fever pitch. Some of our critics thought we were advocating that the architect be excused if they do a poor job with document preparation. That is not the message. What we advocate is the contractor's skill, knowledge, and the supplementary information that is provided through submittals and coordination drawings are necessary in addition to the architect's drawings and specifications. Obviously, you will need to buckle up for this one!

It may surprise some people to hear that the architect's documents cannot be used for construction. Many are of the opinion that the architect prepares the documents and gives them to the contractor, and the contractor takes them and builds the building from the information contained therein. But nothing could be further from the truth.

Then why does the architect place on the documents "Issued for Construction"? Although common practice, this phrase, when affixed to the architect's drawings, can be misunderstood. Nevertheless, this phrase is better than labeling them "100% CD Set," "Final Construction Documents," or something equally misleading. The documents are not issued for construction per se, but instead, they are issued to facilitate construction by expressing the design concept. The documents do not contain sufficient information to construct the project, and much more information is required before the work can be done.

In fact, the architect's documents only represent information sufficient for the contractor to begin "the contractor's required work," which includes the preparation of detailed construction documents, more commonly known as shop drawings and submittals, coordination drawings, and alternate sketches, all of which set out the specific and final details required for procuring and placing the finished work. By contrast, drawings by architects merely reflect the finished design of the work.

This article will examine the role contractor-provided construction documents play in the construction process, along with the other information that is required to complete a project. It will examine why the design professional's documents cannot be used as the actual documents for implementing construction, and it will explore what information is actually used, why it is used, and from where it originates.

# The architect's design is a concept

As defined by *Merriam-Webster's Dictionary*, the term "concept" is "an abstract or generic idea." This definition makes it clear that a concept is not a specific or finite solution with tangible parameters.

The limited content of the architect's drawings is more explicitly addressed in *The Architect's Handbook of Professional Practice*, 14th edition, in a chapter entitled, "Construction Contract Administration," wherein it states: "The construction documents are not intended to be a complete set of instructions on how to construct a building. Construction means, methods, techniques, sequences, procedures, and site safety precautions are customarily assigned as responsibilities of the contractor to give the contractor latitude in preparing bids and carrying out the construction phase."

Similarly, Section 3.12.4 of AIA Document A201-2007, General Conditions of the Contract for Construction, states that the inherently conceptual nature of construction documents prepared by architects and the related responsibilities of the contractor/construction manager for detailed submittals and shop drawings: "Shop Drawings, Product Data, Samples and similar submittals are not contract documents. Their purpose is to demonstrate the way by which the contractor proposes to conform to the information given and the design concept expressed in the contract documents."

Moreover, Section 3.12.6 of A201-2007 addresses the relationship of the contractor's submittals and shop drawings to the contractor's plan for procuring and placing the work: "By submitting Shop Drawings, Product Data, Samples, and similar submittals, the Contractor represents to the Owner and Architect that the Contractor has (1) reviewed and approved them, (2) determined and verified materials, field measurements, and field construction criteria related thereto, or will do so and (3) checked and coordinated the information contained within such submittals with the requirements of the Work and of the Contract Documents."

A201-1997 contains similar language regarding shop drawings and submittals.

This powerful language explicitly requires the contractor to first check each submittal and coordinate it with field conditions and the requirements of the work before submitting it to the architect or engineer to review for conformance with "the information given and the design concept expressed in the contract documents." MASTERSPEC, a product of the AIA and the industry standard for construction specifications, devotes an entire section to project management and coordination (Section 01310, "Project Management and Coordination"). This description of the content of coordination drawings explicitly requires them to be original, detailed comparisons of the various trades, and it recognizes that the architect's drawings will likely be in conflict with selected equipment and required clearances to the extent that coordination is necessary and advisable. The contractor is specifically directed to provide sketches for resolution of such predictable conflicts.

Furthermore, A201 places the contractor in charge of determining how the work will be divided into separate trades, how the work will be bid and purchased, how the purchased products and systems will be coordinated and incorporated into the completed work, and that the work will be in conformance with the design concept expressed in the contract documents.

## When an RFI is not a change order

Although AIA Document A201 makes the lines of responsibility for planning the implementation of the work abundantly clear, and MASTERSPEC sets out specific requirements for accomplishing the task, some assert that a contractor's change order is justified whenever information is not specifically expressed in the architect's documents. As a result, contractors routinely make these assertions through the RFI process and inevitably write change orders to add information to the architect's documents—information never rightfully required or intended to be there in the first place.

For example, an architect has indicated "recessed fire extinguisher cabinet" on an interior wall elevation in the architectural drawings. While no specific dimensions are indicated for the cabinet location, the specifications list several acceptable manufacturers for the cabinet. Still, the contractor submits an RFI: "Please provide detail for cabinet framing in wall."

In this instance, the contractor should provide the final answer, since the size and mounting detail of a recessed fire extinguisher cabinet varies with the manufacturer. The architect could not have precisely detailed the installation without knowing which manufacturer's cabinet was to be used. Also, it is not necessary for the architect to provide a framing detail because the manufacturer's literature describes how the cabinet is to be installed. If the architect answers the RFI with a framing detail, it is likely that the contractor will ask for additional money for the newly detailed framing, alleging that scope was added to the drawings. If the architect doesn't answer the RFI, he or she risks being accused of not being responsive. One appropriate response is to suggest that the contractor honor the manufacturer's instructions for the selected product.

## Benefits of conceptual design drawings

AIA documents have expressly indicated for many years that the architect's drawings are conceptual, and they have required contractors to represent through their review of shop drawings that they have "determined and verified materials, field measurements, and field construction criteria." These actions naturally preclude "scaling" the design drawing directly by attempting to determine dimensions from the drawings with the use of an architect's ruler.

As is obvious to most architects, there are many benefits to the use of conceptual design drawings in the construction process. Some of these benefits are that it:

- Promotes competition. Multiple acceptable manufacturers allow the contractor to obtain the best price or best delivery schedule. It is generally acknowledged that a single-source specified product will be more expensive because of the lack of competition, and that is why it is unlawful on public projects in many states.

- Provides for the latest technology. A manufacturer's product may undergo model and specification changes after the project is designed and before the work is installed. A good example is radiology equipment, where specifications and features change almost monthly, and medical technologists and radiologists desire the latest model for their facility. The architect's conceptual design allows for product procurement with more recent upgrades and developments.
- Allows the trade to determine the final configuration. While architects have a general familiarity with many products, the trade contractor is the expert, knows the product best, and is more capable of determining its ultimate design configuration.
- Places responsibility for means and methods with an experienced provider. Much like the designer's expertise that is accrued from years of experience, the contractor's expertise in the latest construction techniques and how products and buildings go together is a career endeavor. The contractor knows best how to develop a plan for making the design concept a built reality.

## The contractor's plan is critical

The contractor's plan for procuring and placing the work is not always entirely visible to the project team. Although the contractor is required by the construction contract to submit shop drawings, produce coordination drawings, provide sketches to resolve dimensional conflicts, and hold preinstallation conferences—all of which the architect should be aware of and may attend—for the most part, the contractor's work plan is transparent.

Components of the contractor's Plan for the Work are addressed in *Guidelines for a Successful Construction Project,* a joint publication of the Associated General Contractors of America, the American Subcontractors Association, and the American Specialty Contractors. Preinstallation conferences and coordination of subcontractors are addressed in Section D.2.a ("Guideline on Communications"): "Coordination should be assured through regular on-the-job meetings of the general contractor's authorized project representative and the on-site subcontractors' authorized project representatives. Additional meetings may be required for subcontractors whose work might interfere with another at a given time."

This publication—formerly known as the Construction Industry Survival Kit—also includes shop drawings and submittal data and coordination drawings as primary topics for discussion during the preconstruction conference. In Section 6.1 ("Guideline on Preconstruction Conferences"), under Topics for Discussion, is Item 4: "Shop drawing and sample submittal data including procedures for submittal, review, and approval . . . " Item 5 mentions coordination drawings, which are referred to as interference and composite drawings: "Requirements, if any, for interference and/or composite drawings. Who initiates them and what will be the order of progression of these drawings; what is the impact on time for performing the work if composite drawings are required?"

Through such publications, these major construction trade associations acknowledge the role of the contractor in developing and managing the work of coordinating the subcontractors and providing composite coordination drawings. They also recognize that time and planning will be required to coordinate the subcontractors and prepare the drawings necessary to facilitate constructing the work.

The contractor's plan is critical to the success of a project, and it is developed and implemented by the contractor's staff. Yet contractors sometimes reduce staff as they seek to control general conditions costs or because of pressure from owners to reduce expenses. Owners often view these temporary facilities and services as transient, with no sustaining benefit to the project. However, efforts to reduce these costs can be misguided and may adversely affect the project. Staff reductions are not made because planning the work is not required, and consequently the work must be provided by an alternate source. For survey and layout services, a common practice today is to buy layout work from the individual trades performing the work. For example, the plumber may be contracted to measure and lay out the locations of plumbing fixtures and equipment, and the drywall contractor may be contracted to measure and lay out the walls.

Under this scenario, where layout is not provided as a general conditions service, the ability of the contractor to confirm that the plumber's layouts are compatible with the drywall contractor's layouts is reduced. Typically, there are issues of coordination that must be worked through between the two subcontractors. Since the layout process has essentially bypassed the contractor's supervision and control, it is not a part of the work plan, and the subcontractor's source for layout information apparently becomes only the architect's drawings. Consequently, if there is a problem with coordinating the layout between the subcontractors, the architect is often mistakenly viewed as the responsible party.

## The contractor is responsible for subcontractors' work

According to Section 3.3.1 of AIA Document A201-2007, and A201-1997, Article 3.3.2, with similar language, the general contractor is solely responsible for the acts of subcontractors and the coordination of their work: "The Contractor shall be solely responsible for and have control over, construction means, methods, techniques, sequences, and procedures and for coordinating all portions of the Work under the Contract . . . "

Coordination of the subcontractors by the contractor is contractually required, and it is necessary for producing properly placed work. Attempting to transfer the responsibility for coordinating the work to the architect is in conflict with the general conditions, the recommendations of the leading trade associations, and, although it may be a common occurrence, it is not good construction practice.

The issue of pressuring contractors to reduce their general conditions costs has seemingly played a part in causing layout and coordination of the work by the contractors in the field to become a vanishing art. The act of developing a work plan, working with and coordinating subcontractors, and answering their questions has instead evolved into an intensive RFI exchange often designed to force the architect to provide some or all of the contractor's field coordination services under duress. This act of conscripting the architect or engineer is inherently unsuccessful because they do not possess the contractor's skills or contractual authority, and they do not provide supervision. In the construction process, there is simply no substitute for the contractor's work plan.

The following RFI reflects the occasional passive nature of how a contractor might attempt to conscript the services of an architect: "Embeds for the roof screen wall support column bases were set per unapproved shop drawings in the interest of schedule. Please provide a detail for attaching the column base plates with drilled epoxy inserts."

The contractor should have engaged an engineer to design a correction to this placement mistake and proposed an alternate sketch for the engineer of record to review as MASTERSPEC requires. Nevertheless, the design team, in an effort to assist in resolving the problem, responded by sending an Architect's Supplemental Instruction (ASI) with a detail for the inserts as requested. At the end of the project, adding insult to injury, the contractor submitted additional costs in a change order request for "providing inserts per the architect's revised detail" that was attached to the ASI, alleging that the detail was not the most cost-effective solution.

## Systems may be conceptually equal but nominally different

Both the architect's drawings and the contractor's procurement and placement plan, which includes submittals and shop drawings, are affected by the proprietary nature of the specific materials and systems that the contractor decides to purchase. In the absence of a sole-source specification, the architect cannot be expected to know exactly which suppliers, manufacturers, or subcontractors the contractor will select to include in the project. The proprietary nature of today's market dictates that one vendor's product will not exactly match another vendor's product. Thus, the architect details the concept of an installation and specifies the products or systems advertised or known to be conceptually equal in quality. The contractor is responsible for determining and defining specifically how the conceptually equal but nominally different products or systems that have been chosen for use in the project will be incorporated into the work.

An example of a conceptually equal but nominally different product can be found in the case of two popular manufacturers of metal-clad wood windows. Several window manufacturers provide a wood window nominally sized 3 feet-wide by 5 feet-high. However, the actual window provided by one company is 3 feet 1 inches-wide by 4 feet 11 inches-high, and the window provided by another company is 2 feet 11 1/2 inches-wide by 4 feet 11 1/2 inches-high.

Although the windows are of slightly different sizes, the differences do not invalidate the concept of a 3 feet by 5 feet window. Thus, without advance knowledge of exactly which window the contractor will propose to buy, the architect can approximately, but not exactly, represent in the design documents what is required for the project. The subcontractor then indicates in submitted shop drawings exactly how the selected window will be incorporated into the work. The shop drawing, although it is not a "contract document," becomes the document that is actually used for construction. The architect's documents, since they are conceptual, are not and cannot be the actual documents from which construction is performed.

In another example, the conceptually equal but nominally different nature of the final product to be provided is actually of little concern to the architect, provided the contractor coordinates the work of the subcontractors:

> RFI Question: Fire/smoke dampers have been approved as 120 volt. The security system subcontractor has requested permission to change these dampers to 24 volt. Will this change be acceptable?
>
> Engineer's Response: 120 volt or 24 volt is acceptable. Subcontractors shall coordinate per contract.

As long as the dampers are coordinated and function with all related systems, they will be in compliance with the design concept.

## The contractor confirms the architect's dimensions

The purpose of the dimensions given in the architect's drawings is to define the limits of and provide guidance for placement of the elements of the work. If there is a category of information provided in an architect's drawings that must be used directly during the construction process, it is likely to be dimensional information. Nevertheless, the architect's dimensions must be thoroughly examined and verified by the contractor preparing the plan for procuring and placing the work because of the variables in available products and construction techniques.

Therefore, the dimensions provided by the architect are presented only in support of the design concept. Column grids and building limits may be presented and used literally as long as they have been confirmed by the contractor's surveyor. However, standard convention dictates that the architect may use certain nominal dimensions that the contractor must interpret in actual terms. For example, an 8-inch concrete masonry unit is actually 7 5/8-inches tall, and a 2 × 4 wood framing member is actually 1 1/2 inches by 3 1/2 inches.

Dimensions are also impacted by nominal proprietary differences, as in the case of the window size example given above, or in the case of small differences in the actual dimensions of kitchen appliances, plumbing fixtures and accessories, floor tile, elevators, and many other products. These nominally differing dimensions, when they have a critical impact on the layout of the building, must be highlighted in submittals, resolved through the RFI process, or, in most cases, merely coordinated by the contractor or subcontractor on site.

A good example of such a condition is pipe penetrations in the building structural frame. The specifications often require "sleeve layout drawings" to be submitted with the structural shop drawings. The contractor is in the best position to determine specifically where the sleeves for the piping can be placed so as to not interfere with critical structural members such as reinforcing steel or post-tensioning tendons, or with the contractor's provisions for constructability. The architect need not be concerned about the precise location of the sleeve as long as it falls within a wall or chase and meets the requirements of the design concept.

Convention and common sense also allows that some building elements may simply be "conceptually indicated" but not actually dimensioned. Building elements often indicated without dimensions commonly include doors occurring in a long run of wall, electrical outlets whose specific location is not critical, and other such elements. The final "nominal" location of these building elements is rightfully left to the discretion of the contractor.

## How it is supposed to work

When things go the way they are supposed to, the architect's interaction is essentially one of answering questions about design intent and possibly issuing a few supplemental instructions. The contractor significantly marks up submittals, and preinstallation conferences are held at the contractor's request rather than having the meetings required in the specifications. If all went as intended, a project would go something like this:

- Architect designs project and issues design drawings (drawings locate, specifications establish quality).
- Contractor develops plan for procuring the work and allocates work among trades.
- Contractor and trades develop a plan for placing the work and prepare composite coordination drawings and alternate sketches.
- Trades prepare submittals and submit to contractor.
- Contractor coordinates trade submittals with the Plan for the Work, marks up and approves submittals, and submits to architect.
- Architect reviews submittals for conformance with design concept.
- Contractor and trades construct with approved submittals.
- Contractor issues RFIs for questions that cannot be answered from the information given or for questions about discrepancies in the architect's documents.
- The architect responds to RFIs with answers to questions.

If a project was indeed constructed as the AIA documents anticipate, there would be less paperwork, fewer meetings, and fewer conflicts and disagreements. There may be higher general conditions costs to cover the contractor's necessary labor, but there would be fewer coordination issues, fewer reimbursable expenses for the owner to pay, and a shorter period to close out the project. Although the contractor's plan for procuring and placing the work is not a frequent topic of conversation around the job site or in the project meeting, there are contractors that actually prepare such a plan and execute it as the AIA and the leading construction trade associations recommend. The telltale signs are marked-up trade submittals, detailed coordination drawings, fewer RFIs, more installation conferences, and less correspondence in general.

## Architects conceive the concept, contractors plan the work

Contractor-provided construction documents are essential for constructing a project, and it is evident that the architect's drawings alone cannot be used because they are conceptual in nature and inherently inadequate for that purpose. If design drawings were sufficiently complete and adequate for construction, there would be no need for the general contractor. The architect would be providing the plan for putting the work in place. The manufacturer and model along with the precise specifications and physical characteristics of all products and systems in the building would be known and detailed in the drawings in advance. In developing "a complete set of instructions for building the building," the architect would already have determined the means and methods for placing the work. There would be no submittals because all data would be fully anticipated and addressed in the contract documents. There would be no RFIs, no ASIs, and much less correspondence overall. Moreover, project costs would likely increase due to the absence of competition.

While the Building Information Model may improve the coordination process in the future, the need for a contractor's work plan will never go away. Graphically illustrated concepts, desires, and intentions will never precisely match constructed fact. By its very nature, the construction process requires that someone plan, schedule, coordinate, and direct the means and methods necessary for project construction and completion.

Architects will continue to design projects and produce conceptual drawings for the contractor's use. However, until the industry acknowledges the need and demands that contractors plan and coordinate the work, architects will continue to be expected to coordinate both the contractor and the work of the trades. Until owners are enlightened as to the contractor's responsibilities under the AIA documents, the misguided expectation that the architect is responsible for coordinating the work will remain. The legal industry will continue to attempt to hold the architect's conceptual drawings to shop drawing standards, and the number of claims against architects will continue to rise.

---

This article originally appeared in the May/June 2005 issue of *Texas Architect.*

# Chapter 5

## Applications

## A Fistful of Dollars: Surviving Project Buyout

Project buyout has, to a degree, become a killing field for the architect's design, and we just couldn't resist firing a few shots into it ourselves. Licensing statutes are consistent as to who designs a building and who is empowered by law to control the design, but industry behavior doesn't seem to want to acknowledge this. The architect's design is often carved away during project buyout by owners and contractors who make product and material substitutions, and they often want the architect to take sole responsibility if the substitution fails. The primary objective of the architect can become one of simple design survival. Now, put on that flak jacket and issue those documents for bid, so the owner and contractor can start deciding what they want to change!

> A billion here, a billion there, and pretty soon you're talking real money.
>
> —Senator Everett Dirksen

### Introduction

Almost everyone wants to build projects at the lowest cost while maintaining relative quality. Owners generally want the most building for their money, either to buy more scope or to sell the project at a higher margin. The period between the time the cost is fixed, either through an accepted bid or an established guaranteed maximum cost, and the time all of the labor and materials for construction of the building are purchased is called *project buyout*. During this time the contractor can generally increase their profits if they can find a better deal on the specified products and get the architect and owner to accept them. Better yet, if there is a shared savings with the owner on reduced project costs, both the owner and contractor stand to gain.

A popular vehicle for achieving these gains is the substitution process, which is often imposed within a very short time frame, late in the game when time is critical, often causing the architect to render product evaluations without extended research. We touch on substitutions in "Ch-Ch-Changes . . . : Managing Risk in the Change Process" and again in "According to Hoyle: The Submittal Process" later in this chapter. When the substitution requests come in, the architect must scramble to evaluate the proposal and decide if that product or system is as good as what was specified. There is often a great amount of pressure put on the architect to accept the proposed substitution, quality concerns notwithstanding, usually because of cost savings benefits.

This article is about project buyout and the risks involved, including the value analysis/substitution process (or value engineering, if you prefer) and its effect on the owner, architect, and contractor. Since substituting elements of the architect's design involves product evaluation, coordination with related or affected elements, and possible manipulation of the overall building configuration, some posit that owner or contractor selected substitutions constitutes "design" and possibly the practice of architecture. We will provide our observations on this position along with a review of tactics used to get substitutions accepted, and we will offer some suggestions for improving your chances for surviving the substitution assault on your project.

## Prices slashed, today only

> I have enough money to last me the rest of my life, unless I buy something.
>
> —Jackie Mason

The project cost is established by the contractor through the solicitation of quotations from multiple subcontractors. Many contractors and their subs often have long-standing relationships that span many years. These relationships allow subs to submit a price to their "favorite" contractor that is lower than the competition because there are fewer "unknowns" that can equate to risks.

On competitively bid projects, contractors depend on competition among the subs to obtain the lowest price. Many subs, fearful that their competition will find out their number, wait until the final seconds before submitting their final bid. It is common to see "bid runners" standing around with multiple cell phones waiting for that last phone call before bids are submitted. The contractor back at the office gives the final number to the bid runner, who writes in the number just in time to submit it by the deadline.

On guaranteed maximum priced projects, contractors work the numbers in various ways. In addition to basic sub competition, contractors sometimes require subs to absorb project costs in their bids that would ordinarily be in the contractor's general conditions. Such costs can include things like project cleanup, sharing the cost of vertical transportation, or sub-provided bonding in lieu of a contractor-provided bond.

Contractors often hold the sub prices open well into the construction phase, hoping to find a better price before signing the subcontract. This can be perilous, especially if the contractor has gone "hard" on the number in a contract with the owner. Recently, when gasoline prices sharply escalated, some contractors were caught when they had guaranteed the price to the owner, but they had not secured contracts with their subs. When commodity prices suddenly rose, the subs, fearful that increased operating would erode their profit, immediately withdrew their bid numbers leaving the contractors with a contracted GMP and no subcontractor pricing to back it up.

When the subs repriced their work, it was substantially greater than their original bid. Some of the contractors, caught with a GMP shortfall, immediately imposed a vigorous value analysis/substitution effort to get the project costs within the contracted GMP. In spite of such calamities, contractors continue to roll the dice and hold the prices while shopping for lower numbers, attempting to find a better deal before the work must be put in place.

## Shop till you drop

> Whoever said money can't buy happiness simply didn't know where to go shopping.
>
> —Bo Derek

In a typical project buyout, when a better price is found than the one in the bid or guaranteed maximum cost, the contractor often absorbs the difference into their profit without passing it on to the owner. This can be so lucrative that the practice of "bid shopping" has been known to occur in some markets. This is done by revealing the low-bid subcontractor's number to other subs with an offer to give them the job if they submit a lower bid. This practice can be unfair and it is counter to the premise of competitive bidding where a bidder submits a price in good faith.

Shopping, as we use the term, also involves looking at alternative materials and systems. In today's design and construction environment, most building systems and many materials have become highly proprietary and comparable systems are rarely a true equal. We addressed this in "Drawing the Line" in Chapter 4, where we explored the concept of "conceptually equal, but nominally different. Thus, when changes in materials and systems are made, though conceptually equal, they may be physically different enough to require document and even system changes.

## Buyout substitutions

> The insolence of authority is endeavoring to substitute money for ideas.
>
> —Frank Lloyd Wright

For most of the last century, the architect alone determined what products would be included in a project. The architect researched, evaluated, and specified, and that's the way it was. Infrequently, a product would be difficult to obtain in a particular geographic area, and a more available substitution with reasonable equivalency would be selected. More infrequently, a product would no longer be manufactured, and an available similar product was used in its place. Today, the flattening of the earth has greatly reduced these problems.

Thirty-odd years ago, in the quest for cost reduction, contractors began to propose substitutions for the products specified after the construction contract was executed. They offered many reasons for the proposals, but the underlying basis was the reduction of cost. Commonly used slang for their proposals was "value engineering," a term borrowed from an existing value methodology process, although they did not follow the established systematic, multistage approach of actual "value engineering" successfully used in preconstruction phases.

## The Real Value Engineering

Value engineering, originally called "value analysis," was developed at the General Electric Corp. during World War II, and it was defined as "an analysis of the functions of a program, project, system, product, item of equipment, building, facility, service, or supply of an executive agency, performed by qualified agency or contractor personnel, directed at improving performance, reliability, quality, safety, and life cycle costs."

In the 1980s, the U.S. Office of Management and Budget, the president's budget supervisors, began issuing circulars requiring federal departments and agencies to use value engineering (VE) as a management tool, where appropriate, to reduce program and acquisition costs. Organizations such as SAVE International, which purports to be "the premier international society devoted to the advancement and promotion of the value methodology," support and provide certification credentials in the value engineering process.

Although commonly used throughout the industry, the use of the term "value engineering" in proposing cost reductions during the construction phase is misleading, and it is a disservice to the well-established value engineering process that has proven itself over the years and is used throughout U.S. government agencies. In this article we will refer to the value engineering process used during construction as what it actually is: buyout substitutions.

Substitutions are typically proposed after the contract is executed, although some owners require that the bid documents solicit proposed substitutions with the bid. MASTERSPEC sets a time limit on when substitutions will be considered. However, since substitutions are often driven by project buyout, and most owners just can't resist "a better deal" when it is offered, many agree to consider them throughout the construction phase until buyout is completed.

When these "value engineering"/substitution ideas are discussed, and the owner or contractor has shopped prices for alternatives, they often look to the architect to approve the final decision, sometimes on short notice. If the architect is not familiar with the proposed alternative material or system, additional time and fees to conduct an appropriate study may be necessary. Generally, pressure is applied by the owner or contractor to avoid delays, real or imagined. If it is determined that an actual delay has occurred, either through time for study or time to revise the documents, it is possible that the owner or contractor will claim it was caused by the architect's slow response to a reasonable substitution request. Such claims ignore the fact that the architect did not request the change and had no incentive, financial or otherwise, to make it.

The impact of substitution review time on the construction schedule can be used as a strategy by the contractor to force acceptance of a particular product or system. This tactic is addressed in detail in the chapter "Maintaining Design Quality," in the 14th edition of *The Architect's Handbook of Professional Practice.*

To pull it off, the contractor must avoid submitting a submittal schedule indicating anticipated fabrication and shipping time. Unless the architect enforces the submittal schedule requirement, many contractors never "get around" to providing it. The contractor then waits until the last minute to submit the shop drawing and demands a quick approval. When the architect objects that the product does not equal that which was specified, the contractor asserts that preparing a submittal for the product that the architect specified, submitting it for review and waiting for a space in the fabrication line will delay the project. Owner objections are usually quelled by either the threat of delay or perhaps an offer of offsetting compensation for the compromised products. Owners, lured by the monetary incentive and fearful of a project delay, often agree to the compromised and cheaper product.

## What the AIA documents say

> When it's a question of money, everybody is of the same religion.
>
> —Voltaire

Substitutions became so commonplace in the 1990s that they were addressed by the AIA documents in the 1997 document revisions. AIA document A201, General Conditions of the Contract for Construction, states in Section 3.4.2 that substitutions will be added to the work by change order. However, adding the substitution to the work scope does not necessarily require the architect to change the drawings. There is a great difference in risk to the designer of record if the drawings are changed. If the construction documents are revised to include the substituted product or system, the architect will probably be viewed as the primary endorser of the substitution and be found to be responsible as if it had been a part of the original drawings. For this reason, you may elect to not change your construction documents. You have the choice to require the contractor to provide sufficient information for constructing the changed portion of the project using shop drawings, specifications, and/or clarification sketches.

## Potential problems

> So you think that money is the root of all evil. Have you ever asked what is the root of all money?
>
> —Ayn Rand

A good example of a substitution that trapped many architects was the loose-laid, ballasted, single-ply membrane roofing material that was introduced into the market in the early 1980s. Roofing manufacturers marketed the new product directly to owners with a substantial cost savings, and the owners demanded that architects use it on their project. Many architects innocently revised their drawings, incorporating the single-ply system into the project.

Later, when a very strong tropical storm hit the city of Houston, Texas, ballasted single-ply roofs on high-rise buildings downtown began to "gallop" due to the extreme negative pressures at the parapets. The result was displacement of the roof ballast resulting in extensive broken glass in adjacent building curtainwalls.

When claims from the damages were resolved, architects were found to be responsible because they had revised their drawings and certified substantial completion of the single-ply roofs.

Substitutions during project buyout can be beneficial, and they often serve well in bringing projects into budget. Where the architect must be careful is in accepting and incorporating into the documents substitutions that may not perform as expected or may have a greater chance of failure. Should the substitution fail to perform, the architect is almost always blamed or in some way brought in to the dispute.

For example, on a small office building in a northern state during a value engineering/substitution exercise, the contractor proposed to substitute a window system without insulated units or a thermal break for a savings of $7,500 over the originally specified system requiring those characteristics. The owner, who had a very limited budget, accepted the proposal. The architect was asked to change the drawings to reflect the change. The architect revised the drawings, provided an appropriate specification, and issued a change order revising the window system, and the project was built.

Within two years, fuel prices radically increased, and the cost for heating the building in winter was far beyond the expectations of the tenants, and they threatened to move out of the building. They knew business associates in more efficient buildings who were paying much less rent. The owner, upset over the circumstances, sent a demand letter to the architect alleging faulty design and threatened suit. The architect, who felt they had only followed directions, stood their ground and hired a lawyer.

The suit was settled in mediation by the architect agreeing to pay $200,000. The architect's professional liability insurance policy had a deductible of $50,000, which was paid directly by the architect. The architect's culpability arose from the fact that the architect changed their drawings and issued a specification. This was determined to be the same as if the compromised system had been designed and specified by the architect originally. Although the architect proposed an acceptable system, their failure to recommend rejecting the less efficient VE change, or at least voice clear objections while attempting to explain the adverse consequences of the change, obviously created the illusion that the architect was endorsing the change. Of course, a settlement is not a true measure of how a jury may have decided the cause; the outcome of the dispute could have been better, or much worse.

Instead of incorporating the change, the architect can administer it as a substitution, reject it, and refuse to change the drawings. When the owner insists on accepting it, the architect issues a change order for the deduction with the stipulation that the contractor will engineer the system and coordinate it appropriately with the work. The drawings are not revised, and the work is put in place with the contractor-provided documents. The architect may elect to review the shop drawings for the substituted work, but no review stamp should be affixed. Remember, this is not work that the architect designed, specified, detailed, or accepted. An unfortunate outcome in some cases is that the contractor may just refuse to proceed without architect-endorsed documents for the substitution and take the position that the architect's refusal to "cooperate" is delaying the project.

Architects can also ask for a hold-harmless agreement to protect themselves in the event the owner is not happy with the final outcome of the change. Some members of the AIA Large Firm Roundtable, a group of larger architectural firms, incorporate such a hold harmless clause into their contracts.

The substituted system can also be noted on payment certifications and the certificate of substantial completion as owner-accepted nonconforming work. While these actions may seem extreme, they are a viable response to protect the architect's interests when the owner and the contractor wish to play the part of the architect and change the design in a manner the architect believes is unwise.

Additional efforts that can be made to dissuade the owner in accepting the change include a frank discussion, with a consultant present when necessary, to review the impact of the compromised system. The objective is owner enlightenment, and it can be a very effective risk management technique.

Another example involves the substitution of EIFS (exterior insulation and finish systems) for brick on a medical office building. During the value analysis/substitution process, the contractor proposed a less expensive EIFS. The project was extremely over budget, and the architect knew that the change had to be considered. The architect responded by agreeing to detail a more expensive drainable EIFS. This option did not provide a cost reduction as great as the cheaper, more basic EIFS, but it allowed a reduction in overall project cost by using a product that was acceptable to the architect.

A meeting was held with the owner, contractor, subcontractors, and EIFS supplier to review the specified system. A specification was issued that required a preinstallation conference/mockup review. The mockup was necessary to show all design conditions of the EIFS and encourage the trades to coordinate their work with each other. The EIFS supplier was required to visit the site during installation and certify the finished system. The applicator was required to be certified by the manufacturer.

Although the architect elected to change their drawings and issue a specification, the system was noted as a substitution throughout the documents. The owner-contractor agreement had a clause that required the contractor to replace substituted products or systems that fail during the first year after substantial completion. Substitution notations were added to future payment certifications as well as to the certificate of substantial completion.

Within the first year after project completion, leaks were encountered in the exterior wall, but the subcontractor and supplier corrected the failed conditions without incident. End of story. Everyone was happy. Unfortunately, messy disputes arise when contractors and subcontractors refuse to stand behind their work as this subcontractor did.

## Conclusion

> Money often costs too much.
>
> —Ralph Waldo Emerson

Architects will likely always be challenged by project buyout, even if integrated Project Delivery brings enhanced team interaction and cooperation, as many speculate. The primary risk lies in the widely accepted viewpoint that only one person or company is legally responsible for the selection of the products and systems that go into projects. An architect's reputation and financial survival often rests upon his or her ability to select appropriate products and administer their incorporation into the building design effectively.

Owners and contractors are not concerned and do not worry about the architect's license or the responsibilities that go with it. It therefore becomes incumbent upon the architect to provide protection from detrimental compromises in building designs and systems by issuing warnings of the consequences of value engineering, asking for releases of liability, rejecting and refusing to detail the substitutions that are demanded, and noting substitutions as owner-accepted nonconforming work.

These actions and discussions are not always well accepted by owners and contractors because they appear to be detrimental to the cost reduction process and the architect is not viewed as a "team player." The architect can benefit by taking the initiative and informing and educating the contractor and the owner regarding the risks involved, whether they listen or not.

The informed architect could set up an internal process for administering VE/substitution proposals that can be explained to the owner and contractor before the project begins. Some firms have a VE/substitution spokesperson or committee that reviews and clears all substitution proposals. The decision to change or not change the drawings must be made with care, and the architect benefits from being prepared to help the owner and contractor understand why such actions are being taken. Follow-through is important in qualifying change orders, payment certifications, and certificates of substantial completion to adequately document a contested substitution.

This buyout substitution process, cleverly and erroneously disguised as value engineering, has become very popular over the past few decades, and it will likely not go away. Some architects may continue to accept substitution compromises in their designs in good faith and willingly administer them to their detriment. Effective management of substitution compromises requires actions that are not always easily accepted or understood by the owner or contractor.

So as you review with your fellow architects what your recourse will be when the next unacceptable proposed buyout substitution comes around, such as eliminating the waterproofing from the basement wall, think about what you can do to better protect yourself with documentation, think about how you can help the owner and contractor better understand your view of reasonable objectives, obtain the owner's informed consent to the change . . . oh, and of course, don't forget to be careful out there.

# Ch-Ch-Changes . . . : Managing Risk in the Change Process

W e cannot write about risk without writing about changes. They occur on virtually every project, they are no fun, and people just can't seem to remember who caused them. On the other hand, if changes didn't affect the project cost, they would be popular and everyone would like them. That is why well-funded projects are usually happy projects. The operative word for this piece should probably be "contingency," which is an effective way to deal with the unforeseen but inevitable changes. Excuse me, it costs how much?

> Ch-ch-ch-ch-changes
> (Turn and face the strain)
> Ch-ch-changes
> Don't want to be a richer man
>
> —David Bowie

Changes give life to architecture. The ability to change as designs are developed allows our creative work to breathe. The design process tends to be evolutionary, and second thoughts often give way to improvements. It is said that Frank Lloyd Wright perpetually changed Taliesin East, his home in Spring Green, Wisconsin. The art of creativity is vested in the power of fluid thought. Tweak this, tweak that, and move this over there; no, maybe it's better over here.

But this life-giving force comes with a price. Changes are time-consuming, expensive, and disruptive after construction has begun, and there can be risk involved. Because your drawings can never be 100 percent complete or perfectly coordinated, you risk being scrutinized as if they should have been. If changes are extensive on a project, regardless of who caused the need for change, risk of blame becomes elevated.

This article will examine contract changes and the associated risks. We will look at how each project participant can cause changes, along with the potential consequences. We will review the notorious budget bandito and its sidekick, escalating construction costs, followed by the value analysis process and risks associated with substitutions.

We will look at protective measures that can be taken to manage risks better, as well as helpful documentation techniques. Finally, we will examine problems that often arise in the change process and alternative actions to consider.

> Well I tell you that we'll all be looking for changes.
>
> —Paul McCartney

## Who can change things?

All parties involved in a design and construction project can request that changes be made, but only the owner is empowered to approve them.

Changes in the work can be made through a contract modification. The usual forms of contract modification for changes in the work are (1) AIA Document G701, Change Order; (2) AIA Document G714, Construction Change Directive; and (3) AIA Document G710, Architect's Supplemental Instructions. Contrary to popular opinion, responding to a request for information does not constitute a contract modification.

Another popular myth is that an architect can authorize a change in the work through reviewing and marking up shop drawings and submittals. AIA Document A201, General Conditions of the Contract for Construction, clearly states that the architect's approval of shop drawings and submittals does not change the contract unless the contractor has specifically informed the architect in writing of the change, the architect has given written approval, and a modification as described above has been executed authorizing the deviation.

Owners request changes in the work for many reasons. Their program needs may change due to lifestyle changes or new developments in their business. Tastes may change, or they may simply change their mind about what they want or expect from the design. Many owners who have been involved in the construction process give testimonials that they did not really realize what they wanted until they observed it under construction. These same owners often indicate that the more they saw, the better they wanted it to be, and in the end, the costs of changes exceeded their expectations.

Contractors often request changes in response to the marketplace. If a similar product can be obtained at a lower cost, they may propose using it with the intention of increasing profits. Should the contractor propose a product change after the bidding/negotiation phase, it is appropriate to review the change as a substitution as prescribed in MASTERSPEC Section 016000. This section requires the contractor to submit a substitution request using CSI form 13.1A, Substitution Request.

Substitutions carry risk for the architect and owner in that they may not be equal to or better than the originally specified product, and, if they fail, the architect is sometimes blamed. An alternative is not to add the substitution specifications and details to the contract by change order, as it could then be considered the architect's design. Also, if a paragraph similar to the following is added to the specifications, it provides further protection:

> Contractor warrants that substituted material or system will perform same as original specified material or system would have performed. Should accepted substitution fail to perform as required, Contractor shall replace substitute material or system with that specified and bear costs incurred thereby.

This substitution is intended to protect the owner against contractor-proposed products that fail to perform and protects the architect against questionable products incorporated into the work over their objection.

Another way that the contractor can effect a change in the scope is by installing work that is not in conformance with the contract documents yet is accepted by the owner. Although the nonconforming work may be undesirable and may adversely affect other building components, it is frequently accepted by the owner to avoid a delay in project completion or the threat of additional costs.

A201 allows the architect, acting alone, to make minor changes in the work as long as the contract sum or time is not changed. The architect can, and frequently does, recommend a change to the owner to improve the project's functionality or design.

The architect can cause a change by having errors or omissions in the documents that require correction. When this happens, owners may pursue recovery of the change costs. Therefore, the best recourse for the architect when dealing with an E&O issue is to own up to it and diligently pursue remediation. Avoiding or denying these mistakes can cause greater harm such as increased construction costs and damaged owner relationships. Architects are not perfect and will always make some mistakes, but enthusiastic efforts to effect reasonable corrections can bring benefits and minimize impact expenses.

> I'm blind and shaking
> Bound and breaking
> I hope I make it through all these changes
>
> —3 Doors Down

## Changes to reduce cost or quality

The value analysis process, sometimes referred to as value engineering, can impose significant risk on the architect. Architects often spend years developing and improving their understanding of materials, systems, and specifications. They base their designs on familiarity with the performance of products that have served them for many years. Consequently, architects may decide to remove certain products or systems from their specifications if they have performed poorly.

When the value analysis process is initiated, some contractors propose products based solely on their reduced cost instead of an increased value-to-cost ratio. The architect is usually asked to review and pass judgment on these requested changes in a very short time frame. The institutional memory goes out the window, and the owner often receives less value for money spent. Accordingly, such changes should not be accepted without an appropriate reduction in the contract sum.

When the key is turned and the project is delivered to the owner, the realities of the product's true value and performance usually surface. Owner discontent can lead to claims and legal action against the architect based on the argument that the architect allowed the change. For this reason, the importance of not incorporating value analysis changes into the construction contract as substitutions cannot be overly emphasized.

Errors and omissions bring risk to the architect by their very nature. However, many project discrepancies are characterized as errors or omissions when they are not. For this reason, it is important to assist the owner in understanding the actual cause of the problem. For example, in fast track scheduling, architects must make assumptions as to the location, size, and quantity of mechanical sleeves in the building foundation often before the mechanical system has been designed.

These assumptions are seldom precise, and subsequent changes are often required to fulfill final MEP design requirements. Such imperfections are often looked upon by owners as a mistake by the designers, when in reality only the owner benefits from the quest for speed. For more information on the rigors of fast track, see "Managing Fast Track Projects" that we authored in *The Architect's Handbook of Professional Practice*, 14th edition.

> There ain't no good guys, there ain't no bad guys,
> There's only you and me, and we just disagree
>
> —Billy Dean

## And if by chance we disagree

Although owners can change the scope at their preference, problems can arise if the owner approves a change that the architect recommends against. If the change violates a code requirement, a successful argument can usually be made for rejecting it. But if the change is one affecting performance or quality, the architect may not always prevail.

In this case, the architect must determine if the product will likely perform in an acceptable manner. In the event that, after investigation, the architect feels that the product may not meet expectations, he or she should provide the owner with the supporting information and attempt to build a consensus for rejection. Should this attempt prove unsuccessful, an alternative for the architect is to cite the work as nonconforming and refuse to change the drawings. This becomes owner-accepted nonconforming work, and it should be listed as an exception to AIA Document G704, Certificate of Substantial Completion. Otherwise, it may be alleged that the architect approved the change by default.

The architect's refusal to change the drawings may not meet with the owner's approval, and an explanation may be in order. It can be helpful to explain to the owner that the architect is often inappropriately judged by a product's performance, and the proposed product does not meet the quality level that is acceptable. In addition, when the shop drawings are submitted on the nonconforming product, if they are reviewed and approved by the architect, it may be alleged that the architect approved the change. One alternative in this case is to mark the submittal "approved as noted" and affix a note like the one that follows:

This product has been rejected by the architect as nonconforming work. The owner has approved its use in the project, and it has been designated as a substitution under the conditions set forth in the project specifications.

When the project team is not working in harmony, project delivery can suffer. Therefore, if it appears that a compromising value analysis effort is in the offing, the topic should be openly discussed in the preconstruction conference or scheduled project meetings so that the owner and contractor will know in advance what to expect.

> I hold every man a debtor to his profession.
>
> —Francis Bacon

## The rigors of professional practice

The architect is not required by law to perform flawlessly unless the architect promises to do so. The law of professional liability generally recognizes that perfection is frequently sought and often expected, but is rarely achievable. The negligence standard of care applicable to architects requires that we perform our services on par with the services provided by another prudent architect practicing on a similar project in the same community around the same time. When speaking at AIA functions, we have often asked the architects in the room if anyone has made a mistake on a project. Typically, every person in the room raises a hand. Nonetheless, when a mistake is made, and it costs the owner money, there is likelihood that the owner will be unhappy and ask you to pay. This is true although another architect in the same place and time would likely have made the same or similar mistake.

On the other hand, the architect cannot physically observe and be aware of all discrepancies in the work, and, as a result, all nonconforming conditions may not be noted and qualified in the G704. Should a subsequent building survey reveal these discrepancies, the architect could be accused of failing to detect the problems during construction. Therefore, it is important that the architect document nonconforming work he or she is aware of as an exclusion to G704 on an attached list. This issue is addressed in greater detail in "Absolute or Absolution? Observations, Inspections, and the Contractor's Warranty" in Chapter 4, and in "Visible Means: Site Visits and Construction Observation" later in this chapter.

Although changes are an integral part of project delivery, many owners do not understand the conditions that cause them, and consequently they look to others to pay the costs. Many owners believe that the only changes for which they should expect to pay are the changes that they request. However reasonable this may seem to owners and their lawyers, it is not consistent with the standard of care. Neither the owner, contractor, nor architect can perform flawlessly. All projects should include an allowance for correcting mistakes. It can be beneficial to spend time with the owner discussing this aspect of the change process.

And I hear them saying you'll never change things
And no matter what you do it's still the same thing

—Garth Brooks

## Protective measures

There are actions that can be taken to improve success in the change process. For starters, a realistic budget can do much to help avoid cost overruns. However, maintenance of a realistic budget is dependent upon good estimating from the onset and faithful and diligent updating along the way.

Unfortunately, a budget does not always survive on its own. Significant industry changes, such as the recent escalation in copper, steel, oil, and other commodity prices, can send construction costs skyward. This is where contingencies for the unforeseen can serve to neutralize these unfortunate surprises and help keep the project monetarily on track. Success in developing contingences often requires discussions with the owner regarding causational conditions and to help the owner develop a better understanding of construction cost issues.

A very effective method of overall project risk management can be provided by the contractor during the construction phase. When the contractor prepares and executes an effective Work Plan, complex details can be worked out in advance, discrepancies can be discovered and corrected earlier, and the project generally runs more smoothly. The Work Plan can also show where the contractor's means, methods, techniques, sequences, or procedures may reveal the need to make a change in the design to facilitate how the contractor intends to purchase and place the work. This topic is addressed in "Drawing the Line" in Chapter 4.

Finally, a good baseline for navigating the change process is having the right information and knowing who is doing what and when. Knowledge truly is power in a process where the cause of changes may have begun months or years before and manifested over time. A good practice is to discuss the contract change status as a regular agenda item in your project meetings and report them in your meeting reports. A good opportunity to discuss changes with the owner is when the two of you are walking the site together. Keeping changes as a frequently discussed topic will not only keep memories clearer, it may accelerate resolution.

And all the changes keep on changing
And the good old days they say they're gone.

—Harry Chapin

## The change log—for the record

We have emphasized the importance of documentation more than once in past articles, and nothing is more important in the change process. In today's fast-track-prone industry, change origins and causes are frequently called into question. When memories fade or temporary amnesia takes over, good documentation can often provide realistic insight, and problems are more manageable.

The architect may benefit by making efforts to document, as thoroughly as possible, the cause of each change in a change log as it occurs. Team members sometimes do not remember the conditions that gave rise to the change, and when the architect is able to reconstruct the path of events with documentation, the chance of a disagreement is lessened. An effective change log should reflect the following information:

---

### Change Log

| | |
|---|---|
| Date | *December 24, 2007* |
| Description | *Add a door from the conference room into Mr. Smith's office* |
| Purpose/Reason | *More convenient access to the conference room* |
| Requested by | *Mr. Smith* |
| Change Proposal/ Number | *Work Changes Proposal Request, No. 7, dated December 19, 2007* |
| Estimated Cost | *Being developed by the contractor* |
| Modification Document/Number | *Construction Change Directive, No. 4, dated December 23, 2007* |
| Current Status | *Authorized to proceed by Mr. Wright* |

---

Such a log may be viewed as burdensome, but carefully detailed records such as this can be an effective defense against faded memories of past actions and events.

> I'm gonna make him an offer he can't refuse.
>
> —Don Corleone

## Change review meetings

The best practice when reviewing change orders is to do so in an open meeting where all parties can participate in the discussion. This should be done after the architect has had an opportunity to review the contractor's proposal and prepare a draft of G701. Obviously, the architect's review should only take place after the issues involved in the change have been discussed in project meetings; necessary drawings, sketches, and specifications have been prepared; and a proposal or pricing for the change has been submitted by the contractor.

The purpose of the change review meeting is to review cost and time impacts, approve changes, document decisions, and authorize the contractor to proceed with the work. If pricing or time impact information is not available, the parties can discuss authorizing the change through use of a construction change directive. The discussion should include how cost and time are to be resolved in the event of a dispute after the work has been completed.

> If you want to make enemies, try to change something.
> —Woodrow Wilson

## P-P-Problems

A high incidence of nonconforming work and a significantly exceeded budget are two factors that negatively affect the change process.

**Vicarious acceptance of nonconforming work.** When claims are made against architects where defective and nonconforming work is involved, it is often alleged that the architect has responsibility for damages because he or she vicariously "accepted" or "approved" the nonconforming work by signing documents used in administering the work such as AIA Document G702, Application and Certificate for Payment, or G701, Change Order. We have identified this problem in prior articles regarding the architect's certification of substantial completion and payment. Regardless of the presence of the architect's signature on these documents, the nonconforming work is rightfully covered by the contractor's warranty along with the contractor's sole responsibility for complying with the contract documents. This position was delineated in "Absolute or Absolution?" in Chapter 4.

**Vicarious approval of runaway change order costs.** When claims are made against architects on problem projects where the budget is exceeded by a significant margin, regardless of the causes, it is almost always argued that the architect is responsible for damages because he or she vicariously "accepted" or "approved" the contractor's excessive change order costs. The basis for the allegation is because the architect signs G701 along with the owner and the contractor. The architect should be very scrupulous in reviewing the contractor's proposed costs, keeping careful records, and calling the costs into question when necessary. Whenever a change is proposed after the start of construction, it is always beneficial to remind the owner that the work will not be competitively bid and costs are likely to be higher than if included in the original construction documents. We have seen this claim made against architects, although the architect protested for months over the excessive proposed change pricing.

There are limited available options when a contractor quotes excessive prices for changes on a project. One includes the use of a construction change directive, with the contractor performing the work on a time and materials basis. With this approach, be aware that the owner's administrative efforts to monitor the contractor's work time and audit payment records will be increased. Another option is to contract with a separate contractor to do the work. This approach can be problematic should the warranty of the work be affected by the presence of the second contractor. The limited recourse to this unfortunate situation underscores the importance of prequalifying contractors with acceptable performance histories.

Finally, in a circumstance where other parties, such as an owner's representative, a program manager, or a construction manager, are responsible for reviewing and approving costs and/or time, the architect may consider adding a statement to G701 (or G701/CMa, the construction manager-adviser edition) that the architect's signature does not represent an opinion about the construction costs and/or time that are the rightful purview of others.

> When you're finished changing, you're finished.
>
> —Benjamin Franklin

## Conclusion

Changes can originate through all team members deliberately, by default, or by mistake, and their impact on the project relative to time, cost, and quality can profoundly affect how the project outcome is experienced or perceived. All parties can cause damaging impacts to a project.

- The owner can cause damaging impact through failure to understand scope objectives and the program for the project. Too many changes can cause disruption to the project coordination and construction sequencing.
- One of the most damaging impacts on a project is contractor installation of nonconforming work that the owner accepts to save remediation time or avoid forced correction efforts.
- The architect can cause disruption and damaging impact through excessive errors and omissions that can occur when construction documents are poorly prepared and coordinated.

Changes complicate and disrupt the design and construction process. They take up our time and cost us money. They are often controversial, untimely, and provocative. Nonetheless, they are an integral part of architecture and construction, and our skills as architects will be judged on how well we manage them. Changes are usually made under duress when construction is in progress and time is money. Moreover, the owner and contractor may not want to face the tough realities of changes: that they subvert coordination and that administering changes takes valuable time.

Therefore, it is important that architects contribute to managing the change process effectively by explaining the consequences of changes carefully to the owner, frequently monitoring the budget, pushing for the use of contingencies, pursuing the selection of qualified contractors, maintaining good documentation, and insisting that the change order status be a frequent topic of conversation on the project.

So, as you contemplate the owner's most recently requested revisions and consider how you will present your thoughts about increased costs and extended schedules, turn on your computer and update the change log, and always remember to be careful out there.

# According to Hoyle: The Submittal Process

This article was one that we had been itching to write since the series began because the submittal process is not adequately followed on many projects. We used Edmund Hoyle as the example to show that success can be achieved if procedures are strictly adhered to. The article is straightforward, and although the submittal process can be much like a card game, we wrote this one with no cards up our sleeves. Read on and be prepared to effectively administer your submittal process the next time it is your turn to cut the deck.

Any architect who has experienced the construction phase of services will likely agree that contractor submittals are a daunting and risky part of the work. They tend to be numerous, complex, and time-driven. Their success in efficiently traversing the review process is largely dependent on the submitting contractor's scheduling, sequencing, checking, and coordination.

Meanwhile, the contractors are struggling with the prerequisites of subcontractor and vendor selection and product buyout, along with the contracts and purchase orders that follow; all the while trying to comply with the schedules that they submitted at the start of construction.

The architect is often pressured in contract negotiation to reduce the number of submittal review days with the assumption that it will in some way accelerate the project. The reality is that the steps in the process are usually the same no matter what, and if acceleration is desired, effective coordination, timely actions, and established procedures subscribed to by all players will be of greater benefit than hurried actions and eliminated steps.

This article will address the activities that make up the submittal process, along with the complexities and challenges contained therein. It will review the components and activities associated with submittals, as well as offer suggestions for establishing and administering an efficient and effective review process.

Finally, it will offer actions you can take to manage your risks in this area of services. Issues such as how to manage multiple discipline reviewers, what to do when the submittal schedule is late or not provided, how to deal with forced substitutions that are more and more common in submittals, and what actions to take with submittals that are poorly prepared or inadequately reviewed by the contractor will be addressed.

Project success is dependent on the checks and balances inherent in the submittal process, and for it to run smoothly and efficiently, there should be a set of rules and procedures. Like Edmund Hoyle, when he set out the rules for the game of whist in England in 1743 and forever coined the phrase, "According to Hoyle," if a set of rules and procedures is established for submittals, and it is managed accordingly, the chances of reducing risk and achieving success can be greatly improved.

## Responsibility for submittals

The purpose and use of submittals in the design and construction process are not always well understood. To understand fully what submittals are and what they do, we should first review the basics.

**Who prepares submittals?** Submittals are prepared or furnished by the contractor. The architect does not prepare, seal, or issue submittals, and is not responsible for their accuracy or completeness. AIA Document A201-2007 and with similar language in A201-1997, General Conditions of the Contract for Construction, (A201) state:

> 3.12.1 Shop drawings are drawings, diagrams, schedules and other data specially prepared for the Work by the Contractor or a Subcontractor, Sub-subcontractor, manufacturer, supplier or distributor to illustrate some portion of the Work.

**The purpose of submittals.** The purpose of submittals such as shop drawings and the conceptual nature of construction documents prepared by design professionals are addressed in A201:

> 3.12.4 Their **purpose** is to demonstrate **the way by which the Contractor proposes to conform** to the information given and the design concept expressed in the Contract Documents . . .

**Submittals are not contract documents.** The contractor prepares submittals, and the architect prepares contract documents. A201 states:

> 3.12.4 Shop Drawings, Product Data, Samples and similar submittals are not Contract Documents.

**The contractor reviews and approves submittals.** Submittals represent that the contractor has selected and coordinated appropriate products, has reviewed the submittals, and has determined and confirmed the finite details and dimensions required to complete the work. From A201:

> 3.12.6 By submitting . . . submittals, the Contractor represents to the Owner and Architect that the Contractor has (1) reviewed and approved them, (2) determined and verified materials, field measurements and field construction criteria related thereto, or will do so and (3) checked and coordinated the information contained within such submittals with the requirements of the Work and of the Contract Documents.

This common language describes routine procedure throughout the industry. The purpose for the contractor's check is to coordinate and verify that the work, as the contractor has divided it among the trades, will comply with the requirements of the contract documents.

**Submittals are required to do the work.** Submittals are the confirmation of the contractor's intent to comply with the design concept. The importance of this compliance process is emphasized by the prerequisite condition stated in A201:

> 3.12.7: The Contractor shall perform no portion of the Work for which the Contract Documents require submittal and review of Shop Drawings, Product Data, Samples or similar submittals until the respective submittal has been approved by the Architect.

Submittals are not intended to be an opportunity to alter the design concept by either the designer or the contractor. Their purpose is to express how the finished building will be constructed. The contractor reviews submittals to determine if they represent the work as they have purchased and will place it. The architect does not review submittals to determine if the finite details and dimensions are correct because only the contractor has control of or responsibility for the work, the required dimensions, and how all the pieces fit together to form the completed project.

## The architect's role

The architect's role in reviewing submittals is addressed in A201-2007 with similar language in A201-1997:

> 4.2.7 The Architect will review and approve, or take other appropriate action upon, the Contractor's submittals . . . but only for the limited purpose of checking for conformance with information given and the design concept expressed in the Contract Documents.

Although the architect's limited review is clearly stated, Section 4.2.7 continues to clarify what the review is not intended to accomplish:

> 4.2.7 Review of such submittals is not conducted for the purpose of determining the accuracy and completeness of other details such as dimensions and quantities . . . all of which remain the responsibility of the Contractor . . .

The limitations of the architect's review as stated in the general conditions are straightforward. However, for many years some owners and contractors have alleged the architect's review serves as "the architect's guarantee" that the submittal is precisely correct, is coordinated with other submittals, and includes everything required to complete the project. Afterward, should the submittal prove to be incomplete, incorrect, or result in missing or nonconforming work, they allege that it is the architect's fault that the contractor did not fulfill the contractual responsibility to prepare the submittal appropriately. Such allegations fail to acknowledge the contractor's sole responsibility for the work as addressed in A201-2007 and A201-1997:

> 3.12.8 The Work shall be in accordance with approved submittals except **that the Contractor shall not be relieved of responsibility**

for deviations from requirements of the Contract Documents by the Architect's approval of Shop Drawings, Product Data, Samples or similar submittals . . .

This alleged responsibility of the architect for failing to "catch" the contractor's errors flies in the face of AIA general conditions. This mistaken perception was explored in detail in "Absolute or Absolution?" in Chapter 4.

## Types of submittals

There are numerous types of submittals, including shop drawings, product data, and samples, as defined in A201-2007 with similar language in AIA 201-1997:

> 3.12.1 Shop Drawings are drawings, diagrams, schedules and other data specially prepared for the Work by the Contractor . . .
> 3.12.2 Product Data are illustrations, standard schedules, performance charts, instructions, brochures, diagrams and other information furnished by the Contractor . . .
> 3.12.3 Samples are physical examples that illustrate materials, equipment or workmanship and establish standards by which the Work will be judged.

Items and information that fall within these categories can include but are not limited to:

- Physical mockups
- Product, material, or system performance calculations
- Physical product and finish samples
- Coordination drawings
- Key schedules
- Warranties and guarantees
- Record drawings
- Operations manuals

## Submittal requirements

Submittals are an integral part of the contractor's obligation to schedule and coordinate the work and to illustrate to the architect that their finished project will be in accordance with the requirements of the contract documents. A201 states:

> 3.12.5 The Contractor shall review for compliance with the Contract Documents, approve and submit to the Architect Shop Drawings, Product Data, Samples and similar submittals required by the Contract Documents . . .

Similar language is included in AIA Document, A107-2007, Standard Form of Agreement Between Owner and Contractor for a Project of Limited Scope.

## MASTERSPEC

Project specifications customarily address submittals and the submittal review process. For example, MASTERSPEC Section 013300 division 1330 tracks A201 and offers specifics for submittal procedures, including time for review, the number of copies of submittals, and transmittal and tracking documents. For review purposes, MASTERSPEC identifies submittals in two categories: action submittals, which require the architect's responsive action, and informational submittals, which do not require the architect's approval.

## Submittal routing

The contractor submits to the architect, who routes appropriate submittals through consultants, who return the reviewed copy to the architect, who checks for architectural issues and returns copies to the contractor and owner.

## The submittal game

To manage submittals effectively, it is important that the steps in the submittal process be clearly defined to all participants. The following sequence describes the activities and actions that may be used for processing submittals. Project requirements vary, and these steps may not apply to all projects.

**Subcontractor/supplier prepares submittal.** The contractor, subcontractors, and product vendors are usually most informed about the specified product or system. They should prepare, in collaboration with the manufacturer, the detailed drawings that describe precisely how their product will be coordinated with adjacent building products and systems and incorporated into the work. A wise subcontractor will have the manufacturer confirm in writing that the application of the product or system is appropriate.

Unfortunately, perhaps in response to the potential for litigation and the pressures of risk management, there is often a propensity to indicate surrounding materials vaguely and designated as "by others." Although this may provide a vendor or subcontractor with plausible deniability as to the requirements of coordination with surrounding systems, it provides the contractor with little opportunity for effective coordination of the trades. Submittals that do not adequately address the specifics for installation into the project should be rejected by both the contractor and the architect.

**Subcontractor and/or supplier submits to general contractor.** The subcontractor, after a careful review of the submittal, submits the information to the general contractor, with an attached transmittal, in accordance with the accepted submittal schedule.

**General contractor affixes control number.** The general contractor stamps the submittal "received" and affixes a permanent control number in accordance with the project specifications. The submittal is logged into the approved tracking system.

**Contractor reviews and marks up submittal.** The general contractor performs a detailed review of the submittal, coordinating it with adjacent materials and systems, and marks up the submittal to indicate dimensional corrections and specific detail configurations. If the contractor finds the submittal inadequately prepared, the contractor should return the submittal to the subcontractor for revision or correction. The submittal should be forwarded to the architect after it thoroughly and accurately represents how the contractor intends to comply with the contract documents. The contractor remains responsible for compliance with the contract documents without regard of the architect's interaction with the submittals.

Note: The requirement for the contractor to stamp submittals approval was removed in the 2007 document revisions, however, submittal to the architect is a representation that the contractor has reviewed.

**Contractor submits to architect.** Only after the contractor's approval is the submittal sent to the architect with an attached transmittal. The action is logged into the approved tracking system.

**Architect receives submittal and distributes.** The architect stamps the submittal "received" and logs it into the submittal log. If the submittal requires review by a consultant, the submittal is routed to the consultant with an attached transmittal.

**Architect reviews and marks up submittal.** The architect reviews the submittal, but with the limitation stated in A201.

> 4.2.7 . . . only for the limited purpose of checking for conformance with information given and the design concept expressed in the Contract Documents.

The architect marks up the submittal if deemed necessary. If the submittal has been reviewed by a consultant, the architect reviews it for impact on the architectural scope and marks it up accordingly, noting that its review is for architectural scope only.

**Architect stamps submittal.** The architect affixes the review stamp. Options can include approved, approved as noted, revise and resubmit, no action taken, or submittal not required by contract documents.

**Architect returns submittal to contractor.** The architect returns the submittal to the contractor with an attached transmittal, logging submittal description, submittal date, and actions taken.

**Contractor coordinates submittal with work plan and other trades.** The contractor stamps the submittal received and reviews the marked-up submittal, coordinating it with other submittals, adjacent work and the contractor's Work Plan. The issue of the contractor's Work Plan is discussed in the "Drawing the Line" in Chapter 4.

**Contractor returns submittal to subcontractor.** The contractor returns the submittal, with attached transmittal, to the subcontractor to allow fabrication or installation as appropriate.

## Submittal review recommendations

Some steps to take that could improve your experiences with the submittal process are:

- Allow adequate review time in the owner-architect agreement and specifications.
- Require a valid submittal schedule from the contractor so you can plan your commitments.
- Review the submittal process in the preconstruction conference.
- Use a unique control number on each submittal.
- Log and track each submittal.
- Have multiple reviewers use different color markers for tracking.
- Do not review submittals not required by the contract documents.

The key to implementing and managing submittals is to address the issue up front in your contracts and specifications and thoroughly review the process in the preconstruction conference. You should bring your general conditions and specifications to the preconstruction conference and each job meeting and discuss openly the requirements for submittal scheduling, contractor review, submission, and processing.

## Tough cards to play

Regardless of how well a submittal process is planned, issues can arise that challenge efforts and test resolve. Since the same issues are prone to arise on any project, actions can be taken to help reduce the challenges or possibly prevent them from occurring altogether.

The following challenges may be encountered by the architect on a project during the submittal process:

**Inadequate submittal time in contract.** The architect has agreed to an abbreviated submittal review time in the owner-architect agreement. This often results in confrontational tracking of "aged" submittals by the contractor. These aged submittals are often cited by the owner and contractor when they allege delays caused by the "poor performance" of the architect.

**Possible solution.** The best way to allow sufficient time for submittal review is to insist on an adequate duration during contract negotiation. A popular period is a minimum of 10 business days on average. The average time will allow you to bank review time from quickly reviewed submittals to use on those that take longer. This may require an explanation to the owner as to why this average duration is needed, so be ready to make your case. Many contract negotiation issues can be resolved with adequate client enlightenment.

**No submittal schedule.** The absence of a submittal schedule usually indicates that the contractor has not planned and scheduled the sequence of submittals. This often represents a serious flaw in the contractor's Work Plan. A201, Section 3.10.2 and MASTERSPEC Sections 013200 and 013300 require that the schedule be prepared and submitted to the architect. The submittal schedule is required to be coordinated with the overall project construction schedule.

**Possible solution.** If the contractor refuses to provide a submittal schedule, it is advisable to document the event by sending correspondence to the owner noting the issue and advising that all previously agreed-upon review times are suspended until an acceptable submittal schedule is provided. Remember that you have a right to determine if the submittal schedule is acceptable to your administrative schedule. To provide an incentive to the contractor to provide the schedule, you may elect to send AIA Document G716 Request for Information requesting that the contractor provide the schedule. You may wish to track the RFI in a log to document the delay caused by the contractor's failure to submit, as well as insist that the tardy schedule be tracked in the contractor's submittal log.

**Late submittals.** When submittals do not conform to the submittal schedule, it is usually an indication that the schedule is inaccurate or the contractor is behind in project buyout. This sometimes results in pressure applied to the architect to accelerate reviews to make up for the contractor's poor planning.

**Possible solution.** If the contractor is not adhering to the submittal schedule, it is advisable to notify the contractor that they are not in compliance with the requirements of the contract documents. Make an effort to assist them in correcting the problem, but if it persists, you should advise the owner in writing that, until the contractor adheres to the accepted submittal schedule, you cannot comply with your previously agreed-upon review time, and additional costs may be incurred as a result. It is also another opportunity to send and track an RFI requesting the information.

**Forced substitutions in submittals.** A tactic sometimes used by the contractor to force a substitution involves waiting until a submittal is due or past due and the construction schedule is being threatened. A substituted product or system is proposed with the premise that there is insufficient time to prepare and submit the specified item, alleging that the project will be delayed unless the substitution is accepted. Owners and architects are often forced to acquiesce to the substitution because of these time constraints.

**Possible solution.** Should the contractor attempt to wait until the last minute and submit a substituted product or system in the form of shop drawings, it is recommended that the submittal be rejected as nonconforming work and the contractor be reminded of the substitution requirements in the specifications. MASTERSPEC requires that substitutions be requested within a specified time after the notice to proceed. If the owner elects to accept the substitution, unless you feel that it is equal to or better than the originally specified product or system, you should advise the owner that it will be considered owner-approved nonconforming work and will likely be listed as an exception in the certificate of substantial completion.

The issue of forced substitutions in submittals is addressed in *The Architect's Handbook of Professional Practice*, 14th edition in an article entitled "Maintaining Design Quality."

**Work performed without an approved submittal.** Some contractors elect to put the work in place before the submittal has been approved, possibly to accelerate the work, or because there was no submittal or the contractor neglected to resubmit a previously rejected submittal. Regardless, placing work without an approved submittal is strictly prohibited by A201:

> 3.12.7 The Contractor shall perform no portion of the Work for which the Contract Documents require submittal and review of Shop Drawings, Product Data, Samples or similar submittals until the respective submittal has been approved by the Architect.

**Possible solution.** If the contractor refuses to resubmit a submittal that has been noted for this action, you may wish to remind the contractor in writing of the requirements of A201 cited above which prohibits the contractor from performing work without a required submittal. You may choose to copy the owner on the notice. This is also an appropriate opportunity to submit an RFI to the contractor requesting resubmittal.

When claims are levied against architects, it is often argued that the architect most be aware of and prevent the contractor from installing work without approved shop drawings. A201, Section 3.12.7, and the fact that submittals are part of the "Work" make it clear that the contractor is solely responsible for work performed in the absence of approved submittals.

## Submittals are a part of the work

The contractor is paid to produce shop drawings and submittals because they are a part of the Work as defined in A201:

> 1.1.3 The term "Work" means the construction and services required by the Contract Documents . . . and includes all other labor, materials, equipment and services provided or to be provided by the Contractor to fulfill the Contractor's obligations.

As a part of the Work, we believe they come under the terms of the contractor's warranty as reflected in A201-2007 with similar language in A201-1997:

> 3.5 The Contractor warrants to the Owner and Architect that . . . the Work will conform to the requirements of the Contract Documents . . .

Many contractors diligently administer the submittal process, and when they do there are usually few problems that result. However, it is advisable to decide your alternative courses of action and be prepared to respond to challenging submittal issues should they arise.

## Blind nello

The contractor's responsibilities for submittals notwithstanding, the architect should diligently manage its portion of the submittal review process. The architect is expected to review the submittals in the context of the requirements of the contract documents and review them so as to cause no unreasonable delay in the work. An architect could fail to meet these responsibilities if he or she started redesigning the project or changing the scope of the work through review redlines and comments made on the submittals.

The architect could also incur risk if he or she marks through the contractor's submittal information and provides alternate information that is inaccurate. For example, a contractor provides a window submittal with exact dimensional information given; the architect, believing the dimensions are inaccurate, marks through the contractor's dimensions and provides alternate dimensions. As the work is installed, it becomes apparent that the architect's dimensions are incorrect. In this instance, the architect could be held responsible for the architect's erroneous dimension markups. A better form of communication in this instance would be to provide a notation requesting the contractor to confirm the dimensions shown on the submittal.

## Calling the hand

Over 250 years ago, Edmund Hoyle evaluated the game of whist and set out rules and procedures for players to follow. His rules of games have prevailed over time to the extent that his authority is now communicated through a catchphrase that is applied to all activities that benefit from a set of rules. The submittal process is dependent on following the rules, and success is best achieved, especially in the submittal process, when it is followed according to Hoyle.

The checks and balances inherent in the submittal process contemplated by A201 are designed to promote successful projects. Submittals are the most explicit indication of how the contractor has interpreted the design concept expressed in the contract documents. They indicate the extent to which the contractor has organized, coordinated, and developed their work plan. The speed and efficiency with which the architect can review and approve submittals is to a great extent dependent on how well the project team prepares and performs.

The best approach is to plan well and plan early. The preconstruction conference provides an opportunity to discuss how the submittal process will flow. Discussions should include document media, number of copies, review mark colors, control number format, and routing. One firm produces a project procedures manual, which includes a flow diagram for submittals. If all aspects of the process are agreed upon in advance, the chance of misunderstandings and poor participation are lessened.

As the architect, you should consider tracking submittal progress with your own log rather than relying only on the contractor's tracking. Most contracts these days have a designated review time, and the process should be managed to stay on schedule. An effective logging system can track the contractor's actions as well as your own. It seems that more and more project meetings these days include an adversarial and confrontational display of the architect's shortcomings through illustrations from the contractor's submittal log. The contractor's shortcomings of inadequate reviews and late or missing submittals are not generally tracked in the contractor's tracking logs. Efficient and proactive submittal management is necessary to stay on top of the game.

As we move toward more integrated project deliveries, the submittal process may change, but it will never go away. Architects will continue to produce conceptual documents, and contractors will interpret the concept through submittals. The process will likely continue to be the most critical time-driven activity in the construction process.

Set down that cup of coffee and unroll that submittal on your desk. Check to see that the contractor has affixed and signed their approved stamp, and look to see that the control number is correct. And, as you reach for your received stamp, don't forget to be careful out there.

# Visible Means: Site Visits and Construction Observation

I n this article, we provide all the basics for conducting and reporting site observations. We leaned away from the archaic term "field observation" because projects today are not always in a "field." The operative words for this piece are "work observed," and we discuss the issue of "concealed and nonconforming work." The essence of the article is that you can't see everything constructed on a project, and we are gratified that the 2007 AIA document changes reinforce this position. Now where did I put my hard hat?

One of the more rewarding experiences in architecture is to see your project under construction. Nothing is more exciting than to visit a busy job site, smell freshly cut wood, and observe the trades as they perform their skills and artistry.

The construction phase, as we have noted before, carries a high level of risk. Architects are judged not only by the accuracy of their documents, but also by how quickly they respond and the actions they take. It is understandable that most claims against architects arise during this time.

Site visits should not be approached casually and, above all, should not be eliminated from contracted services. Some states now require that a registered architect be retained to provide construction contract administration services if an architect was required to provide the building design. Many firms have a policy of refusing to eliminate construction contract administration from professional service contracts.

On the other hand, providing construction services can also bring opportunities. Should errors or omissions become evident, the architect is available to provide timely solutions and corrections that can preserve the design intent and potentially minimize claims for damages.

This article will focus on site visits and on-site activities during the construction phase. It will explore important activities, such as attending and reporting project meetings, reviewing applications for payment, conducting preinstallation conferences, and providing inspections for substantial and final completion. It will address the preparation of site observation reports and some effective ways to communicate the project status to the owner. Visits to the site should be enjoyable, but we should not forget the primary purpose for traveling there.

## Preparation

AIA Document G612-2001, Owner's Instructions to the Architect Regarding the Construction Contract, Parts A, B and C, is a useful form for addressing important issues—such as construction to be performed by the owner's own forces, fast-track scheduling, phased occupancy, and bond and insurance information—in addition to information required for the bidding process. The information on the form should be gathered from the owner at the start of the project.

The next step in preparation is to read the contracts. The owner-architect agreement contains your service requirements during the construction phase, and the owner-contractor agreement and general conditions document provide information on the contractor's duties. You should be aware that most of the AIA's Owner-Architect Agreements incorporate by reference the architect's construction phase services described in a particular general conditions document. It is important to determine if the requirements of the owner-architect agreement and the owner-contractor contract are consistent. There is a greater likelihood that the documents will be consistent if they are AIA documents. Unfortunately, some owners prefer to use non-AIA documents, or AIA documents that have been extensively modified.

Variations in the documents could cause misunderstandings and discord, and you could be prevented from providing contracted services. For example, if you have typical basic services during construction in your contract, you will be required to review and certify contractor applications for payment. In the event this requirement is not in the contractor's agreement, you could be bypassed in the process. Although this may be advantageous from a risk standpoint, you will not be providing services according to your contract. Unless the documents can be made consistent through the change process, you should advise the owner in writing of the discrepancy. This will document that the owner has been made aware that you will not be performing the services.

When you have determined the contract requirements, you should assemble the necessary items to do your job. These could include the following:

- Owner-architect agreement with atypical conditions noted
- Owner-contractor agreement, general conditions, and supplementary conditions with atypical conditions noted

- Drawings and specifications
- Consistent filing protocol for documents
- Laptop computer
- Cell phone
- BlackBerry or other PDA
- Digital camera
- Sketch pad or journal
- Hard hat
- Appropriate shoes
- Safety vest
- Goggles
- Measuring tape
- Flashlight
- Mirror

## Site visits

Site visits can be time-consuming and labor-intensive, and they should be planned and executed efficiently. If your contract does not stipulate a structured sequence or time for visits, discuss with the contractor during the preconstruction conference which day of the week is best for the visit. Contractor Work Plans, when the contractor has actually prepared one, are usually organized around weekly subcontractor meetings, and team members often prefer the project meeting to be held on the same day at the same time each week, every two weeks, or at such interval as agreed upon with the owner.

AIA Document A201-2007, General Conditions of the Contract for Construction (A201), addresses site visit requirements:

> 4.2.2 The Architect will visit the site at intervals appropriate to the stage of construction . . . to become generally familiar with the progress and quality of the portion of the Work completed, and to determine in general if the Work observed is being performed in a manner indicating that the Work, when fully completed, will be in accordance with the Contract Documents.

These three objectives, (1) to report the progress and quality of the work to the owner, (2) to report any observed deficiencies, and (3) to assess conformance of completed work to the contract, are the contracted reasons for visiting the site. The wording "endeavor to guard", which appears in the 1997 AIA document revisions, is used by claimants in attempts to establish that the architect has an overriding duty to guard the owner from defects and deficiencies in the work. This phrase was removed in the 2007 AIA document revisions.

In addition to these contracted services, there are other administrative tasks that can be performed during the visit. Determining the "appropriate" time to visit can be accomplished in several ways. If the contract does not stipulate a specific time or interval, scheduled visits can be determined during the preconstruction conference. The complexity and sequencing of the project may influence the number and frequency of visits. The level of activity may also influence the visit interval. For example, you may visit the site less frequently during excavation and site preparation than during erection of the primary structure. On complex projects, it is important to determine before contract negotiation if a high number of visits will be required.

Structural consultants will conduct their site visits at the beginning of the project, and mechanical, electrical, and plumbing consultants will visit less often in the beginning, with visits increasing as more of their work is installed. Special consultants, such as curtainwall or roofing consultants, will schedule visits as their products or systems are installed. One must always be prepared to go to the site when circumstances demand, but it is more desirable to make scheduled visits and tend to business in an orderly fashion on each occasion.

Site visits are typically scheduled to coincide with the project meeting, also referred to as the owner-architect-contractor (OAC) meeting. OAC meetings are often held at the project site to allow reviews of ongoing construction issues and challenges, presenting an opportunity to "walk the job" with the owner and contractor.

Other activities in addition to site observations that are conducted during site visits include the review of a "pencil copy" of the contractor payment applications, review of pending change orders, review of the contractor's as-built drawings, and, most importantly, spending time with the owner. Some clients are not familiar with the construction process, and walking the site to review and explain construction issues and details can put them at ease, in addition to cultivating a relationship.

## Site observations

Site observations have a limited purpose, and that purpose is misunderstood by many. A201 requires that we become "generally familiar" with the work. This is not a requirement to know everything that is going on. While developing this general familiarity, we are to report deficiencies if any are observed and determine generally if the completed work conforms or will conform to the contract requirements. Owners and contractors frequently want to believe that site observations are thorough inspections of each element of the project by the architect, but that is simply not the case.

For the reason cited above, construction observation carries increased risk and should be undertaken by the most qualified people available for the assignment. Some firms elect to have nonarchitectural experienced personnel who have knowledge of construction make the site visits under the supervision of a registered architect. However, this approach can be challenging when design problems arise that require immediate resolution. For this reason, it is desirable to have site visits conducted by the partner, project manager, project architect, or other person who has construction contract administration experience. Larger firms may use a dedicated construction services department to accomplish this task.

Some architects prefer to walk the site prior to the OAC meeting to become familiar with the progress of the work. They may note questionable issues or conditions that warrant discussion in the meeting. They will also be able to report the general progress of the work to the owner. When such opinions about the progress of the work are presented to the owner, whatever the venue, it is preferable that the architect document the discussions for their records, even if reported orally. When claims of negligence are filed against architects, it is often alleged that the architect was not adequately keeping the owner informed. Good records of discussions can help defend against this form of amnesia. Many firms have a policy that a written report is issued after every visit to the site.

Many owners look forward to the opportunity to walk the site with the architect, and an invitation should be offered accordingly. It is also common in conjunction with the OAC meeting for the contractor to request observations of specific issues and conditions that may require an interpretation by the architect. If the issue cannot be resolved immediately, the architect should be prepared to document the condition for resolution back at the office.

Preparation for walking the site can include a digital camera, a set of drawings for reference, a sketch pad or journal, a measuring tape, and a flashlight. Some architects like to take a mirror for peering into dark or hard-to-access spaces. If a particular product or system is being observed, it is helpful to have the appropriate shop drawing or product data. Business attire is usually not appropriate if you are walking around formwork and wet paint or entering dusty work areas.

Interaction on the site with the contractor and subcontractors should not be confrontational or argumentative. It can be challenging for the architect to maintain a neutral posture if approached by the contractor or subcontractor on difficult issues. Remember that the overall objective is the same for everyone: to deliver successfully a completed project that conforms to the design concept. Construction administration issues and attitudes are addressed in the article "Zen and the Art of Construction Administration" in Chapter 3.

The contractor is required to provide a safe workplace and give the architect access to the work. Safety, these days, may involve protective goggles and a brightly colored safety vest in addition to a hard hat and appropriate footwear. Some project sites prohibit shorts, as well as women's skirts and heels, and require viewing of a safety film before entering the work area. These precautions are definitely beneficial, but they are also a testament to the increase in personal injury claims on projects.

Some subcontractors have requested architects to sign a release before entering temporary structures such as scaffolding. AIA documents typically require that the contractor provide a safe workplace and give the architect access to the work. Should you be approached to sign a release, advise the general contractor of the issue, and ask how you will be given safe access to the work. You should consult your attorney before signing such a document.

## Concealed and nonconforming work

Observation of the work prior to it being concealed by subsequent work, if possible within the framework of the project schedule, may require some level of orchestration. It is advisable to discuss this issue with the contractor in the preconstruction conference so that site visits can be planned accordingly. On healthcare and other projects with complex building systems, an "above ceiling punch" is often done, and timing of the site visit is necessary to coordinate with available completed spaces. Given the limited nature of the time the architect spends on site, it may not be possible to review all work before it is concealed. If you have a special interest in a portion of the work that may be covered before your next visit, discuss schedule options with the contractor and owner.

In the event work is concealed before the architect has had a chance to make an observation, if the work is suspect, it may be necessary to have the work uncovered. If the observation was discussed in advance, and the contractor concealed work that the architect requested to see without prior notification to the architect, Section 12.1.1 of A201 requires the contractor to uncover the work at his or her own expense if requested to do so.

When there is no prior understanding that the work is to be left exposed by the contractor until the observations are made, the contractor can be required to uncover the work, but if it is found to be acceptable, the owner may have to pay for the costs involved under A201 Section 12.1.2. If the work is found to be not in conformance with the contract documents, the contractor may have to pick up the tab. With the possibility of disputed costs involved, the decision to uncover concealed work should be discussed openly and in detail with all involved parties. And, you guessed it, discussions should be documented thoroughly.

When nonconforming work is encountered, the contractor should be notified in writing. Although the defects may be discovered with the contractor present, they should nonetheless be documented to allow future confirmation of resolution. Documentation can be accomplished through a field observation report, an OAC meeting report, a memorandum, or a letter. When you cite nonconforming work and ask that it be remedied, be prepared for resistance, because replacing work already in place is an unpleasant event for everyone. This issue of replacing installed work is addressed in "Gimme Shelter: The Building Exterior Wall" in Chapter 7.

## Inspections

A201-2007 and A201-1997 require the architect to make only two inspections on each project:

> 4.2.9 The Architect will conduct inspections to determine the date or dates of Substantial Completion and the date of final completion . . .

These two inspections differ from a scheduled site observation. In the first of these two inspections, the architect is looking at the "completed" work to determine if it appears to be "substantially" complete. Completed work conceals many supporting elements, and there is no way to know if those portions of the project are correctly installed unless the architect witnessed every piece of the project as it was installed. Even though these two events are called "inspections," it serves to remember that they are based on becoming "generally familiar" with the work and are not based on exhaustive inspections. This complex and often misunderstood event is addressed in "Substantial Completion, Where Art Thou? A Challenging and Elusive Milestone" later in this chapter.

Substantial completion marks the beginning of the closeout phase of the project, and adequate preparation will allow for greater efficiency and fewer misunderstandings as the project comes to an end. A good way to begin is with a pre-closeout conference. The conference should be attended by the full project team. Discussions can include level of quality expected, required closeout documents, the punch list review schedule, and owner-accepted nonconforming work. Project closeout is addressed in an article entitled "Project Closeouts" in the 14th edition of *The Architect's Handbook of Professional Practice*.

## Reporting

The status of construction can be reported in multiple formats. Most written formats are acceptable as long as they are issued timely. Some project management software programs include an observation report form.

AIA Document G711-1972, Architect's Field Report, is one of the most common formats for reporting the work progress. The architect usually walks the project—drawings and digital camera in hand—and takes notes or dictates the work that is observed. Images of site conditions can be included in the published report and e-mailed to the recipients. Before images are included, the architect might consider thoroughly examining the image to determine that it is representative of the discussion included in the report and that unreported nonconforming work is not readily visible in the image. Ideally, if nonconforming work is visible in the image, it should be noted in the report.

Other formats can include incorporating reporting of observations into the OAC meeting report or simply sending an e-mail, a letter, or a memorandum. In any case, it is important to report on the status of the work in accordance with your services agreement.

The contents of the report could include a date and sequential number, notations of work conformance, and general comments of work in progress. G711 contains a distribution check box at the top; however, a mass e-mail transmittal with all project member names and addresses included can save time. The form also has a place for weather, temperature range, and percentage of completion. With the availability of the National Weather Service, and since your contract likely does not require you to assess the percentage of construction completion, you may choose to leave these blank. The same goes for the listing of those present at the site, since those statistics are typically maintained by the project superintendent.

Your observations on the work status probably should not contain finite descriptions. For example, if you state that "the brickwork is completed," and it is not completed in every conceivable detail, you may be accused of misrepresenting the conditions. It is safer to use phrases such as "the brickwork appears to be completed."

Communication about any subject, particularly about defective or nonconforming work, should include "truths." While it is true that no one likes to have their work failures aired out for all to see, it is also true that known defective or nonconforming work must be reported and perhaps remedied. For this reason, your comments on defects and deficiencies should be straightforward and declaratory. Comments such as "repair scratch on door or replace door" conveys the required actions better than "the door has a scratch" or "the scratch on the door needs to be fixed." It is a truer statement in the context of the responsibilities of the contractor that the scratch must be repaired than it is that the scratch exists on the door.

## Preinstallation conferences

These meetings are held to go over how the contractor and the contractor's subs are going to put a specific product or system together or how the construction of two or more products or systems will affect each other. Frequently, these meetings cause the contractors to think through what they are going to do on the project in a way that exposes coordination or installation difficulties that have not been previously considered. These meetings also frequently bring about disclosure of substitutions planned by a subcontractor that may not have been brought to the contractor's or architect's attention. Some examples of the subjects for such meetings are exterior wall systems and windows, skylights, roofing, waterproofing, sealants, and other critical and complex assemblies involving coordination between materials or subcontractors. Attending these meetings with the owner, contractor, and subcontractors allows a contemporaneous review of issues related to each system.

## Mockup reviews

Even very small projects can benefit from a mockup that tests how a complicated or critical system will be installed. From simple mockups like tile grout or cabinet doors to complex mockups like brick veneer and metal stud walls, important communication occurs through constructing and discussing a mockup. When the mockup is viewed in the company of the owner, contractor, and subcontractor, all critical parties have an opportunity to discuss their expectations for the assembly.

Keep a record of when the mockup reviews occurred and who was present. Photographs and narrative descriptions of decisions or modifications can also be beneficial.

## Construction is a team sport

It is exciting to travel to the site and observe your project under construction. The tedious hours in the design phase seem more worthwhile when you can see the tangible result. The legacy of an architect is a built structure for people to see and use and hopefully appreciate and admire.

The construction process today can be risky, and most claims arise from actions or activities that occur during this time. Effective planning, good relationships, and proactive contract administration can reduce risks and make the job a lot easier. As we have emphasized in past articles, the owner will likely remember their experiences during construction much more than the other phases of service. Repeat business can be fostered by an owner's comfort with your construction contract administration services.

In positioning for success, the objectives for site visits should ideally go beyond the three requirements of A201. Spending time with the owner and discussing the issues of the construction process can be worthwhile at a time when their money is being spent at a high rate and time pressures bear. Developing a win-win relationship with the contractors can foster understanding and assistance when the flaws of human nature manifest in the work.

Success with these objectives requires preparation and planning. An effective preconstruction conference and productive project meetings can enable the team to achieve their goals and have more fun in the process.

That phone call just now was the owner, and she wants to you to meet her today at the site to discuss the redesign of the building entrance. Grab your hard hat and journal, and be sure you have some extra pencils. And don't forget to be careful out there.

# A Certifiable Risk: Cautions and Strategies in the Payment Certification Process

Architects have been certifying payment for many years, but only in recent times has this practice begun to elevate risk. This article takes a look at the history of certifying payment and the documents that have evolved in the process. It examines the growing tendency by some to attempt to hold the architect strictly accountable for any variation or discrepancy although he or she is only a part-time visitor at the job site. Our examination also emphasizes the contractor's certification that the work is in accordance with the contract documents. Some complained that we were criticizing the certification process. Since it *is* risky, we should talk about it. Oh, and by the way, sign here please, and fill in the amount you are certifying.

The architect's certification of contractor applications for payment can be perhaps the most perplexing of all the architect's construction phase responsibilities. Although architects are neither accountants nor construction experts and do not observe each piece of work as it is put in place, they are nonetheless generally expected to provide a professional certification that the contractor's application for payment has been verified and is correct.

This is done although the architect is only intermittently present at the job site, and the knowledge required to "verify" a particular status of construction completion often comes through information provided by other parties, upon which the architect must rely. Yet some owners claim that the architect's certification is absolute, and should questions subsequently arise about the state of completeness or money dispersed, they look upon the architect to be in some way—and often solely—responsible.

## To certify

What does it mean to certify something? *Black's Law Dictionary* defines *to certify* as "to authenticate or verify in writing; to attest as being true or meeting certain criteria." Similarly, *The Architect's Handbook of Professional Practice* defines *certificate for payment* as "a statement from the architect to the owner confirming the amount of money due the contractor for work accomplished or materials and equipment suitably stored. . ."

The terms *verify* and *confirming*, used in both definitions, tend to establish the architect as an authority. *Merriam-Webster Online* defines *verify* as "to establish the truth, accuracy, or reality of" and confirm as "to give new assurance of the validity of." (In acknowledging the risks associated with certifications, *The CSI Manual of Practice* suggests substituting the word *certify* with *recommend*, which according to *Merriam-Webster Online* means "to present as worthy of acceptance or trial.")

Nonetheless, certifications in the payment process have been around for a long time, and over the years the AIA has wisely included valuable qualifications for tempering the absolute connotations.

The first edition of *The Architect's Handbook of Professional Practice*, published in 1920, contains Exhibit 24: Certificate of Payment and Statement of Account. Although certificates were likely used prior to that time, this is the first such document that we could find that was published as a form and recommended for use by architects. This form is strikingly similar to the current AIA form G702-1992, Application and Certificate for Payment. In addition, Chapter 39 of the first *Handbook* provides a fairly detailed set of instructions for the architect to follow in "ascertaining the amount to be paid." Particularly modern in concept, considerations included "extras and omissions, cash allowances, deductions for uncorrected work, deduction for liquidated damages."

A separate form, Exhibit 23: Application for a Certificate of Payment, was available in the first *Handbook* for the contractor to submit with the promise that ". . . he will forthwith pay the several subcontractors . . ." upon receiving payment. The contractor unconditionally "certified" applications for payment back then, although a notary seal and signature were not required.

Forms G702 for the Application and G703 for the Certification first appeared in the 8th edition of *The Architect's Handbook of Professional Practice*, published in 1958. The documents were merged into a single form in the 10th-edition *Handbook*, published in 1983, which required the contractor's sworn signature and notary seal. Revised in 1992, form G702 remains current today.

Thus, it appears that the requirement for the architect to "certify" the contractor's payment application has been around at least since 1920, and possibly longer. Certainly, the risk in certifying was not as great in the early part of the 20th century, but something caused protective changes in the documents to be made sometime between the mid-1960s and early 1980s. It may have been the same circumstances that prompted the invention of professional liability insurance in 1957, or maybe it was the insurance itself, because up until that time the architect did not possess that potential revenue target. At any rate, the time following the emergence of professional liability insurance coincides with the emergence of these protective changes. That coincidence raises the question: Did the insurance policy generate the rise in claims, or did the increase in claims generate the emergence of professional liability insurance?

## Significant changes

Most likely, these two documents were consolidated into one document for convenience. There was, however, a most interesting change that occurred: the requirement of a notary confirmation for the contractor's sworn signature. A notary attests that a third party has witnessed the contractor's signature, and it is confirmed with a seal and witness signature. This requirement was possibly added to give the architect further assurance of the veracity of the contractor's statements regarding compliance with the requirements of the contract documents.

The changes made were not entirely for the protection of the architect, as the contractor's certification of the application was changed from an unqualified certification to one based on the contractor's "best knowledge." However, in today's practice, the payment application certification can be viewed as superseded by the contractor's warranty to the owner and the architect that the work is in conformance with the contract documents.

At the same time, a similar "best knowledge" qualification was added to the architect's certification. Nonetheless, the architect certifies the accuracy of the contractor's payment application and, in so doing, provides what some wish to consider a binding, absolute, and all-knowing representation of the status of the project. Claims alleging that the architect erred in certifying a payment can consequently give way to attorney rhetoric that holds the architect responsible, regardless of logic or reason, for not knowing what he or she "should have known" about the contractor's application for payment.

## Lessening risk

Suppose your client has decided to skydive, and he has asked you to "certify" the dependability of the parachute. You didn't pack it, and you cannot know for sure if it is packed correctly. It looks OK, and you used the qualifying language to the best of your knowledge, information, and belief in your certification. But if the parachute doesn't open, are you liable?

A201 requires in Section 9 many actions by the architect for processing payment to the contractor. First, the contractor must submit a schedule of values "in such form and supported by such data as the Architect may require." The architect can object to the schedule, but it may not be revised to his or her satisfaction. But with the exception of major variations in values, how is the architect really going to know if the schedule is accurate beyond relying primarily on the contractor's representations?

*The CSI Manual of Practice* advises caution when reviewing the schedule of values: "Front end loading is a deceptive technique, raising the amount of early work to improve contractor cash flow." If this illicit activity is prevalent enough to be cautioned against in *The CSI Manual of Practice*, how can the architect be sure it does not exist on any project? Absent an audit by an accounting firm with in-depth construction contracting knowledge, how can it be known?

Then there is the issue of stored materials and ownership. Materials must be suitably stored on site or, if agreed to in writing, stored in an acceptable location off site. Payment is contingent upon ". . . procedures satisfactory to the Owner to establish the Owner's title to such materials and equipment. . ." In the absence of specific "procedures" to establish ownership, the owner has but to rely on the architect's "certification" that ownership has actually transferred and the architect must rely on the contractor for the same.

## Contractor's representations

The contractor's representation as to the amount applied for in G702 is stated as follows: "The undersigned Contractor certifies that to the best of the Contractor's knowledge, information and belief the Work covered by this Application for payment has been completed in accordance with the Contract Documents. . ."

This brings us to consider the fundamental issue as to whether the architect should be permitted to rely upon the contractor's sworn certification of the amounts due that the work is substantially in accordance with the requirements of the contract documents. We have observed on several occasions that the contractor is on the site daily, complying with the contractor's obligations to supervise, direct, coordinate, and inspect the work. The architect is on the site from time to time, gaining general knowledge about the construction. The contractor is the only party in a position to observe the complete work as it is put in place and actually know if it is in conformance.

*Black's Law Dictionary* defines *express warranty* as "a written statement . . . to which the manufacturer, distributor, or retailer undertakes to preserve or maintain the utility or performance of the consumer good or provide compensation if there is a failure in utility or performance." By this definition the contractor promises to pay for any damages caused by any nonconforming work. Yet owners frequently claim that the architect should reimburse them for the full value of the cost of remedying a contractor's defective work, presumably justified because the architect has "certified" payment for that defective work. These claims suggest that the architect is not entitled to rely upon the contractor's sworn representation included in the application for payment, but instead must perform some act of verification beyond what reasonably can be ascertained.

This point of view is without merit, for this would place the architect in the position of being the ultimate surety with absolute responsibility for guaranteeing the work performed by the contractor. Furthermore, if no party is aware of defective work, then the owner's claim is likewise unreasonable because it implies that only the architect should have known of defects in the contractor's work. Undoubtedly, the contractors and subcontractors would have had a better chance to know the actual condition of the work they performed than did the architect.

## Conclusion

It is not possible for the architect to know in every way if the work is completely acceptable or has been constructed in accordance with the contract documents. Accordingly, it is also not possible to determine if amounts of payment requested and sworn to by the contractor precisely represent the work in place or materials stored or that some portion of the work is nonconforming. Yet architects provide a certification that some allege constitutes an absolute authentication or verification of the contractor's request. We do this with best efforts, justifiably relying upon sworn representations given by the contractor and based on limited firsthand knowledge of what actually makes up the constructed work.

It can be helpful to inform and enlighten owners of the realities of our actions. The fact that our actions are based on our best knowledge, information, and belief—that is, we do not see all of the work as it is put in place and we must rely on the contractor's sworn certification—is a qualification that makes it possible for certifications for payment to be issued.

When the first certificates for payment were issued early in the last century, the risks associated with these actions obviously did not carry the broad range of legal implications that are manifest in claims made against architects today. But as claims increased over the years, it became necessary to qualify and temper the certification language to match the actions taken.

So, as you sign your certificates for payment and prepare your letters of transmittal for dispersal to the owner and contractor, be mindful of the way others may look upon your actions. And while you're at it, remember to be careful out there.

This article is reprinted with permission from the May/June 2007 issue of *Texas Architect*.

# Substantial Completion, Where Art Thou?
# A Challenging and Elusive Milestone

The often erratic and contentious issue of substantial completion seemed to us to be a good topic for examination. But much like the 1969 movie, *Butch Cassidy and the Sundance Kid,* where they put too much dynamite in the mail car to blow open the safe, we didn't realize how many opinions this piece would detonate. We've proved several times that we are willing to swim in the shark tank when we must.

The hallmark of successful project delivery is substantial completion. It is a milestone that can bring reward and satisfaction, or it can be the source of frustration and discord. It is sometimes elusive and difficult to achieve, can be complex, and is often viewed with very different expectations by members of the project team. Substantial completion is the brass ring for which everyone reaches, the Holy Grail that is diligently pursued. The projected date is typically written into the owner-contractor agreement, and the contractor's work plan is prepared in anticipation of achieving it.

Substantial completion is defined in AIA Document A201-2007, General Conditions of the Contract for Construction, in Section 9.8.1, and similar language in AIA Document A201-1997 and G704-2000, Architect's Certificate of Substantial Completion, as:

> . . . the stage in the progress of the Work when the Work or designated portion therefore is sufficiently complete in accordance with the Contract Documents so that the Owner can occupy or utilize the Work for its intended use.

This date of reckoning defines the conditions that profoundly affect the risks and rewards of the owner, the architect, and the contractor. It decides when the owner will assume responsibility for operating and maintaining the building. It starts the clock on the statutes of limitation and repose for the architect's liability unless agreed otherwise. It initiates the warranties by the contractor for certain building products and systems, and it often determines obligations of the contractor for a penalty resulting from late completion or a bonus for finishing early.

It chronicles the projected end date of the architect's basic services, which occurs 60 days after substantial completion; it bequeaths a substantial portion of retainage to the contractor; and, for owners and plaintiffs' lawyers, it supposes a representation of completeness by the design professional, which, if not essentially correct, can bring increased risk.

When vested interests of the players are pitted against one another, this celebrated occasion can become a target-rich environment for mischievous activities as the parties attempt to reconcile their cost of doing business. Liquidated damage assessments, withheld payments, delayed guarantees, and debated utility bills are but a few of the moves that are sometimes made.

Substantial completion is not an issue to be taken lightly. It is an occasion that demands accuracy, compliance, and fair dealing. It is an undertaking that brings risks, but it is likewise a process from which one can achieve deliverance. This article will explore the realities of substantial completion, the risks associated with it, the all-too-common challenges that accompany it, and the opportunities to guard against these risks and rise above the claims and financial penalties that are its occasional companions.

## A tale of two purposes

It is understood in the design and construction industry that at least one purpose of the certificate is to substantiate the point in time when the building is nearly complete and available to be used. Less obvious and less commonly discussed is the collateral purpose that substantiates that the building is built nearly in accordance with the contract documents. The contractor warrants in A201-2007 in paragraph 3.5, and A201-1997, with similar language, that the project will be in accordance with the requirements of the contract documents, but, in reality, no design can ever be exactly matched by constructed fact. For this reason, a court or arbitrator could reasonably construe "substantial completion" to mean the building is not only substantially complete in terms of physical quantity and utility, but also that it is substantially, but not completely, in accordance with the contract documents for all material purposes.

## What is substantial completion?

AIA Document G704-2000, Architect's Certificate of Substantial Completion, offers some insight as to both the architect's responsibility and the definition of substantial completion. The first important duty of the architect is:

> The Work performed under this Contract has been reviewed and found, to the Architect's best knowledge, information and belief, to be substantially complete.

As addressed in Rogetsthesarus.com, synonyms for the adverb "substantially" convey the following meaning: "essentially, largely, mainly . . ."

Also, we have already seen that the definition of substantial completion contained within the language of the certificate involves a finding concerning the building condition as:

> . . . sufficiently complete in accordance with the Contract Documents so that the Owner can occupy or utilize the Work for its intended use.

Once again, turning to *Roget's Thesaurus,* the word *sufficiently* means: "adequately, acceptably, appropriately, well enough . . . "

As used in the certificate, the words *substantially* and *sufficiently* are not intended to convey the meaning of absolute exactness but to convey the concept of almost being complete, and that the state of completion is materially so to the extent that the building can serve the intended use. The language in the certificate is not intended to convey that the building is either completely or precisely "in accordance with the contract documents."

## Construction observations and inspections

Because G704 functions as a companion to both A201, General Conditions of the Contract for Construction, and to the AIA Owner-Architect Agreements, the condition of "the architect's knowledge, information and belief" supporting the determination of substantial completion is derived from the architect's observations for general conformance as well as from the first of only two "inspections" that are performed by the architect. The owner-architect agreements generally state:

The Architect will visit the site at intervals appropriate to the stage of construction ... to become **generally** familiar with the progress and quality of the portion of the Work completed, and to **determine, in general,** if the Work observed is being performed in a manner indicating that the Work, **when fully completed,** will be in accordance with the Contract Documents. However, **the Architect shall not be required to make exhaustive or continuous on-site inspections** to check the quality or quantity of the Work.

This language makes it clear that the architect's review of the work is made in anticipation of the completion of the project. As stated above, in addition to observations at the job site as construction is progressing, the architect conducts two inspections. The first is to determine the date of substantial completion so that a certificate of substantial completion can be issued, and the second is to determine if the architect agrees with the contractor's representation that the work has been completed.

## Contract documents

It is important to remember that contract documents are a living and constantly changing body of information. Not only are contract documents composed of the contracts, conditions, drawings, and specifications that were originally issued, but they also include changes, supplementary instructions, value analysis amendments, and other documents developed during the construction process. All parties must recognize that clarification documents such as requests for information, construction change directives, and proposal requests can become contract documents if incorporated by change order. Architect's supplemental instructions and change orders are contract documents by definition. On the other hand, when documentation of changes in the contract is considered, the owner, contractor, and design professionals must remain aware that shop drawings and submittals are not contract documents. Making changes on shop drawings and submittals will not incorporate the changes into the contract, except perhaps in the limited condition where the architect adds comments regarding a contractor's specific request for a change, and the change does not involve a change in time or cost. A contract change can only be accomplished by a contract modification document as addressed in Article 7 of A201.

## Profound realities

The issues associated with substantial completion can have a great effect on all team players in both good and bad ways.

**Implications for the contractor.** The date of substantial completion is typically established at the onset of the project, and it is a milestone that the contractor is required by contract to achieve. The project schedule is predicated on this achievement, and the contractor's work plan is formulated and managed to that end. If substantial completion is not achieved on the designated date, it can trigger damages if provided for in the contract. If the date should be in jeopardy, contractors frequently seek time extensions on the alleged basis of discrepancies in the construction documents and slow responses by the design professionals.

Contractor penalties and bonuses are often written into construction contracts in an effort to increase incentive for completion, and contractors and design professionals may not escape owner recovery efforts if penalties are assessed. Substantial completion is the affirming evidence that the completion date was or was not met.

Substantial completion also triggers payments to the contractors. When a project reaches this milestone, it is customary to release all retainage except for an amount that can safely cover the cost of work remaining for correction or completion. In many cases, this remaining money equates to the contractors' profit. This occasion also allows the contractor to reassign team members to other projects, leaving only a skeleton crew to complete the work and administer closeout, thus reducing overhead and general conditions costs.

**Implications for the architect.** For the design professionals, substantial completion typically marks the beginning of the statutes of limitation and repose. The statute of limitation is the time that a claim can be legally made after the condition giving rise to the claim is first discovered. The statute of repose is the time within which discovery of such conditions will allow a claim to be made. Some states, such as Texas, have a 10-year statute of repose with a 2-year statute of limitation for professional negligence. This means that a claimant has 10 years to discover conditions and 2 years after discovery to take legal action. Therefore, for 12 years after substantial completion, the architect is exposed to potential claims for negligence.

Design professionals also have exposure to damages resulting from late completion of construction. It is common for owners and contractors to blame project delays on deficiencies in the drawings and specifications or slow responses, alleging that the substantial completion date was adversely affected by the design professional's actions.

Some owners claim that the architect's issuance of a certificate of substantial completion is de facto approval of any remaining nonconforming work placed by the contractor. They often believe the architect is at fault, although the contract documents clearly state that the contractor is solely responsible. The contractor's warranty to the architect and the owner that the work will be free of defects further reinforces their sole responsibility for work completion and conformance.

Accordingly, the owner's occupancy or use of the project does not constitute acceptance of nonconforming work, as is succinctly stated in A201, in paragraphs 9.6.6 and 9.9.3.

**Implications for the owner.** Regarding substantial completion, the greatest damage experienced by owners is usually the loss of use caused by a delayed opening. If project use produces revenue, such as a hotel, casino, professional sports facility, or hospital, damages can mount up quickly. Other damages from a delayed opening can be extended loan costs, increased operating costs due to maintaining two facilities, and labor burden costs for increased employees hired in anticipation of moving into the new facility.

## Risk considerations

When administering substantial completion, architects should be mindful of the inherent risks involved. Consider the following in your management activities.

**You do not control the date.** When architects negotiate their services contracts, they typically apply a fee based on the prevailing market rate. The portion of their fee that is allocated for the construction phase is not based on the length of time required for construction unless the fee basis is time-driven. When a contractor comes on board, the construction time is typically negotiated in the construction contract with a projected date of substantial completion. The architect may be made aware of the contractor's proposed completion date but is rarely consulted regarding the appropriateness of that date.

Therefore, it is advantageous to address substantial completion with the owner at the beginning of the project to establish that your construction phase services are finite. If you fail to do this, the owner will likely expect you to provide construction phase services without additional compensation for as long as the project continues. One way to control your risks in this area is to stipulate a set number of site visits within your initial fee and designate a cost per site visit for any in excess of the original number. You will more likely be successful in achieving this if your cost per visit is quoted on your direct and overhead cost without excessive profit markup. This way, the owner will feel that you are being fair, and you will be protected against uncontrolled losses caused by a time for construction that you do not control.

The contractor's proposed completion date may significantly differ from the date originally anticipated by the architect. And variables such as phased construction and adverse climatic conditions can greatly affect total construction time. It is good practice to compare the two dates to determine if additional construction phase fees are appropriate for accelerated services if the date is earlier or extended services if the date is later. The architect's costs, just like the contractor's, increase if too little or too much time is scheduled.

**You are assessing work conformance.** The AIA documents require the architect to determine general conformance of the work to the contract documents, but they do not require the architect to assess work quantity or completeness. The reason for this is that the contractor is responsible for putting the work in place and, therefore, the contractor controls the quantity. This is why architects do not issue a certificate of final completion as a part of their services. To do so would constitute a representation by the architect that the work is 100 percent complete in every way, a condition that is warranted by the contractor and for which the contractor is solely responsible.

It is important, therefore, that design professionals use care in assessing work conformance and completion. We have addressed the importance of avoiding quantitative statements in field observation reports and other communications in Chapter 3, in our article entitled "Project Manager or Risk Manager?" There is no requirement contained in the AIA documents or in MASTERSPEC that requires the architect to quantify the work in place. However, certifications of contractor applications for payment are often inappropriately viewed by owners as a de facto representation of work-in-place quantities as well as work quality.

Your assessment is a certification. According to *Black's Law Dictionary*, a certification is "a formal assertion in writing of some fact."

A fact, according to *Black's* is "an actual and absolute reality, as distinguished from mere supposition or opinion."

Therefore, certifications by a design professional can carry risks that rise above your contracted responsibilities should you use improper wording or misleading connotations. You should be aware of words to avoid and stick with the recommendations provided in *The Architect's Handbook of Professional Practice* and the wording suggested in the AIA documents. You should consult legal counsel in all cases involving certifications containing language that differs from the wording contained in the AIA documents, or when otherwise prudent.

An example of certification required in addition to what is prescribed in the AIA documents is when the project lender or title agency desires certification from the architect. Such certifications often contain wording that goes beyond what the architect is obligated to do within the contract and within the accepted standard of care. The entities that seek this additional certification are typically not concerned with your level of risk exposure.

**The owner and contractor may have conflicting priorities.** Contradiction and complexity are sometimes introduced into the substantial completion process should the owner and the contractor have conflicting priorities. In the event there are liquated damages stipulated in the owner-contractor agreement, and the project is being completed late, the owner will want the substantial completion date to be later rather than sooner and the contractor will desire the opposite determination. This can result in a disputed date, so you should always thoroughly document your reasoning for the date you certify.

Even when penalties are not a part of completion, an owner may challenge the substantial completion date to delay paying for utility costs or tolling the beginning of warranties. Substantial completion is a milestone in the project delivery process that profoundly affects many parties and, as a result, often does not occur without disputes and extenuating circumstances.

**Your certification may be taken literally.** When certifying substantial completion, it is easy, and even common, for the architect to view the occasion as a routine event in the course of project delivery that requires only a review of the punch list and a signature on a form. Unfortunately, should the certification be scrutinized in a claim or litigation, it may be evaluated only on its literal representation. If the certification does not cite and quantify any nonconforming or incomplete work, such as an attached punch list or log of nonconforming work, the courts may assess that the architect has found the project to be substantially complete in every way. Even though most projects have some portion of their scope that does not conform to the documents, if these portions are significant, you could be adjudged to have misrepresented the state of project completion.

To effectively manage this dilemma, you should keep track of any nonconforming work you observe during the course of the construction phase.

Nonconforming work can arise from contractor error, which the owner can accept, if the owner chooses, or it can survive because the owner has accepted alternatives the architect does not agree with, both of which are allowed in A201 General Conditions of the Contract for Construction.

Disputes can also arise when you qualify owner-accepted nonconforming work in your certificate and the owner is not expecting it. Therefore, it is important to keep all parties advised when it is likely that the certificate will contain such qualifications. A review of actions to take regarding owner-accepted nonconforming work during project closeout is addressed in *The Architect's Handbook of Professional Practice,* 14th edition, in "Project Closeouts."

## Completion challenges

Substantial completion, because of the myriad conflicting priorities and objectives of the parties involved, can be a difficult experience. The financial penalties and rewards that hang in the balance can cause discord among the parties, and the issues involved, as noted below, can be quite complex.

**Liquidated damages.** Most owners want to gain access to their project on the earliest possible date. Whether it be for their business operations or to allow their tenant contractor to start the interior build-out, they typically want the work finished and the contractor out. To achieve this end, they sometimes use financial incentives to coerce completion. Liquidated damages can be quantified in the owner-contractor agreement. This is typically an amount of money charged per day for each day after substantial completion that the project is late. It is intended as an offset to owner costs for loss of use. Including such an amount in the contract avoids the process of trying to determine actual damages after the fact.

As you can imagine, the potential for liquidated damages can significantly motivate the contractor; however, the potential for making themselves financially whole also carries motivation for some owners. Unfortunately, the end result is often a dispute over the substantial completion date involving finger-pointing and a search for parties to blame.

**Separate contractors.** Another matter that sometimes complicates the picture is separate contractors hired by the owner. They work on the project at the same time and in the same location as the general contractor. While A201 requires the general contractor to "cooperate" with separate contractors, their presence provides an opportunity for the general contractor to claim damages should they feel that the separate contractors have interfered with their work.

**Early occupancy.** Early occupancy of some portion of the project by the owner can present a common challenge to substantial completion. Whether it is because of the owner's desire to perform separate work such as interior finish out or because of actual move-in, occupancy of the project before it is substantially finished requires careful coordination and documentation.

For example, if an owner occupies a building before the punch list has been completed, there will likely be disagreement between the owner and contractor over dents and scratches. In the case of separate contractors, there can be disputes over the completeness and acceptability of the work prior to being covered up or changed. It is advisable to discuss early project occupancy in advance with the owner to avoid misunderstandings and allow for appropriate coordination.

**Punch list coordination.** The completion of a project may not always be on time, and the final portion of work sometimes includes compressed activities. Therefore, it is important that the contractor and architect coordinate with each other on the punch list review. Much time can be wasted if areas are not ready to punch when scheduled, and much money can be spent if a "SWAT team" is required for the design team to review substantial completion in an abbreviated time period.

A good general rule is that the design team should make two trips through the building as part of basic services: one to determine what work remains for completion or correction and one to determine when that work has been completed or corrected. It is important to remind the contractor that additional trips will result in additional fees. These charges should rightfully be invoiced to the owner; therefore the owner must be apprised of any delay by the contractor and any resulting delay in preparing the punch list. The contractor, in accordance with Section 12.2.1. of A201, is responsible for these additional service charges. The lack of a contractual relationship will prevent the architect from submitting an invoice for additional services to the contractor. Even in the absence of an invoice sent to the owner, the causes for delayed or prolonged punch list activities should be documented.

**Contractor's failure to complete or correct the work.** Problems can arise should the contractor fail to complete or correct all of the work on the punch list in a timely manner. In addition to extra trips by the design professional to the building site, the owner may have to hire another contractor to finish the work, and the new contractor may not be able to complete the work as efficiently as the original contractor. Allowing for these additional costs is why money is often retained that is a greater amount than the determined value of the work remaining for completion or correction.

A significant problem arises when there may no longer be enough money remaining in the contract to pay for the remaining uncompleted work. Contractors submit general conditions costs with each application for payment, and if the project is delayed long enough, the contract balance can erode to the point that there is more work remaining to do than there is money to pay for it.

Should this occur, the architect is empowered to withhold certification to protect the owner as stipulated in A201-2007, and A201-1997, with similar language, Section 9.5, "Decisions to Withhold Certification," which states:

> The Architect may withhold a Certificate for Payment in whole or in part, to the extent reasonably necessary to protect the Owner . . .

This section of A201 also allows for the withholding of a certification for other reasons, including defective work not remedied, damage to the owner, and persistent failure to carry out the work. When a certification is withheld or a previous certification is nullified, it is generally appropriate to notify the contractor's surety of your actions if the contractor is covered by a performance and payment bond. The surety must give consent to final payment, and AIA Document G707-1994, Consent of Surety to Final Payment, is available for this purpose.

Withholding of a certification should not be approached lightly or casually. Because this condition usually results in the contractor having to work without receiving payment, it can result in the contractor's refusal to work and the initiation of legal action. Therefore, this action should be taken only if *absolutely* necessary, and the reasons for taking it thoroughly documented. Project delays should be discussed with the affected parties as soon as they occur. A201 and the owner-contractor agreements require that the contractor take necessary measures to get back on schedule, and if appropriate actions are taken, the withholding of a certification may be avoided.

## Consultant certifications

The architect's consultants are required to "assist" the architect in determining the date or dates of substantial completion for their portion of the work. This is stipulated in Section 4.5.14 of AIA Document C141-1997, Standard Form of Agreement Between Architect and Consultant.

> The Consultant shall assist the Architect in conducting inspections . . . to determine the date or dates of Substantial Completion and the date of final completion. . . .

The 2007 AIA document revisions changed this document to C401-2007, Standard Form of Agreement Between Architect and Consultant. It does not contain the same wording as its 1997 predecessor. Instead, in Section 1.3 it states:

> To the extent that provisions of the Prime Agreement apply to This Portion of the Project . . . the Consultant shall assume toward the Architect all obligations and responsibilities that the Architect assumes toward the Owner.

Since the architect is obligated to conduct inspections for substantial and final completion, the consultant is likewise obligated. To complete the documentation, C401-2007, Section 1.1 states:

> A copy of the Architect's agreement with the Owner, known as the Prime Agreement . . . is attached . . .

AIA Document G704–2000, Architect's Certificate of Substantial Completion, is available for the architect to document substantial completion of the entire project.

There are several options for documenting substantial completion by the architect's consultants. Minimum efforts could include their signatures adjacent to the architect's on Document G704. A more comprehensive approach could be to prepare a separate consultant's certification and attach it to the architect's certificate. In any case, written confirmation of their opinions and an actual certification is advisable. One architecture firm has prepared its own form entitled Consultant's Certificate of Substantial Completion. It includes only the consultant's signature and is attached to the architect's certificate at the time of issuance.

## A perfect world

There are times when substantial completion occurs on schedule and punch list review time is reasonable. When substantial completion is successful, it is usually because of the following:

- Reasonable original project schedule
- Reasonable original contract sum
- Deliberate and adequate contractor's work plan
- Capable team of trade contractors
- Stable and timely sequence of owner decisions
- Candid series of discussions among all parties
- Well-documented construction process
- Thorough and effective punch list schedule
- Commitment to adequate work quality
- Preplanned closeout phase

## The beginning of the end

Thus, substantial completion can be both a curse and a cure. Although substantial completion is a significant milestone of project delivery—the anticipated beginning of the end of contract obligations—it is often disputed and prone toward complexity. It is an event of conflicting priorities for all involved. The contractor usually wants it earlier rather than later. The owner often views it as later as regards costs and warranties, although they desire it to be earlier so they can use the building. The architect wants the date not to move, but it almost always does. Money hangs in the balance, profits realized or denied. It is the starting bell for money recovery attempts, and posturing and mischievous activities sometimes are a factor.

It is also the beginning of closeout activities. Testing, equipment start-up, operations training, and the plethora of record documentation are a part of making it down the home stretch. It is an event that can be successful and borderline enjoyable, provided that advance preparation and execution remain intact. When the project team is in sync and obligations are met, it can be a shining moment before the owner for both the contractor and designer.

When all goes as planned, it can be a time for pride and profit. The ribbon can be cut and the building dedicated, the project documents can be archived, and the job cost report can be finalized. Once again, the project manager can begin his or her next assignment. And when the owner-contractor agreement is executed, substantial completion will again become the brass ring—the most anticipated and pursued milestone in the project schedule.

So grab your camera, clipboard, half-sized drawings, punch list, and digital recorder. Put on your hard hat and safety gear, and begin your substantial completion inspection.

Oh, and while you're at it . . . don't forget to be careful out there.

# Chapter 6

## The Architect's Lament

### Your Grandfather's Working Drawings: A Nostalgic Look at the Past; Observations of the Present

This is the first "lament" article of several in the series. It brought everyone to their feet; some in praise and some in protest. Such healthy interaction is one reason we write. Some "old-timers" have actually broken down as they have told us of their appreciation of "grandfather." Some young folks have called us nostalgic old fools. Indeed, we do reflect nostalgically on the chief draftsman and the days of lead and Mylar. But the more forceful message is that most of the protégés of the chief can't do digital drafting. This leaves us with what we call an "upside-down experience quotient." We also ponder the idea that apprenticeship for architects may be failing in modern practice. These problems may ultimately be resolved, but much can be done in the interim. Now put your head down and keep drafting!

Architects and their instruments of service have become a target for disputes and litigation at an increasing rate in recent years. Rarely is there a major project where the drawings and specifications are not subjected to scrutiny by parties claiming to be harmed by the documents or looking to find a source of harm within them.

Design professionals are greatly challenged by this turn of events, and we ask why and how it is happening. What has changed about architecture and our services? Do professionals have fewer skills than in years past? Or is it that contractors are not as experienced or skillful and thus unable to build from architectural drawings? Are CAD drawings inherently less thorough than documents of the past? Perhaps the appearance of accuracy implied by CAD has changed owners' and contractors' expectations? Or is it that there are simply too many lawyers?

This article will explore the profound impact of CAD on the way that our drawings are produced today. It will begin by looking at the purpose of our drawings and their intended use. It will examine the management void left by the change from manual artistry to digital and its effect on our work product and how it is perceived and used. It will conclude with suggestions for what firm principals and managers can do to bridge this gap and improve how the work of architects is perceived.

# These are not your grandfather's working drawings

Baby boomer architects may recall the drafting room environment of the past. A common fixture was the chief draftsman. (They were called draftsmen back then and not draftspersons as they are today.) The chief draftsman reigned with an iron hand and a quick temper over the drafting room, which later was renamed the studio. The documents used for construction were called working drawings, and mastery of their creation was an unending career objective.

Junior draftsmen, also referred to as cubs, were expected to keep their heads down and their tails up. They were expected to labor with precision and cleanliness over tracings made on Mylar or Clearprint 1000H drafting velum. The medium of choice was wax lead, or H and 2H graphite lead, or Rapidograph ink pens, and tracings were kept free of smears and lead buildup by using Pounce or other drafting powders. Their most useful computer was an Add-Feet Jr. that added feet and inches much like the ancient abacus. Baby boomer architects can also tell you war stories of having their hair lifted by a stern chief draftsman when mistakes were discovered in their work. The worst days for apprentice architects were the days when the chief draftsman reviewed and redlined their drawings. The rebuke was almost unbearable as the limitations of their professional skills were exposed for all to see, and often for all to hear.

If you find that this world seems alien and contrasts with your workplace of today, then it is safe to assume that today's products of service are not your grandfather's working drawings. Today, the strict discipline that old-timers apprenticed under would likely be considered harassment, and it might even be prohibited by law.

Unfortunately, for all practical purposes, the chief draftsman has long become extinct. Working drawings today are prepared almost entirely on computers. Reverence for and possessive feelings about drawn construction document "artwork" seems to be vanishing, or possibly has already vanished. The intelligence of computer-generated drawings has begun to replace the draftsman's knowledge. Young architects serve their apprenticeship to their Dell, IBM, Hewlett-Packard, or Sony. Details, instead of being constructed thoughtfully line by line, are pulled from recent projects or a library of existing details, then picked and dragged to a place on the computer screen. Redlines, when offered as a criticism of drafted work, are made on impersonal and disconnected "plots" and are transferred onto the electronic ether, bypassing the emotional importance of an ownership in a work of art. Criticism is presented to young architects with more thought of not offending than of teaching.

These days, senior project leaders, unable to comprehend fully the story of the building in the limiting context of a computer screen, and not usually proficient with CAD, rely on younger architects to do the drafting. They can no longer mentor and coach in the artistry of drawing organization and detail composition. This can lead to drawings that are issued for construction unchecked by more experienced eyes. The result all too often is incomplete, unworkable, or, worse, un-constructible designs depicted on drawings that must be revised to a sufficient and acceptable level of quality while under fire on the job site. It is not always clear who is teaching whom about the technical arts in architecture. It appears that, in a number of cases, the experience quotient has essentially turned upside down.

## How about them Apples? . . . or Dells? . . . or Sonys? . . .

The computer emerged as a great solution to the laborious manual endeavor of crafting our designs line-by-line on a two-dimensional surface. CAD opened the door for infinite reusable backgrounds and detail libraries. Today we have virtually instantaneous transfer of drawings through the Internet. But, unfortunately, with these innovations came isolation. All too commonly, we no longer have one-on-one discussions with a supervisor even as the apprentice architect crafts the wall section. We no longer discuss the reason that the flashing must terminate where it does, or why the caulking is placed as it is. Change, a thought-filled and laborious endeavor in a hand-crafted tracing, is now widely thought to be accomplished with the casual push of a button. The result is a serious disconnect in our intellectual transfer. The universal knowledge of our firms is sitting dormant as the youngsters surf and select, pick and drag, and cut and paste.

We should try to reconnect the circuit. Try to reestablish intellectual communications among ourselves. To do that we must begin by going back to one-on-one learning opportunities, taken advantage of at the point of need: at the drafting table, or the modern equivalent thereof. We must stop worrying about the perpetual receipt of e-mails through our BlackBerry and whether our phone mail greeting is current. There are more important things. Things like taking the time to sit with the young architects, our apprentices, to talk about the basic elements of our documents and how they are used.

## The purpose and effect of documents

A valuable exercise is to gather the staff over lunch and get back to the basics by discussing the fundamental purpose of construction drawings. One way is to begin by making lists of the simple things. Emphasize the idea that working drawings should depict the building design in its final desired form. Prepare your cubs by explaining the *Architect's Handbook of Professional Practice* position that working drawings are not intended to be a complete set of instructions on how to build the building. Even so, the drawings must explain the design concept thoroughly.

The "water runs downhill" approach is a good way to have fun beginning at the base level. Encourage questions about building systems and details. CAD or manual, the building system is the same. Explain that projects go more smoothly and clients are happier when the final scope of the project is adequately represented in the drawings and specifications.

Take your cubs to the job site. There is nothing more instructive than the work itself. Copy them on site observation reports, and explain site conditions requiring an answer to a request for information from the contractor. More importantly, explain what was not adequately expressed in the documents that would have prevented the RFI in the first place. Let them develop their own answers to an RFI. If you have been involved in a lawsuit, let your cubs read the Plaintiff's Original Complaint or the Defendant's First Set of Interrogatories.

The purpose of these exercises and discussions is to let the gravity of the purpose and effect of working drawings settle upon the people who are preparing them. These are the essential lessons that were so personally and effectively conveyed by the old chief draftsman—the lessons that modern young architects desire and need, but to which they are less and less exposed because of our impersonal digital environment.

## The relationship of drawings and specifications

The relationship of working drawings and specifications is too often misunderstood. The specifications help define the quality of the materials and systems to be used in a project. The drawings help define the layout, location, and quantity of the primary elements and materials in a project. Even so, the specifications may list the quantity of certain elements, such as the number and type of fasteners to be used in a particular assembly.

It is general practice today to not use a specific manufacturer's name or product model number on the drawings, leaving that information to be indicated by the specifications. However, the preparation of construction documents is a matter of individualized professional judgment, and this rule should be bypassed if the professional feels it necessary to provide a more clear and understandable message in the drawing. Nevertheless, drawings are an incomplete story without the companion specifications.

## The functional use of working drawings

The best way to address the functional use of working drawings is to first look at how and for what purpose drawings are used in each phase of services. Although drawing phases tend to be blurred by CAD and will be so even more by integrated project delivery, understanding drawings by phase is essential.

**Schematic design phase.** The primary purpose of schematic design drawings is to explain the design concept to the owner. Although the design is not yet entirely represented, the schematics can demonstrate basic spaces and relationships. Due to the elemental aspects of this graphic illustration, the architect will need to explain verbally what is not apparent to the owner. This will require paying close attention to the owner's reactions and asking confirming questions.

For the architect, the schematic design drawings are often a catalytic influence for further exploration of the design concept. Finally, these drawings may provide the contractor or estimator with a basic scope for formulating a very rough cost estimate. The overriding function of schematic drawings, however, inures to the benefit of the architect and owner.

**Design development phase.** The purpose of design development drawings is to focus in the design more of the technical aspects of materials and building systems. Although this phase allows the architect to finalize space and function to a great degree, the primary achievement is to enable the owner to understand how the project will function, as well as to give more detail about what it will look like. Again, this will require the architect to observe carefully the owner's reaction and ask confirming questions.

A second beneficiary is the contractor who can become more comfortable with the scope of the building and proposed materials and systems. During this phase the architect continues to explore yet more refined design solutions.

Sometimes the purpose of design development drawings is misunderstood, such as when owners expect them to serve as the basis for a "guaranteed price" or when architects use them as a beginning for construction documents. Design development documents do not reflect the full story required for constructing the building and rarely can serve as the only base information for developing a complete "maximum price." They may indeed serve as an efficient starting point for construction documents, but CAD technology creates the illusion of accuracy and completeness beyond their intended scope.

**Construction documents phase.** The audience for "working drawings" is the contractor, its subcontractors, and code enforcement officials. The purpose of construction documents is to communicate in detail the requirements of the design concept. The detail must be sufficient to allow the contractors that will build the project to implement their plan for pricing, contracting for, procuring, and placing the work.

## The impact on budgets and schedules

Construction documents can impact project schedules in several ways. One significant impact is that a reasonable amount of time is required to prepare construction documents. In a traditional project schedule, construction documents are prepared before construction is begun. When owners desire to start construction earlier, they often request a shorter construction documents preparation time frame or elect to fast track the project.

Shortened preparation times hasten the preparation of the documents and leave less time for checking and coordination. Working faster causes speed-induced errors to creep into the documents. Fast-track project scheduling where construction is begun before construction documents are complete can also lead to speed-induced errors as well as scope gaps in the individual partial packages of construction documents. Fast-track delivery can also be complicated by an owner's desire to know the estimated cost of construction before construction is started. It can be very difficult to use packages of incomplete documents for defining the ultimate cost of construction. Shortened or hastened time frames carry increased risks for both the design professionals and the owner, and frequently the contractors as well.

The errors and omissions that are usually contained in construction documents can also cause the documents to impact the budget and schedule.

Errors and omissions often cause unanticipated construction costs, which usually result in some element of delay or extended schedules. When errors and omissions are found in the documents prior to construction of a building element, there is less likelihood that the budget and schedule will be affected, especially if the contractor or subcontractor has not been selected. However, the negative impact of errors and omissions found during construction usually increases dramatically as the job progresses toward completion.

## The "complete" documents myth

There is no accepted industry definition of "complete" construction documents. If such a definition did exist, it would obviously be a valuable tool for architects, owners, and contractors. One reason that documents cannot be complete is that projects tend to be one-of-a-kind creations. Another reason is that the documents are conveying a design concept and not a finite assembly. (In "Drawing the Line," in Chapter 4, we explored the limitations of the architect's drawings and the additional information and work required of the contractor to actually build the building.)

The uniqueness of an architectural project is the custom design and assembly of thousands, perhaps millions of parts and pieces incorporated into a project through a progressive series of strategic decisions. The preparation of architectural drawings is a process that is substantially infused with subjectivity. Although somewhat objective rules can be applied to some of the process, the majority of decisions and actions involve the subjective application of professional judgment, which varies from project to project, professional to professional, region to region, circumstance to circumstance, and time to time.

Accordingly, architects cannot prepare complete or entirely correct construction documents. What an architect can do is prepare documents that are sufficient for supporting the construction process. Incompleteness, conflicts, coordination miscues, errors, and omissions can and will occur in all documents prepared by human hands. The surviving discrepancies are corrected during construction through communications with the contractor, requests for information, and the change process.

We have reviewed in our past articles that a design professional cannot be reasonably expected, and is not generally required by law, to provide perfect services. Accordingly, an architect cannot be expected to provide the undefined and indefinable perfect set of completed construction documents.

## The impact of CAD

An analysis of the impact of CAD on the preparation of architectural construction documents would fill volumes. In this article we have observed that CAD has essentially been a young architect's game since the onset of its application. The skill of creating graphic architectural illustrations cannot be taught by industry elders as it was during the time when your grandfather's drawings were prepared.

Another distinct disadvantage of CAD is the illusion of greater accuracy and completeness early in the project. Because of the crispness and the ease with which CAD allows architects to embellish documents, schematic design and design development phase drawings appear to contain information beyond their state of research and development. This appearance in turn causes owners and contractors to believe that the drawings contain information that allows uses beyond their limits.

Unfortunately, this illusion prevails with architects as well. Architects should be cautioned not to issue documents before they are sufficient for their intended purpose. Although schematic design and design development drawings may look very accurate and complete, and it may be easy to add a small modicum of information to increase this illusion, the reality is that they are not yet sufficiently developed for use as bidding or construction documents. Perhaps one solution would be to present our CAD schematic and design development phase drawings in "freehand" or "sketch" presentation mode to subliminally reinforce their conceptual nature.

Today, in the studio, you are as likely to hear discussions of controversy about layers, line weights, pen tables, and font sizes and styles in a drawing as you are to hear debate about the building details. These discussions come under the heading of "CAD Standards" and are viewed as so important that we not only have a national CAD standard but a host of others as well. In our drafting room of the past, our drawings had just two layers, a front and a back. Our line weights and pen tables were limited only by the artistry of the draftsman. Our fonts, also the subject of artistry, were developed throughout a career and were a benchmark of personal pride. On a manual tracing prepared by more than one person, you might find two or more "pen tables" and more than one "font," yet the drawing would be legible and usable. Time was spent learning and focusing on architecture, and not as much on CAD standards.

CAD drawings do, however, offer some very positive benefits. It is possible to achieve a much greater level of accuracy by drawing building elements at their actual size rather than drawing them to a scale, as required by manually prepared drawings. CAD offers the promise and fulfillment of speed in preparation and change unattainable with manual drawings. CAD also offers the opportunity to develop and store details that can be used on subsequent projects with great ease.

These details, sometimes characterized as standard details, or a detail library, can allow a younger team to apply the benefits of experience that otherwise may not be available. However, such standard details must be rigorously maintained for accuracy and current application so that they do not become outdated or are inadvertently used erroneously on repetitive projects. They must be touched periodically by experienced eyes.

When the manual draftsman drew a detail from the office standard files, the detail was completely recrafted on each new drawing and the chief draftsman guided and critiqued with each new use. Today, details are often picked and dragged from the detail library without sufficient scrutiny as to how and if the detail applies.

# Back to the future

The matter of the upside-down experience quotient has had and continues to have a significant impact on the preparation of working drawings. However, this impact may resolve itself as the younger generations of CAD-capable architects mature and move into positions of leadership, assuming that newer generations of CAD, such as BIM, don't continue to turn the quotient upside down again and again and again. If BIM develops to its apparent potential, the kind of knowledge required to design and place virtual data and components in three dimensions may actually improve the experience quotient. Firms have already found opportunities to add senior architects to their 3D CAD studios to coach in how a building goes together, since constructing a building in 3D CAD benefits from a steady application of that knowledge.

For now, more experienced architects must make a concerted effort to develop and modify their leadership skills and habits so that the transfer of information and experience regarding the creation of working drawings can occur with the same ease and effectiveness with which it occurred with our grandfathers. The goal should be future project leaders with the skills and mentoring abilities of the old chief draftsman—skills of divining and explaining, day by day, the quality and state of completeness of the construction documents for which they are responsible.

Architects should also strive to review their documents in the same context as the audience who will be using them. Documents cannot be developed and checked solely on a computer screen if the contractors who will be using them on site will be working from paper copies. Someday in the future, it may be that documents will be provided to the contractors on video tablets or through computerized goggles, and this requirement will no longer be necessary. But for now, checks and balances implemented through a paper medium should remain a part of our document development process.

Those who can remember back when CAD was emerging would likely never have guessed that such a wonderfully accurate and time-saving innovation would interfere with the age-old mentoring process. Nevertheless, we must confront the challenges and take action to restore the stabilizing transfer of knowledge and experience. Architects must endeavor to be more effective in passing on to succeeding generations their knowledge and experience on how buildings and systems go together. We must impart what we know through our years of experience to those whose primary contact with our profession is now through a computer screen.

Younger architects must be mentored by more experienced architects concerning the purpose for preparation of construction documents as well as how to understand and use the various components of the documents. And more experienced architects who may be less skillful in the use of CAD must endeavor to understand more thoroughly how construction documents are digitally created.

Architects must also explain to owners and contractors that even under the most perfect circumstances, the documents will be neither complete nor entirely correct. This reality must be explained in order for owner's and contractor's expectations of the architect's instruments of services to be realistic. Under the best of circumstances, documents will require clarifications and additional information to be suitable for construction. Just as they always have.

The basic model of our grandfathers was sound. The closest thing most of them had to a detail library was a plastic toilet fixture template, a modular brick scale, and a stainless steel eraser shield. As they moved through the drafting room in their green Josam drafting aprons, they believed that mere observation of existing details and drawn works was not enough. They believed that explanation and step-by-step discussion was required. This belief endured even when their explanation was presented with the stern expectation that you would heed what they said.

If we are to return to a course of excellence in working drawings, we must apply our grandfather's model to our electronic environment. We must print out the detail library and paste it on the wall. We must take out our red pens and brainstorm the parts and pieces through interactive discussions. Before the young architects put their hands on the mouse, they should first know why they have chosen that detail, how they need to change it to make it work, and how to coordinate it with related components and systems.

Our grandfather's drawings were produced in a time of simpler building systems and less proprietary differentiation of building materials. Nevertheless, our grandfathers arguably produced a better-quality working drawing, using a time-honored apprenticeship process that we can learn from today. Regardless of the promise of new and improved methods of CAD, such as BIM, the need for architects to understand the requirements for organizing and producing working drawings and applying professional judgment in meeting those requirements will remain. Perhaps the past is as much a part of the future as the future itself. Perhaps, even against the backdrop of today's computer technology, the primary goal in performing our services should be to produce our grandfather's working drawings.

And, as you consider these nostalgic thoughts about the past, and ponder the future, we'd like to remind you to be careful out there.

# The Speed of Life: Preserving Your Personal Life in a Hectic World

This is the second "lament" article in the series. It is impossible to address how things have changed without including what they have changed from. And to a degree, the article is about blinking. We blink, and 10 years have passed. Technology in the business world is constantly accelerating the way we work and reducing the amount of time we have between working. The speed increases and the roses we wish to smell become a blur along the way. It is up to us to regulate our lives among the chaos and enjoy the things we consider meaningful. We offer some observations about this challenge and a few suggestions for pursuit. Meanwhile, keep your priorities in line, and don't blink, for your opportunities will be gone.

We're holdin' on tight (holdin' on tight)
(We're) travelin' at twice the speed of life.

—Sugarland

We are in a time of prosperity seldom equaled in our profession. For most of us, work is abundant, and working hours have been expanded to accommodate the demand. There is much less time available to practice architecture as we once did, always thought we would, and hoped that we could. Passing ourselves coming and going, we worry with recruiting new employees while hoping to keep the ones we have. We struggle to believe we are providing top-notch services to reliable repeat clients, while we worry that we may not be able to accept that new commission we have worked so hard to earn. We are awash in emerging technology that promises to change our profession in many ways. We have too many e-mails to answer and constantly fidget with our PDAs and cell phones. We risk burning out ourselves and our coworkers with each passing day.

By the mid-1900s, architecture, in terms of managing design delivery, had changed very little for more than a century. The modern firm of the 1970s, struggling to recover from the devastating recession of the early 1970s that almost decimated many old-line firms, attempted to adapt to new ideas designed to speed up the metabolism of architecture practice. This included learning to incorporate new technologies in a rapidly changing world of architecture. The need to study productivity and various methods for producing work faster and more efficiently became a priority.

The world is a rose; smell it and pass it to your friends.

—Persian Proverb

Newer technologies took the pencil from our hands and replaced it with a keyboard. Electronic innovations allowed us to work faster and accomplish more, but the spaces of time between routine business activities began to compress, and the time for leisurely interaction in our work became harder to find. Work time as we know it today no longer offers us time to smell the roses.

This article will examine the significant change that has developed in architecture over the past generation and its impact on our personal lives. We will look at the facets of our business that have put us in overdrive, increasing the speed of life and robbing us of much of our time once allocated for observing, pondering, discussing, and, yes, listening.

## As soon as possible

Time, time, time is on my side, yes it is.

—The Rolling Stones, 1964

The time-honored methods of delivering architectural information before the 1970s were land-line rotary dial telephones, hand deliveries direct from the blueprint shop, and the United States Postal Service. An architect could always call the client and discuss the project, but transmission or shipping of drawings and images was a slow process. In a dire emergency, an architect could get on an airplane and deliver promised drawings in person. The exchange of information was much slower, as were the expectations of those participating.

When facsimile machines and overnight deliveries entered the picture, the speed of life began to gain a faster pace.

## Just the fax

Facsimile transmission technology was introduced in the 1970s, but it was not widely used until the early 1980s. By the time the 1990s rolled around, it was routine to send a fax of 30 to 40 pages or even larger. The first commercially viable fax machines were cumbersome and designed to send only a few pages. Telephone transmission technology at the time consisted of land lines communicating through analog switches. It was common to experience dropped calls, resulting in incomplete faxes. A typical fax session involving the transmission of 10 pages could go something like this:

You pick up the receiver and dial the fax number, hoping that someone is at the other end to answer. If they answer, you hurriedly jam the receiver into the rubber fax receptacle, while the person on the other end does the same. You listen to the high-pitched sounds until they stop, hold your breath while the sheets begin to feed, curse when the telephone company drops the call, and start the infernal process all over again . . . This endeavor could often absorb an hour. The great benefit of this exhausting effort was that the client or consultant received information that would otherwise have required two days or more for delivery.

These spaces of time between tasks, imposed by technical limitations, gave us more time for contemplation and creativity. We were able to give more time to our work, and obligated deadlines were more forgiving. As technical advances began to encroach upon our sacred spaces, the speed of life began to erode the luxurious time between tasks, robbing us of this once-respected commodity.

## Overnight deliveries

Although it is the abbreviated name and trademark of a well-known package delivery company, FedEx became a part of the architect's lexicon as the generic name for overnight shipping. Overnight delivery was one of the innovations, along with computers and e-mail, that has made the most dramatic difference in the speed of an architect's life. The regular mail expectation of four days to the East or West Coast and two days from Chicago to New York or Dallas to Houston became one day. Waiting time for review of printed material and the intervals waiting for critical reviews or decisions were slashed. An architect could work until the day before a drawing package was due and ship it overnight to the recipient with the assurance that it would be received on time. We discovered it was often faster to send an overnight package across town than to use the mail.

The development of faster communications and deliveries had a systemic effect on our phases of service. With overnight deliveries came overnight responses. This caused us to push on the competitive edge by promising accelerated services. The roses, waiting to be smelled, became red blurs along the way.

## Personal communications

> The more elaborate our means of communication, the less we communicate.
>
> —Joseph Priestley

The telephone was a necessary fixture in business commerce almost from the day it was invented. There is no one living today who did not grow up with this remarkable device. Nonetheless, its early use had significant limitations compared to today's technology.

Once upon a time, a phone could not be answered while it was in use, and the six to eight messages received while you were out of the office were handwritten on pink memo pads by your secretary. You returned the calls and talked to your clients and business associates about the tasks and questions at hand. It could take a day or two to get in touch with each other, and when you did, you conversed in detail, exchanging as much information as possible, knowing that future communications would be just as cumbersome.

Eventually, rotary lines were developed and your "secretary" could actually take a message for you while you were talking on another line. Now, only one phone call was necessary to leave the message. The development of cellular technology and improved electronics has brought efficiency and the speed of life to new heights. When voice mail arrived on the scene, a new form of telephone etiquette emerged. Social interaction no longer required a live conversation. Business could now be transacted through the exchange of messages without the human component of warm spontaneous interaction.

E-mail, although it existed long before it achieved its current market penetration, served to speed up life dramatically, but it also significantly reduced the culture of personal communications. Replacing to a great extent the role of the telephone in business, it is now common to receive 50 or 60 e-mails a day, compared with 8 or 10 telephone calls of 20 years ago. The use of e-mail as a substitute for personal communications is now so pervasive that it is common to send an e-mail to a person sitting 20 feet away rather than walk over to his or her desk and have a conversation. The preference for and reliance upon e-mail as a substitute for personal communications is more poignant when observing an office when their e-mail server is down . . . employees become restless and angry and vent their helpless feelings brought about by those "idiots" in IT.

As a result of voice mail and e-mail, we have all become accustomed to communicating without personal contact. Human interaction is now a second priority. In fact, many people prefer this approach. Many find it tempting to put off returning a phone call until lunchtime or after work, leaving a voice mail message rather than actually talking to a person. This has become all the easier since the development of caller ID. The culture of people speaking real time to other people has greatly diminished.

Now that e-mail has been coupled with PDF technology, fax machines and overnight deliveries have been pushed aside by the ability to e-mail large documents around the world in a matter of seconds. Not just an enemy of personal communications, e-mail is now serving to reduce even more the space between tasks, and the roses are almost rendered unseen.

## The path of artistry

> God is in the details.
>
> —Ludwig Mies van der Rohe

When computer-assisted drafting emerged as a usable technology, the great fear was that creativity would vanish. There was great concern that artistic sketches and flowing thoughts capable of becoming unique designs would give way to electronic libraries of static details that would yield only monotonous design regurgitations. Fortunately, great designs continue to come forth, but they often still begin with blank paper and pencil. Etch-A-Sketch® technology has not completely taken the pencil from our hands. Not yet.

Integrated project delivery anticipates more interaction among all industry players. Design teams are already obtaining 3D data from manufacturers and vendors. Rather than draft medical casework from scratch, the supplier can e-mail you their equipment already drawn. A laboratory interior can be completed in minutes.

This practice offers the supplier a leg up on the competition because of proprietary nuances, and it is being adapted by all building component manufacturers. It is possible that the entire building exterior could become an accumulation of components supplied, already drafted in 3D, for the architect to drag into place. Could this spell the end of learning how walls weep and flashing channels water? What about the artistry? Will artistry be forced to compete with what manufacturers have available?

While these practices may improve quality control overall, they could possibly dumb us down even more. The spaces of time required for researching products and understanding how they perform may be deemed unnecessary. When was the last time you flipped through a volume of Sweets® just to study the details and learn about products? Or the last time you did it, was it done on the Web with a search of unemotional but surgical precision? Balancing the thick book and marking all those pages was once a part of the process. It took more time, which allowed more thought and deliberation. As we flipped the pages, we tended to learn unexpected things along the way.

Yet BIM is in all likelihood the next great catalyst of change for the profession of architecture. It is a catalyst that offers the promise of moving us closer to a practice integrated with all of the participants in the design and construction process. It may also be a tool that allows great advances in the way architects view and accomplish design. That is, if we do not allow it to compress and eliminate further our precious spaces of time.

## The speed of life—conclusion

> Be aware of wonder. Live a balanced life—learn some and think some and draw and paint and sing and dance and play and work every day some.
>
> —Robert Fulghum

Architecture was a little more fun when the speed of practice allowed for a little more contemplation of the tasks at hand. Many times we have risen from the drafting table confident that a good night's sleep would help reveal the solution to a gnarly design problem. Contemplation, introspection, and discussion among comrades often has revealed the path to a solution. The way we do architecture today, with CAD and e-mail and cell phones and PDFs . . . well, it has infused us and our clients with the expectation that "fast and furious with great precision" is just a day's work.

We seem no longer to think of the possibility that a significant measure of the craft and artistry that has been so much a part of architecture has in many ways taken a back seat to technology and speed. Is the message that the introspection quotient has turned upside down? Or is the message that the speed of life is leaving the artistry of architecture behind? We believe these important messages should be considered as one approaches daily tasks and ponders the future.

As you zip through all those e-mails, deleting some before reading and pecking out your responses in terse, abbreviated replies, take a moment to think about what that framed diploma or license hanging on your wall really means to you. If you have been around awhile, think back and ask: Has your speed of life evolved as you hoped? Is it giving you the time you really want and need? You can adjust the speed, you know. Or, if you are just starting out, think about what you want your speed of life to be and be conscious of trying to make it so.

> It is never too late to become what you might have been.
>
> —George Eliot

Everyone needs to reflect upon what we want to accomplish in the architecture of the future in this promising time of great change. We need to think about our spaces of time and how we want to live them. It is never too late to follow a road of our own making.

Do we have an answer for how the speed of life is impacting our love for architecture? We can answer only for ourselves. How we deal with the speed of life is ultimately up to us as individuals. But we can offer that it is an awe-inspiring thing, smelling the roses. And, lest we forget, as you ponder your plans and contemplate your speed of life . . . try to be careful out there.

# Raiders of the Lost Art: The Vanished Treasures of Architecture

This is another of our "lament" chronicles that looks back at what we like to think of as the golden years. From Rapidograph pens to paper sepias to pin bars, we seek to draw one more tear from the old-timer and perhaps cause the youngster to wonder, if but for a second, if it really was better back then. We also look to the future and the amazing developments that our successors have at their disposal. Without doubt, some day, they will wax nostalgic about a ground-breaking software program or a legendary file transfer process, and they, too, may shed a tear for their vanished treasures. Can we borrow your handkerchief?

> It was the best of times, it was the worst of times, it was the age of wisdom, it was the age of foolishness, it was the epoch of belief, it was the epoch of incredulity.
>
> —Charles Dickens, *A Tale of Two Cities*

These past few years have challenged our profession. We have experienced a surge in work like never before. It has tested our resources, and it has had a catalytic effect on the way we practice and view what we do professionally.

We now use electronic tools to deliver our services. The way we work and communicate has changed dramatically for most architects. Our telephone does not have a cord anymore, and the Architect Registration Examination can no longer be taken with a number 2 pencil. These changes have brought us to the threshold of a new and profoundly different way to work. Alas, BIM!

Earlier in the chapter, in "Your Grandfather's Working Drawings" and "The Speed of Life," we gazed nostalgically upon "the way it was." We now find ourselves worn thin by work, and we succumb to the urge to take yet another look both back and forward at the wonder and promise of our profession and the ensuing changes over the years.

## Substance in all experiences

It is easy to feel that much of the artistry in our practice has been raided over the years by advances in technology and changing priorities; the passing of the chief draftsman's one-on-one mentoring, the longer spaces between communications and mail deliveries that gave us more time to contemplate, discuss, and ponder.

Our commentary in "Your Grandfather's Working Drawings" took on mixed reviews, some opining sentimental banality and others grateful for the fond look at past experiences. Responses were divided essentially by age group, of course. We were grateful for all these observations, since our core purpose is to stimulate.

Accordingly, we believe that there is substance in all experiences, in our losses as well our gains, so buckle up, and get ready for a look at the architectural practice of our apprenticeship, the vanished treasures, and those from whom we learned.

# The beginning of the New Age

> There will come a time when you believe everything is finished. That
> will be the beginning.
>
> —Louis L'Amour

We both grew up in the rural South, drinking sweet tea and eating sand-
wiches made from "light bread." Staples at the dinner table were red beans
and rice, fried chicken, and mashed potatoes. Our parents had a flickering
old black-and-white TV on which we perpetually adjusted the outside
antenna as we struggled to watch cartoons on Saturday morning. The lingering shock and misery of World War II and Korea caused adults to speak
in hushed tones because memories of fallen loved ones hovered close by
and pictures were still displayed on the mantel. We got Lionel and American
Flyer train sets and Strombecker slot car tracks for Christmas. For all those
enchanting memories at home, so it was with architecture.

## 1. The reign of the chief

Back then the world within an architecture office was ruled with an iron
hand by the chief draftsman. There was no "studio director" or "senior
designer," or even a "project manager." You were expected to get your butt on
your stool (right, there weren't any "brand name" office chairs) by 8:00 A.M.
and keep your head down and elbows up until quitting time, which would
be decided by the chief. The "coffee bar" had yet to be named, and it certainly
was not a place for gathering.

Not long after "modern" practice began to emerge in the late 1970s, it
became clear that the reign of the old chief draftsman was coming to a close.
The modern studio began to emerge as an office organizational concept,
and for many firms the "departmental" distinction between disciplines
began to blur. Aesthetic pursuits, or "design," always important, became a
dominant idea even in venerable old "production" firms. The days of the old
chief draftsman, already numbered, continued to dwindle, and essentially
he was gone.

## 2. A lost art—Rapidograph

Drafting with ink required the use of reservoir ink pens such as those made
by Mars or Koh-I-Noor (Rapidograph). For a young draftsperson in the
late '60s and early '70s, a rite of passage was obtaining your first drafting
pen. The best choices for school design studios were an "0" (aught), a "1" or
"2," and a "3." These numerical designations delineate the width of the line
drawn by each pen, though an artistically qualified draftsman's repertoire of
line widths was in reality limited only by the imagination.

These numerical designations are also the genesis of the modern term
"pen table," that portion of a CAD program where "line weights" are specified. Most draftsmen (no politically correct "draftspersons" back then)
developed unique techniques for the combinations of lead, wax, and ink

lines used in their drawings. These techniques would realistically be viewed as artistry.

A boring duty, yet in retrospect an introspective treasure, was the need to regularly clean your pens. There was often a longer line at the sink by the coffee pot for pen cleaning than for refreshment.

## 3. Another lost art—standing on a stool

Contemplation of the artistry of drawings was once a prevailing idea in the architect's mind. Taking the time to contemplate and worry about the quality of the communication aspects of a drawing was an inherent part of document preparation. No supervisor questioned why these communication skills were of concern. It was common in the drafting room to look down a row of drafting tables and see someone standing on their stool squinting down at their drawing. Drawings were taped to the angled surface of the drafting board, and the best vantage point for scrutiny was up on the stool.

Stool standers included designers squinting at their renderings as well as draftsmen who viewed their technical drawings as essential presentations of their art. No one laughed or found this curious, and someone else would soon be up on their stool, squinting down. A draftsman standing on a stool was accepted as reverent recognition of the concern for communication quality. Today, one does not see draftspersons, or CAD operators, standing on their stool squinting at their computer screen.

## 4. The New Age—sepia tones

> They that will not apply new remedies must expect new evils.
> —Francis Bacon

It was common at one time for the beginning draftsman to serve some time as a "tracer," tracing what were then the standard details and backgrounds of practice. Standard details were maintained in a notebook and could be taped under a sheet of tracing medium—tracing paper, Mylar, or linen—and traced over by the draftsman. Similarly, the initial floor plan background would be drawn by an experienced draftsman, then additional copies for consultants or for reflected ceiling plans could be traced above the original. The experienced architects in an office would frequently visit with the "copy boys" explaining the nuances of the details, floor plans, and backgrounds. Construction materials and products were largely generic and changed slowly so the detail book was easily kept up-to-date. Eventually ammonia process sepia tracings were developed and replaced the need to replicate details and plans by tracing. With this invention an essential element of drafting apprenticeship vanished.

Sepia "eradicator" was used to erase a part of the sepia image from the back of the paper or Mylar, and new drawing elements were drawn on the front. The sepia print often picked up heavy background from the original tracing, and the eradicator removed it, leaving unsightly white smears around the revised detail on "blueline" reproductions. Nevertheless, sepias helped speed up the practice by allowing drawings to be easily and inexpensively replicated.

## 5. Pin bar—layers and levels

Original tracing and sepia copies shared the characteristic of having just two layers, a front and a back. This limitation of layers ruled the organization of drawing components for many years. Still, the tracing media of the time offered one more layer than the papyrus of ancient times. Drawings were thought of as artistic compositions and were considered to be proprietary to the artisan—the architect or draftsman who prepared them. Consequently, a drawing sheet was usually prepared by one or just a few draftsmen who controlled drawing preparation and content.

A desire for speed and the erosion of the artisan's control brought about a new phase with "pin bar" drafting. Several sheets of tracings were registered on a pin bar, a flat strip of metal with vertical pins that aligned with holes along the edge of the Mylar sheet. Stacking the sheets on the pin bar aligned the sheets and allowed one background to serve as the basis for several different drawings. For example, a single original background sheet could become the base drawing for both a floor plan and a reflected ceiling plan. Due to the limitations of the light source in a vacuum frame printer, only about four tracings were all that could be overlaid. Nonetheless, drawing on eight layers was a great improvement over the traditional two. With pin bar, the artisan lost proprietary control of at least some of the composite drawing, and another essential element of apprenticeship was gone.

CAD technology arrived amid incredible controversy, and drawing preparation became faster still. Communications between people with more experience and people with less experience lessened, and teaching and counseling in the ways of the old chief draftsman were pushed even further from the profession's collective memory. The turning of the experience quotient for apprentice architects entered full swing.

## 6. Placeholders

A practice common in CAD drafting today is to imbue a drawing with "placeholders" to mark the location for information that has not been developed or is not yet known. This is a modern practice facilitated by the fact that CAD drawings are very easy to copy and to change. Popular to the point of being cultural in many firms, placeholders offer the impression that a drawing represents a state of completion that doesn't actually exist. The drawing is thus, at least partially, an illusion.

Drawings drawn by hand, in graphite, wax, and ink seldom incorporated an excessive number of placeholders, if any at all. Everyone understood all too well the limitations of the drafting medium as not being tolerant of excessive changes. Through the generations the technique of drawing construction lines was developed. These lightweight construction lines made it possible to ghost in an area of the drawing without risking ruining the "tooth" on the surface of the linen, paper, or Mylar. Lines were not finalized until design knowledge was sufficient to allow completion of the drawing, and accordingly, the drawings did not become illusory. Moreover, communication of reliable information was more enhanced then than it is now.

## 7. Proprietary endeavors

Architectural practice has been significantly complicated by the fact that construction materials, products, and systems aren't as generic as they used to be. Addressed in detail in "Drawing the Line" in Chapter 4, products and systems these days tend to be very proprietary. This serves to create an environment where products and systems, although "conceptually equal," are actually "nominally different." Architects have more products and systems available on the market from which to choose, and therefore they are not as familiar with the specifics of how each product or system can be incorporated into their buildings. This causes the architect to yield some control over their designs to vendors and subcontractors who furnish and install the product or system. This diminished level of communications extends to the builders as well.

## 8. CAD—vanishing spaces

When drawings were drawn with pen or pencil by the artisan's hand, they were drawn in a conventional drafting room. People sat side by side and talked to each other, face to face, about the designs they developed and the physical documents they prepared. Today, in our electronic environment, drawings are commonly prepared by multiple parties, drawn at life size, in a "room" that is limited only by the extent of the universe.

There is no longer a tangible edge to the paper in the computer world. The drafters of documents today seldom communicate by actually speaking to each other; indeed, they may share only the language of the software they use and they may not know who their coworkers are. CAD is a marvelous tool that has profoundly changed our profession, but as we opined in "Your Grandfather's Working Drawings," it has contributed a great deal to turning the experience quotient upside down. Many architects today may understand computer drafting, but they may not understand buildings or the art of communication.

## The future

> The future ain't what it used to be.
>
> —Yogi Berra

Building information modeling promises to be an even more marvelous tool than CAD. We believe that a process wherein the architect's design evolves contemporaneously with the contractor's plan for construction will foster a closer collaboration among architects, consultants, contractors, subcontractors, and vendors, the inevitable outcome of which can serve to return the application of experience and detailed knowledge to its rightful place within the design process. This, in turn, may foster an increased opportunity and perhaps a desire for more open communication and interaction.

Yet, despite the need we all feel to work together, to be seen as eager and adaptable and to not be perceived as a detractor, BIM can also be viewed by some as a cloud on the horizon. These concerns for the future must not be shouted down or swept aside if architecture of the future is to benefit from its promise and potential. The most important issue, in the vein of "Your Grandfather's Working Drawings," is that the upside-down experience quotient in our profession today places those who understand this technology the least, the leadership of integrated project delivery, closest to the threshold of the future. Concerns we have about the future development of architecture include:

- The generations who will inherit our profession must be the prime movers into BIM and integrated project delivery.
- The profession is presently mired in lawsuits that are becoming increasingly more aggressive in blaming architects for every conceivable thing that goes on during construction.
- Potential liability issues involved in sharing the BIM "model" are significant.
- Training is more difficult, for today at least, as BIM requires a way of thinking about designs, building, and drawings that differs significantly from the two-dimensional world of today's CAD and our current drawing culture.
- Penetration into the marketplace is presently somewhat minimal, and in the vendor and subcontractor market, it is likely to remain minimal for smaller companies for quite some time.

We are not detractors, we are believers. But just as much as we believe in BIM, find it fascinating, and have each delivered projects with this technology, we also believe in facing reality.

## Conclusion

> The universe is change; our life is what our thoughts make it.
> —Marcus Aurelius Antoninus, AD 180

Architecture as a profession has traditionally been steeped in effective and thorough communication. Bricks don't care much about communication; they just like to be laid straight, true, and plumb. Water doesn't care much about communication, as long as its "users" understand that it does very much like to run downhill. Without effective communications among each other, architecture is a lost cause. Without effective communications between each of us and the profession we love, there are no effective architects and, hence, no meaningful architecture. Life as an architect cannot devolve into a constant race to do things faster and more efficiently. There is a limit beyond which it cannot go. Life as an architect must involve contemplation of the art, loving caresses of the medium, and never-ending introspection about how we can effectively communicate with ourselves and others who interact with us.

When we were young, we thought that we were different from and could not understand our parents and grandparents. Now we find that we are not understandable or recognizable by our children. The more seasoned among us actually emulate our elders, if we'll allow ourselves a look inside. The apprentices among us are just as certain as we were of our forebears that we don't understand them at all. The future has always been what the future was. That is, except for Rapidograph pens, 1000H Clearprint drafting paper, and that little can of Pounce. The loss of the treasures of our past sends us a profound message that, if recognized, can strengthen us for the present and the future. Most things will never be as they were, but one undeniable constant remains. Like it or not, change is our future . . . for us, all of us.

As you put on your coat and gather up your briefcase headed to your next meeting, amble by the digital sender, or stop by an intern's computer station, and gaze at what is before you. And as you observe, understand that in an instant, it all can and will change. Then head for the door and try to be careful out there.

# Chapter 7

## Introspection

## Who Are You? Defining the Architect

We are continually frustrated at the lack of understanding of architects by the general public. This article is as much a call to arms as it is a definition. We are convinced that our risks would be less if everyone better understood what an architect is and does. The operative word for this piece is "communicate," since who people think we are is greatly determined by who we lead them to believe we are. Are you one who wants them to know who you really are? Are you?

Why is it that many people do not understand what architects do? For some reason, the practice of architecture is generally not well understood outside the profession. As a result, the expectations of owners and the public do not always align with actual outcomes. A significant part of the problem is that most people think they know who architects are and what they do, but their perception is not entirely accurate.

*Merriam-Webster's*, defines an architect as, "A person who designs buildings and advises in their construction." While this is true, it does not convey the essence of the actual practice of architecture. Moreover, by its simplicity, it is misleading. It suggests that an architect knows everything there is to know about designing and constructing a building. Perhaps that is one reason why we frequently get sued for the contractor's misdeeds.

Architects have struggled for decades to convey our identity to the public. As the profession has evolved from the nonlitigious days of the combination architect and constructor that marked the days of the master builder, we have yet to shed the identity of being the only professional in charge. This lack of understanding of what we do continues even though the AIA has produced literature explaining what an architect is so that clients can find out more about the services they are obtaining. Meanwhile, to add confusion to naiveté, software developers are running around calling themselves architects, and computers run on "architecture." No wonder the help desk treats us the way they do.

We have pondered whether young people enrolling in architecture school really know what an architect is. We were somewhat uninformed when we started out. For many, architecture school was not what we expected it to be. Many architects have pondered at some point in their career whether the long hours and relatively low pay during their early professional life was really what they bargained for.

This article will explore the architect's misunderstood status and the challenges and frustrations that it can bring. We will examine how the public has been exposed to architects, and what they tend to expect of us. Finally we will look at some alternatives and potential opportunities for improving awareness.

> Oh I'm just a friend.
> That's all I've ever been.
> Cause you don't know me.
>
> —Ray Charles

## The eye of the public

If people in general derive their understanding of architects from what they see in the movies, consider the material that is available. Most everyone should remember *The Fountainhead,* where Gary Cooper is Howard Roark, an architect who blows up his own project because the owner and contractor are not adhering to the design concept. Imagine that. So he takes the law into his own hands and vaporizes his design. Do real-life architects do that? Not if they want to stay in business and out of jail.

There is also *The Towering Inferno,* where architect Paul Newman stumbles through his fire-engulfed high-rise on opening night, discovering construction atrocities committed by the contractor, yet the architect internalizes the blame in the name of poor design. Then, adding to the misinformation and fantasy, he rides the elevators into the inferno, an act that is not only stupid but unrealistic. No wonder the public has doubts about us.

Then there is *Intersection,* where Richard Gere's architect character spends most of the movie having an affair, as does an architect played by Wesley Snipes in Spike Lee's *Jungle Fever.* Isn't that a wonderful image of architects? All we need is for the public to believe that architects are philandering losers.

In *The Belly of an Architect,* Brian Dennehy plays an architect who goes off the deep end and messes up his family and career. In the *Death Wish* series, an architect played by Charles Bronson becomes a berserk vigilante.

For a profession of well-meaning people who just want to create cool places for people to be in and enjoy, we tend to be portrayed poorly or to be overly romanticized in the public eye. It's no wonder our identity is flapping in the breeze.

## Raising public awareness

The AIA goes to respectable lengths to educate the public on architects and architecture. *You and Your Architect* is downloadable online at www.aia.org and addresses some of what an architect does, as well as how to find and hire one. Most of the architect association Web sites around the world provide informative links—such as the RIBA's "What Architects Do" and the AIA's

"What an Architect Can Do for You"—in efforts to enlighten and educate the public. Yet what architects are and do continue to be largely misunderstood by many.

This fundamental misperception of what architects are and the services they provide produces unrealistic expectations that result in dissatisfaction and discord. Although you may do a near perfect job, if what you do is not what the owner expects, you may still be in trouble. Owners who perceive unfulfilled promises often pursue recovery through legal means.

Claire Gallagher, EdD, Assoc. AIA, an architecture/design educator who has devoted her career to working toward raising public awareness and making architecture more widely understood outside the profession, wrote on Architectureweek.com in June 2001, "It is a loss both to the profession and to society that architectural process is shrouded in mystery."

> But I'm just a soul whose intentions are good
> Oh Lord, please don't let me be misunderstood
> —Eric Burdon and the Animals

## Perceptions and expectations

Many owners are under the misguided perception that architects are obligated under their contract to search out and find defects and deficiencies in the contractor's work. We explored this topic in detail in "Absolute or Absolution?" in Chapter 4.

AIA Document B141-1997, in Section 2.6.2.1, states, "The Architect, as a representative of the Owner, shall . . . endeavor to guard the Owner against defects and deficiencies in the Work . . . " This language, "endeavor to guard," has been misconstrued by some to mean that the architect has the ability to prevent defects by catching the contractor's mistakes and making the contractor correct them. Consequently, when problems are discovered in the completed work, the architect may be accused of causing construction defects, rather than the contractor who performed the work, in spite of the fact that the contractor provided an express warranty that the work would be free from defects.

The language "endeavor to guard" has been popular among plaintiff attorneys in court pleadings when claiming against architects, and consequently it was removed from the AIA documents in the 2007 revisions. However, its absence will likely not decrease or eliminate attorney motivations to allege architect negligence in discovering and reporting building defects and deficiencies.

Meanwhile, many contractors do not know much more about architects than owners do—especially if the architects they encounter concentrate their efforts primarily on design issues and issue insufficient or uncoordinated construction documents or take a passive approach to construction contract administration (CCA). When a contractor works with an architect who does not produce adequate construction documents or does not proactively provide CCA, the contractor assumes that all architects typically opt to pay little attention to details and construction. Especially when architects are not visible on the job during construction, the contractor and owner cannot be aware of the services that an architect can provide. It was Woody Allen who said, "Eighty percent of success is showing up." The importance of proactive construction administration is addressed in "Visible Means: Site Visits and Construction Observation" in Chapter 5.

> Cellophane, Mister Cellophane
> Shoulda been my name, Mister Cellophane
> Cause you can look right through me
> Walk right by me, And never know I'm there.
> —Soundtrack to the musical *Chicago*

## Alternatives and opportunities

Gallagher's solution to our anonymity is to " . . . bring architecture and what architects do into elementary and secondary school classrooms." She adds, " . . . once they begin incorporating design into their teaching, architecture will cease to be a mystery to the public."

Gallagher's systemic approach will likely improve things over time, but architects can help themselves individually by taking action. We must stop acting like we are just another profession, like a lawyer or a dentist, whom everyone automatically knows a lot about. After all, those professionals are often portrayed on television or in movies acting as heroes and are not usually portrayed blowing up buildings or committing revenge murders. We must face the fact that people are no more familiar with us than they are with rocket scientists, like the people at NASA who do those mysterious things to get rockets into space. Perhaps, in that respect, architecture *is* like rocket science!

We have to accept the fact that, generally, people just don't know what we do. We must factor this into our daily activities and within our work routines. With sensitivity to avoid the condescending, we must actively work to enlighten people around us to the greatest extent possible.

We should make ourselves completely available to the owner. We can provide the owner with information on the specifics of project issues and our profession. Looking cool, dressed in that black sports coat and matching turtleneck sweater, delivering that crisp, clean 3D model of the project simply does not enlighten as well as subjecting the owner to your piles of bumwad sketches and countless red-marked drawings. When it comes to what we do, presenting laser-sharp whiz-bang technologies in the boardroom is a poor substitute for exposing the owner to the creative power and probing realities of the "back room" where we spend most of our time in search of our designs.

Let's face it; owners are no different from you and me. We like the mom-and-pop restaurant where the menu is on a chalkboard, the tables are plastic laminate, and you can see Pop cooking in the kitchen. We like to see the manual innards of a business. When we can see the backroom disarray, we can understand more about the process and we appreciate how the product gets to the table.

Guiding the owner through the document preparation progress in the back room, or traipsing through the dusty formwork on a hot day and laboring over details of the fascia substrate, is a quantum improvement over anonymous status reports. If you are there, and if you are responsive, and if you have answers, you can gain trusted advisor status and actually demonstrate to the owner in real time what an architect is and does, as well as the limitations inherent in the process.

## What they really think

You can truly observe what owners and contractors really think architects do by looking at what they say we were responsible for when they file claims against us. Some of the following language, stylized from a series of actual claims against architects, reflects the unreal views of what others think we do, or should have done:

> ... most, if not all, of the issues noted are the result of nonconforming work performed by the contractor. These problems were exacerbated by the Architect's failure to observe nonconforming work and require that the work be redone.

In this instance, the claimant and their lawyer clearly do not understand that the contractor's obligation to perform the work well is not overridden by placing a stronger obligation on the architect to "catch him if he doesn't." They also do not understand that the architect has limited power or authority to force the contractor to correct nonconforming work, but can only reject the nonconforming work. A201 requires the contractor to correct work the architect has rejected.

In another example, the perceived power of the architect is more extreme:

> At the time that contractor's defective work was performed, Architect was supervising the work at the site. Additionally, the work was performed while Architect was in charge of the work.

In this instance, there are several misunderstandings. Architects do not "supervise" the work on the site unless they have signed a contract specifically to provide such services. The AIA Contract Documents define supervision" as a construction activity, not as an architectural service.

The most extreme misunderstanding in this claim is that the architect was somehow "in charge" of the work. Sections 4.2.2 and 4.2.3 of the A201, General Conditions, specifically state that the architect will not have control over or charge of the work.

Both of these instances reflect poor communication of the real duties, responsibilities, and actions of the architect. Although the claims may be defensible based on contracted duties as well as standard of care, the misunderstandings that are the foundation of the claims could have benefited from better communication about what architects do.

## Anything but guaranteed

Architects often seem to have a need to be seen as respected professionals, along the lines that it is perceived that physicians and attorneys are respected. Yet, inherent in the practice of medicine and law is the patient's or client's knowledge that success is anything but guaranteed as a result of the professional services that physicians and attorneys provide.

Although a physician does not frequently ask you to sign a release for a simple office visit, any serious and more complex procedure will nearly always be accompanied by the request that you sign an informed-consent release attesting to your understanding that success is not guaranteed and that there are well-known risks and side effects that may arise out of the physician's efforts.

Likewise, your lawyer will sit with you and offer counsel about the risks inherent in a legal proceeding or contract that you may be contemplating. You, like other parties, hire lawyers to help you understand and mitigate these inherent risks.

Yet architects generally do a poor job when it comes to being open and forthright about the risks inherent in designing and constructing a building. Whether it be the risk of increased costs or lengthened schedules inherent in the fast-track process or the probability, if not the certainty, of errors and omissions committed by the human beings that provide architectural services, architects are reluctant to talk about the things that can go wrong. Physicians and attorneys, ostensibly respected professionals, aren't reluctant to set realistic expectations for their clients, while architects, wanting to be perceived as respected professionals, are. Perhaps competition for commissions is a cause of this behavior in our profession.

> Can you see the real me, can you?
>
> —The Who, 1973

## Getting to know you

Who are we? We owe it to ourselves to do our best to reveal our profession to the public. We design the building, we produce the construction drawings, and we administer the construction contract. We make thousands of decisions and spend countless hours toiling away in the obscurity of our back room. Just like every other human being, we are not perfect and some of what we do doesn't turn out like we hope it will. Nonetheless, most of what we do produces results that are not only sufficient, but exciting. If everyone really knew what we actually do, our work would be more appreciated and better respected.

This problem of unrealistic and inaccurate perceptions about what we do did not happen overnight, and it will not be resolved in another night. We can blame the system and we can blame the players, but we must primarily blame ourselves. We must decide that we want to be understood. We must start by learning to talk about what we do. In the course of delivering our services, we must be able to explain our process and our actions as we go along. We must invite our owners into the back room and let them experience the "moving parts" of our operation. Schedule site visits with the owner and walk the job together. The more of our process the owner can see and experience, the more they will understand who we are.

We must also maintain our presence with the contractors. This can be done by conducting or at least being an active participant in the project meeting, walking the site, and spending time in their back room. We should schedule extra time to spend with the contractor on site visits. These actions represent good project management, but they also enlighten and inform. As you take time out from what you are doing to walk to the coffee bar, stop a few steps away and look back at your workspace. Contemplate what you see, and muse how you would explain to the owner what you have been doing in the past hour. Explaining the benefits of your actions to the client and the project will reveal to the client a little bit more about who you are. Go on now and get that cup of joe, and as you do . . . remember to be careful out there.

# Who's on First? Covering Your Bases in a Resource-Challenged Industry

We discussed and debated this topic at length before we began writing. It is a sensitive subject in that no one wants to admit that they are short-handed or have been challenged at assigning the best people to a project. And when you refuse to admit it, the discussion doesn't last very long. We wrote the piece with mixed emotions. Although not having and assigning the best people carries a risk, the alternative of not enough work and too many people is much less desirable and more risky. It's almost as confounding as the renowned Abbott and Costello sketch. Who? That's what I said!

> Abbott: I say Who's on first, What's on second, I Don't Know's on third. . .
> Costello: Well then, who's on first?
> Abbott: Yes.
> Costello: I mean the fellow's name.
> Abbott: Who.
> Costello: The guy on first . . .
> Abbott: Who is on first!
> Costello: I'm asking YOU who's on first.
> —"Who's on First?" Bud Abbott and Lou Costello

A reality in the design, development, and construction industry is that we are only as good as our project team. Accordingly, we strive to assign and staff our projects in a way that will be most beneficial for the client and the scope of work. However, in this extended active economy, available personnel for owners, architects, and contractors alike have been significantly tapped. Even the small practitioner who relies on occasional contract labor may have difficulty in finding help when that larger commission arrives.

The response for many firms has been extensive overtime, a marked increase in average salaries, and less experienced employees promoted early to management-level positions. This issue spans the breadth of our industry, and more and more owner, architect, and contractor project managers are running projects for the very first time. Most participants in the developmental, design, and construction business today are experiencing some form of the "Walk before you crawl" (or at least walk not long after you crawl) scenario in their offices today.

The overall result in some cases is understaffed project teams, with limited experience, struggling to keep pace with project demands. For clients this may result in owner representatives with less experience at managing building programs, understanding construction costs, and working with architects and contractors. Contractor project managers may have less experience at preparing the contractor's work plan and directing or coordinating the subcontractors. The design professional's project manager may struggle with document completion and coordination, or coping with client expectations.

Meanwhile, those of us involved with risk management are waiting for the inevitable ballooning of claims that has happened in the past when such conditions were experienced.

## Good news, bad news

The good news is that most everyone is busy and profits are reaching record levels. The bad news is that the expensive days of claim defense and settlement will likely fall in later years of lower workload and lesser profits. Other bad news is that many of those recently hired employees could be laid off. Those of us in the business for the past few decades have seen this event at least two times before, and if we hang in there long enough, we will likely see it again.

This article is about ways to cover your bases in these days of increased work and limited employees. We will examine alternatives for improving your work production with your current staff, ways to outsource your work, and ways to minimize future layoffs. Don't be bashful about evaluating these options and testing them in your firm. You are not alone in your workload status, and your competition is likely already using some of these alternatives. Also, do not be bashful about suggesting alternatives we may not have considered or of offering criticism of those we have.

## The hole in the workforce

The last recessive time of significance occurred in the late 1980s. It followed a building boom that had caused many firms to expand, both in offices and employees. As the work began to dry up, the first responses were usually a freeze on raises and hiring. Then we held our breaths and hoped that new work would come or that natural attrition would assist in balancing staff.

But the new work did not come. Times would be lean for several years. Around our town, hundreds of architects and interns lost their jobs, and that devastation replayed through the cities of our nation. Everyone was touched:

owners, architects, and contractors alike. From the early to mid-1990s, the industry hired very few employees, some firms continued layoffs in their struggle to survive, and some firms did not survive.

Many promising employees sought alternative careers just to have a job. As a result, managers who would have been hired and trained during that time would now be 10- to 15-year veteran managers who could handle a large or complex project. The recession of the early 1990s continues to impact the profession because today, when we desperately need this talent pool, they are not here in the numbers we need.

The damage from this unfortunate event was exacerbated by the emergence of CAD. These managers would have developed their careers on the computer, and they would be mentoring and teaching younger CAD operators how buildings go together. Their absence plays a part in why the experience quotient in our profession has turned upside down as we espouse in "Your Grandfather's Working Drawings" in Chapter 6.

We all face today's busy times with a hole in the workforce. Owners, architects, and contractors struggle to maintain this vital management element. Competing firms steal from each other in hiring wars that only serve to drive up base salaries. For all participants in the design and construction industry, the mid-level manager is the most sought-after employee.

## Alternatives

> When you come to a fork in the road, take it.
>
> —Yogi Berra

Everyone is now being forced to make decisions about how to cope with the strain on the workforce. The easy way out would be to stop taking on new work, but this approach does not conform to the mindset of our feast-or-famine industry. The natural response is to keep taking on work and then worry about who is going to produce it. After all, we have always managed to get the work done somehow, haven't we?

### Positive action

These times require specific actions if we wish to improve upon the challenging conditions. Some of these actions can include:

**Communicate closely with your client.** Products of these working conditions can include missed deadlines and incomplete or uncoordinated work, which can result in owner frustration and disappointment. On the other hand, most clients will understand if you keep them closely informed of your work status. A client who does not know who's on first on their project will be less confident about the working relationship and may be more difficult to satisfy. Owner expectations may also be more difficult to manage during these times. If you have to tell a client you are going to miss a deadline because you are understaffed, early is better than later, because bad news does not get better with age.

**Focus on your employees.** Strive to improve overall employee comfort level. Everyone wants optimum performance from their staff every day, but when workload is up and staffing levels are down, higher employee comfort and satisfaction can help offset demanding schedules. The long working hours that are required can be tempered with amenities to soothe and reward. Historically, firms have offered unlimited coffee and tea to employees, but lately firms have added baskets of fruit by the front door for employees to snack on, gourmet coffee and tea service, chair massages, and the like. One architect came up with an afternoon tea break with warm, moist towels to refresh.

Entertainment can also make the employee's long day more enjoyable: movies at noon, tickets to the game or theater. Flex time can allow employees to control and enjoy their personal life better. To maximize flexibility and help minimize paid time off, one firm asks all employees to be in the office between 10:00 a.m. and 3:00 p.m. It is the employee's option for the remaining time as long as it is contiguous and meets a minimum number of hours.

**Plan for the future. Get serious about training.** Although training should be a continuing concern, it is especially important when you are asking less experienced employees to take on assignments for the first time. AIA member surveys have consistently indicated project management training as one of the most requested topics at conventions and conferences. Many of the larger firms are contracting with training companies to provide management and leadership training on a continuing basis. Project manager boot camps designed specifically for architects are available from several sources.

Larger firms are moving past the basic human resources structure to organization development. This program takes employee needs to a higher level by including HR, skills, and leadership training and employee performance assessment into a coordinated strategic initiative. This approach has existed for many years in large blue-chip corporations, and the design and construction industry is now discovering its applications and benefits.

One firm's initiative is called People and Organization Development, and it is designed to improve all employees throughout their working experience. A curriculum has been developed for each job description so that skills training is better understood and career paths are more visible. A curriculum was also developed for future leaders, which include management and leadership training.

A shorter-term improvement that can assist in maintaining management quality is to stack your management structure. A strong, experienced project manager with lesser experienced managers assigned to him or her can oversee more projects through monitoring, mentoring, and teaching. This approach can be effective for all participants under all industry conditions, and it is reminiscent of the old chief draftsman whom we talked about in Chapter 6.

### Going outside

    Costello: Now suppose that I'm catching. Tomorrow's pitching on my team and their heavy hitter gets up.

    Abbott: Yes.

    Costello: Tomorrow throws the ball. The batter bunts the ball . . . I wanna throw the guy out at first base. So I pick up the ball and throw it to who?

Abbott: Now that's the first thing you've said right.

Costello: I don't even know what I'm talkin' about!

Workforce levels tend to follow workload, and, in busy times, many practitioners find themselves scrambling to balance the two. Since tapped-out employee resources tend to reduce the chances of walk-in candidates, a stronger program for employee recruiting is often pursued.

Architecture schools produce a consistent and predictable workforce at the entry level, and structured school visits and recruiting can be beneficial. Larger firms use school recruiting for summer internships, which can facilitate full-time job offers at graduation time.

For more experienced employees such as the much-sought-after mid-level manager, recruiting agencies can be helpful. However, be aware that the use of recruiters can contribute to hiring wars among competing firms. When the mid-level workforce is depleted in a local area, it is not uncommon to see owners stealing managers from architects and contractors, or vice versa. We all struggle to remain civil and resist retaliation as we face workforce shortages amid departing employees.

A potentially more benevolent approach to staffing is employee sharing. Firms in the same geographical area with differing work loads have been known to lend out employees. This retains their employee through lean times while benefiting the other firm with an experienced, temporary employee. It is advisable, however, that the two firms be good friends and have the same work philosophy.

All of these staffing approaches can benefit from the assistance of a strong human resources department, and recruiting typically at least touches a part of HR and organization development.

Yet another option is the use of consultants. Another architecture firm can be used to share in the work. However, unless the firm was proposed at the onset, consideration should be given relative to the owner's awareness of the team makeup.

If the entire workforce is severely depleted, as is the case in many U.S. cities, some of these ideas may not be workable, which leads us to another emerging option.

### Going further outside

An alternative that is growing in popularity is outsourcing offshore to other countries, where fees can be very competitive. After a few years of monitoring this emerging service model, the AIA International Committee hosted a roundtable in September 2006 to examine current industry practices in this area.

More than 35 invited experts, practitioners, AIA leaders, and representatives of organizations and software companies aired questions, shared perspectives, and discussed the challenges.

The 2006 AIA Firm Survey revealed that over 60 percent of architecture firms outsource work some of the time, and 8 percent of those firms have sent domestic project work offshore. Based in part on Forrester Research findings, the consulting firm Larsen Associates has projected that as much as

20 to 30 percent of architecture jobs will be offshore by the year 2015. This survey, presented at the 2006 AIA National Convention in Los Angeles, also reported that offshore costs were a tenth to a third of domestic costs.

Findings and recommendations of the AIA Offshore Outsourcing Roundtable were published in a report that is available from the AIA International Committee Web site.

## Steps to control workload

As the development, design, and construction marketplace has heated up, and in many markets overheated, everyone has looked for ways to control workload without offending valued clients or potential new clients. Many such techniques applied by architects have been successful, but not for every firm. We'll look at a few:

**Go/no go marketing.** When your workload exceeds your labor capacity, it is wise to focus your marketing strategy on those projects for which you are most qualified and on which you are most proficient and profitable. Times such as these are not always best for exploring new markets.

Some firms have developed "go/no go" criteria to concentrate efforts on the most reasonable commissions. Such measures can include minimum project size, specific locales, specific building types, or repeat versus new clients. One firm with a high repeat client percentage decided to work only for their existing clients unless a new client's project was a preferred project type, exceeded a minimum size, or included broader market area potential.

With your existing clients, you might wish to pursue those who value you and your services most highly and decline those who reject the concept of brand loyalty or who have been historically difficult to work with.

**Increasing fees.** Some firms have increased fees in a polite attempt to avoid turning down a commission, and stories abound of clients having accepted the higher fee without complaint or hesitation. This has resulted in an opportunity for many owners, architects, and contractors to experience increased profits, but it has done little to help manage workloads. On the other hand, the higher fees have helped soften the blow of increased overtime work and rising salaries.

**Extending delivery times.** Some firms have taken the direct approach and have quoted extended delivery times, either by setting a later start date or by increasing the amount of time required to produce the work. Historically, when a developer, architect, or contractor has been awarded a commission, the expectation is that the work will commence fairly soon. If staff is not available to start "soon," then repositioning the project's start or completion time may be the only reasonable way a firm can accept a new commission.

**Turning down work.** This option tends to run counter to the culture of architects who have endured the "feast to famine" reality of the design and construction business. Nonetheless, in this time of limited resources, saying no to a new project may be the only viable option. Many architects come from a background of "never say die," and, like us, are struggling to cope with a business environment where turning down a new project can ever be a viable option. We know that we are not alone with our feelings. However, we are confident that many of you have considered or will consider projects that you probably should turn down because of your workload. Even if "...we have always managed to get the work done somehow, haven't we?"

## Conclusion

> Costello: . . . I throw the ball to first base. Whoever it is grabs the ball, so the guy runs to second. Who picks up the ball and throws it to What, What throws it to I Don't Know, I Don't Know throws it back to Tomorrow—triple play.
> Abbott: Yes.
> Costello: Another guy gets up—it's a long fly ball to Because. Why? I don't know. He's on third and I don't give a darn!
> Abbott: What was that?
> Costello: I said I don't give a darn!
> Abbott: Oh, that's our shortstop.

The development, design, and construction industry will always ebb and flow with the state of our economy, and, accordingly, our business will always be a "feast to famine" endeavor. Hopefully, times will never again be as bad as they were during the Great Depression of the last century when there was no labor shortage because there was no work at all.

These challenging conditions will visit us from time to time as they did in the early to mid-1970s when few architecture graduates could find jobs, and again as they did in the mid-1980s and early 1990s when layoffs were the rule. But since we have had a strong economy and plentiful work for more than a decade, a large portion of our work force has never felt the sting of "famine."

We have presented a few options for managing these busy times, and we hope you find them helpful. But be forever mindful that change is always on the horizon, and those ideas may morph with other concerns and present new challenges. What challenges? Will the workload of today perpetuate and become a way of life? Many of us have been looking for signs of a turndown in work for years, and as we write this article, it does appear that signs are on the horizon. Of course, we may only be seeing what we wish to see. Mixed in among the challenges of delivering today's work and looking out for tomorrow's work is the certainty that BIM and integrated project delivery are going to alter not only how we deliver our services but our relationships with owners and builders as well.

Metaphorically, these can be confusing times. Who's on first? Naturally! As you sign the owner-architect agreement for that new project and ponder, maybe even worry a little, about how you are going to cover your bases, be grateful that it is a time of feast, take comfort that you are not the only one facing the same or similar challenges, and remember to be careful out there.

# Little Boxes: The Challenges of Producing Original Design

This article required a good amount of research to seek out the historic details of the buildings cited, but it turned out to be both fun and educational, a combination that does not always occur. We most appreciated the universality of the message and its application to everyone involved in architecture. We struggled with a title for this piece, and a Martin D18 guitar hanging on the wall reminded us of Pete Seeger singing Malvina Reynolds' "Little Boxes." Does anybody have a pick?

Success in architecture is nurtured by originality. The famous designs of the world, by definition, exist only in one place. There is not a subdivision of Fallingwater, and every cityscape does not contain a Chrysler Building. These are designs that never before existed and are not intended to be replicated.

Mediocrity, on the other hand, is viewed by most architects as the kiss of death. But originality does not come easy; it takes collaboration and teamwork to produce engaging designs. Effective collaboration and teamwork means that those designers in their bright clothes and funny eyeglasses must rely on us "tech people." And we must often accept leadership from them (as much as it hurts to admit).

Unexciting designs can be a great disappointment. Pete Seeger sang it best in Malvina Reynolds' 1962 song, "Little Boxes."

> Little boxes on the hillside,
> Little boxes made of ticky-tacky,
> Little boxes, little boxes,
> Little boxes, all the same.
> There's a green one and a pink one
> And a blue one and a yellow one
> And they're all made out of ticky-tacky
> And they all look just the same.

However, efforts to produce innovative designs sometimes are challenged by the limitations of technology. Frank Lloyd Wright's mushroom-shaped columns in the S. C. Johnson Wax Company building deviated from conventional design so much that the Wisconsin Industrial Commission challenged their ability to perform. A column was tested to failure to prove that the design was adequate, and it was found to support five times the calculated design test load. Such critical reviews of designs are necessary to make our projects successful. Catastrophic failures such as the 2004 roof collapse at Paris's Charles de Gaulle International Airport validate this need and will serve to fuel more intense scrutiny on designs in the future.

## Dichotomy of priorities

Design interpretations in our drawings, while hopefully not catastrophic, are nonetheless often challenging. If you practice on the technical side of architecture, you may have experienced an occasion where artistry and technology collided. A striking design creation, although breathtaking and unique, may have trodden beyond conventional achievement and technology. A design that may have played well in the presentation later proved to defy the limitations of logic or engineering; the slender cantilever jutting from the parapet was far too shallow to hold itself up using any reasonable materials currently known to humankind.

These challenges often test our limits, but it is what original architecture is all about.

There is an inherent dichotomy of priorities in the development of design in architecture. As designers we want to create something that has never before existed, while the technicians seek to use tried and proven building materials and systems to stay out of trouble. Sometimes these priorities conflict and the built design fails, performs inefficiently, or, although perhaps generally viewed as successful, falls short of expectations. Leaking walls or cracking floors will tend to ruin everyone's day.

This article explores affirmative measures for dealing with the *unique-idea-to-built-reality* challenge. From close team communications to product performance awareness, it will address essentials helpful in delivering designs that are constructible, workable, and durable while accommodating the uniqueness of original design. It will explore how we can develop cohesive project deliveries that meet both the designer's and the deliverer's objectives and keep discord and disappointment among the project team to a minimum.

Designers who read this article may be indignant that project managers and project architects do not understand the challenges they face in dealing with those "straight-edgers" in the back room. The deliverers (technical practitioners) will likely be frustrated that we do not understand why their talents are not valued highly enough. Meanwhile, as well-intentioned antagonists, we will strive to stay in the middle of that two-way street.

## Historical design limitations and solutions

Designs have been challenged since the beginning of our built environment; however, developments and advances in construction technology have on occasion brutally reconciled those limitations.

In 1284, builders of the Cathedral Saint-Pierre de Beauvais attempted to build the exterior walls higher than structural masonry technology would allow, resulting in a catastrophic failure. The Torre Pendente di Pisa is perhaps the most famous of all building failures. In 1174, geotechnical engineering did not exist, and the bell tower was constructed over an ancient river bed using an apparently inadequate foundation design. The result was uneven settlement of the foundation during construction, and presto! The Leaning Tower of Pisa. The tower continued to lean over the years until measures were recently taken to counterbalance the foundation and arrest the failure, allowing this icon of imperfection to survive its design inadequacies.

A celebrated success in construction technology was Brunelleschi's dome at Santa Maria del Fiore. The project was started in 1296, but the dome was not constructed until 1420 after the tension ring was developed. The ring resisted the outward pressures at the base of the dome. Since the dome was built without the aid of formwork, which had been absolutely necessary in all previous Roman and Gothic construction, Brunelleschi built a 1:12 model in brick to demonstrate his proposed construction method. This has to be one of the first preinstallation conference/mockup reviews.

Another great success of that era was the flying buttress. Cathedral Saint-Pierre de Beauvais had confirmed the limitations on free-standing load-bearing masonry walls, and buttresses, attached perpendicular to an exterior wall, transferred the loads laterally and stabilized the wall, allowing the wall to be taller, thin, and with windows, instead of the thick masonry that could be as much as 8 feet wide at the base.

## Modern design failures

Design failures have persisted in modern times. Most architecture and engineering students have seen the 1940 film of the collapse of the Tacoma Narrows Bridge. Hailed as a great achievement in bridge aesthetics, the design concept was constructed in what proved to be an unsympathetic condition of constant wind. The result was wind-generated harmonic oscillations compounded by the sail effect on the mass of the bridge, resulting in a catastrophic failure soon after the bridge was completed.

More recent are the multiple failures of the 60-story John Hancock Tower in Boston, constructed in 1976. Efforts to reduce the building mass and lighten the building frame, relying primarily on stiffness, proved inadequate for wind loads, resulting in excessive sway causing nausea to inhabitants. Corrective measures included the installation of two 300-ton tuned mass dampers at the 58th floor to counteract the movement. Most people remember the tower for its breaking glass. However, the glass breakage has been found to be a problem involving lead sealer adhering (and transferring differential-movement cracks) to anodized glass; all unrelated to the building movement—but still related to aesthetic intent versus unknown physical properties.

The most devastating United States' building design failure in terms of loss of life and injuries was the 1981 Kansas City Hyatt walkway collapse. Suspended walkways in an atrium failed during an event attended by approximately 2,000 people, killing 117 and injuring more than 200. In this instance, the original design of the hanger rod connections was found to be adequate; however, it was changed during construction to a configuration that was easier to construct and less expensive, resulting in a doubling of loads. This event emphasizes the reality that design and technical collaboration may sometimes need to go beyond the documents phase.

More recent was the 2004 collapse of a portion of Paris's Charles de Gaulle Terminal 2E Concourse. The concourse was a flat, tube-shaped concrete roof structure, 2,100 feet long with no supporting pillars. It collapsed 11 months after completion, killing four travelers. Calculations indicated that the structure was overstressed. The terminal is being torn down and replaced with a more traditional steel and glass structure at a cost of 100 million Euros. Construction is scheduled to complete by summer 2008.

# Design solution basics

Our ability to construct designs that are not just little boxes on the hillside will be challenged as long as we strive to create what has never been built before. Our success in architecture will depend on reasonable design concepts and how well we manage the design development process. The risks associated with daring, original designs can be managed more effectively by concentrating on the following basics:

1. **Communications.** If the design concept is to be adequately understood by the entire project delivery staff, effective communications are essential. Frequent meetings and discussions about new, innovative products that are planned for the design will help prepare the team for preparing construction documents. Your engineers should attend the meetings to discuss design achievability. Copy all team members with design meeting reports. Require interactive participation during design development among all project team members. If a product is being used in an innovative way, have the manufacturer's representative attend the meetings and give advice on the product's limitations.

2. **Verification.** Perform constructability back-checks frequently during the design development phase. If a limitation can be identified early, it can save many hours wasted in producing details that will later be redesigned or even discarded. Some firms conduct in-house design critiques at the end of design development to gather opinions from the other design studios. Team experiences can offer valuable insight.

   If you are struggling to reach a comfort level with constructability by the time construction document preparation begins, call in an outside consultant for a constructability review. Some contractors offer these services as a part of their business development. Verification by an expert can save time and money at this critical juncture. A criticism of the Charles de Gaulle failure was that the owner was also the contractor, and this "closed loop" did not permit effective scrutiny by other parties.

3. **Awareness.** Keeping up-to-date on building products and systems can assist greatly in developing a realistic technical design. If your team is aware of how products perform, they will solve the technical issues with greater efficiency. A habit of ongoing product research will in itself keep your ability to solve design concepts at a higher level.

   It goes without saying that consulting manufacturers and vendors offer the best way to know what their products and systems can do. Don't be hesitant to accept their offers to do a show-and-tell brown bag lunch. The more aware your staff is about products on the market, the more able they are to understand a design concept. Also, be sure to take advantage of the Best Practices reviews provided by the AIA. Gainful information is available from practitioners who provide these insightful articles.

4. **Document production.** The preparation of construction documents is the last chance to determine final design configurations before the stakes start to increase. Changes to the documents after they are published and bid nearly always result in increased cost and possibly delays in project delivery. Angst among team participants increases markedly if the construction documents should come under fire.

5. **Teaming.** Do not produce your documents in a vacuum. Scheduled "brainstorming" reviews involving the entire design team will sustain the balance between designers, project managers, and project deliverers. It could prove beneficial to develop multiple solutions to design configurations and evaluate each scheme on concept achievement, feasibility, and value. The axiom by Robert Kriegel and Louis Patler, "If it ain't broke, break it," could provide a worthwhile approach for testing design interpretations. Remember, at this point, those pretty conceptual details are on paper, and not constructed and hanging in the air. It is far more desirable to debate your details among your coworkers and consultants than to defend them under duress when something has gone wrong in the field.

6. **Frequent technical feedback.** As stated previously, manufacturers and vendors know more about their products and systems than anyone else. Use their resources to confirm that your use of their product is acceptable to them. Do not be shy about including them in the design development process: They may be able to provide a design solution within the limitations of their product that has never been previously done. You also can gain insight on the success of your details and coordination efforts by paying attention to how well the project goes together during construction, as we propound in "Lemons to Lemonade," later in this chapter.

7. **Quality design through technical delivery.** In reality, architects lose clients or get claimed more frequently because of poor technical follow-through rather than because they have produced poor aesthetic designs. The appearance of a building generally involves a subjective assessment. On the other hand, technical failures, such as leaking windows, will more likely involve an objective assessment. It is much easier to identify the aspects of a technical failure than an aesthetic one.

To create a holistic design culture, you must first consciously define your approach of how projects will move through your office. You must set priorities for technical delivery as well as for your design aesthetic. Whether your office is large or small, there will be times when design must rule and times when technical efforts must rule. Technical efforts must involve decisions on not just how you will use computers and software, but also how you will detail windows and roofs and coordinate with your engineers or specifications writers.

The bottom line is that to be successful, you must establish a solid technical review process for integrating design and technical goals equally. Even if you are a sole practitioner, you must decide to set aside time to review how the project will be detailed and delivered. A large, nationally recognized firm recently established a "Legacy Award" for technical excellence, which they present at their annual internal design awards program. This recognition reinforces their belief that quality design is best achieved through celebrating technical coordination and delivery.

A single person may be able to perform a successful project review in a smaller firm, but as the firm's size increases, it often becomes desirable to involve more team members. Should a firm's management be solely design-centered or solely business/technical-centered, it may be necessary to use a moderator to facilitate project reviews. And, as we mentioned before, as the project moves through the construction documents phase, it can be effective to get construction experts to participate in the reviews.

8. **Implementation.** When implementing quality design through technical delivery, you should consider the process to be a vital part of performing architectural services. You may wish to celebrate it as a special program within your firm. You should integrate related activities such as design reviews, technical reviews, and constructability reviews

---

# Case Study | Team Brainstorming Agenda

Following is a possible case study agenda for a teaming session to merge design ideas with technical goals.

### Design Goals

- Recognizing importance of aligning horizontal stone band with windows
- Aligning porte cochere with north roof edge
- Maintaining planning aesthetic in individual units

### Overview of Primary Building Systems

- Masonry details: parapet; cast-stone accent band
- 12" window setback; jamb/sill waterproofing/flashing
- Screening, roof mounted, mechanical
- Detailing of "razor" profile roof edge at north elevation
- Thin profile porte cochere structure depth

### Project Schedule

- Lobby lighting plan
- Lobby floor design
- Finalize unit review with owner

### CAD

- Set up layer standards for DD/CD drawings

---

into your project delivery schedule. It is helpful to keep records of the decisions and agreements made during these reviews and use the records to measure how well goals are achieved. Ask the technicians on your team if they feel that they are important and are being heard. Celebrate your team's accomplishments in achieving higher overall project quality by presenting design awards to the technical deliverers as well as to the designers.

## And they all look just the same

Our chances to become a recognized award-winning architect depend on our ability to produce unique, innovative designs. If all our projects look alike, we will surely fall into the unrewarding realm of mediocrity. It is our designers' free thinking and risk taking that can provide us with a landmark design. It is incumbent upon the people who provide technical services to match unique and innovative design ideas with equally innovative project management and technical follow-through.

### How to avoid ticky-tacky

Our objective should be to approach our designs with our heads up and always be cognizant of the process required to deal effectively with the challenges that arise. We have only to look at the recent past to gain a chilling awareness of potentially adverse outcomes. We can improve our chances for producing successful designs if we strive to maintain awareness of construction technology and the limitations of materials. This can best be accomplished by using the resources available to the project team and within the industry.

We can also benefit by developing and maintaining an internal program for technical adequacy in design delivery. Close communications, frequent back-checks, and scheduled consultation with appropriate consultants and vendors can be valuable components to this process.

Hopefully, you have read our unglamorous but nostalgic retrospective of the drafting chief in the back room in that old green Josam apron in "Your Grandfather's Working Drawings." Not many people would consider the drafting chief to be a "designer," even though that person spent day in and day out designing details required for successful project delivery, much like the project managers, project architects, job captains, and draftspersons do in our offices today. The important objective is to be aware constantly of the conflicts within technology that sometimes appear and manage the development of the design concept to accommodate these challenges. And, with sufficient organization and effort, hopefully, your little box on the hillside will not look the same as the others around it.

> Little boxes on the hillside,
> Little boxes made of ticky-tacky,
> Little boxes, little boxes,
> Little boxes, all the same.

While you work late, contemplating how you are going to detail that slender, wispy icon pointing skyward from the roof, remember to be careful out there.

# Gimme Shelter: The Building Exterior Wall

his is a straightforward "water runs downhill" piece, and it should be meaningful to every practitioner. It takes a look at some basic wall types and window systems, and it notes the challenges in achieving adequate wall design and construction in the industry today. It cites available resources for designing and specifying wall systems, along with important mockup and review requirements needed in the construction phase. Move that can over where the drip is falling; does anybody have an umbrella?

> Ooh, a storm is threatening my very life today,
> If I don't get some shelter, oh yeah I'm gonna fade away
> —The Rolling Stones, 1969

Our professional lives are threatened today by moisture intrusion. Professional liability insurance specialist Victor O. Schinnerer reports that almost one quarter of claims against insured architects allege problems with waterproofing or a component of the building exterior closure. Many of these claims are related to failures in the exterior wall. These failures generally result from water intrusion directly through the wall and water vapor transmission and condensation on or within the wall. When unwanted water and water vapor come in contact with materials and finishes not designed to resist or accommodate moisture, damage occurs. The end result can include staining, material degradation, mold, and lawsuits.

## The rain in Spain falls mainly on the buildings

What is it about water and the exterior walls that both designers and builders are struggling with today? In the industry there seems to be more maneuvering to manage risks or blame others than efforts spent designing and building exterior walls that accommodate and manage moisture. This includes architects, constructors, manufacturers, and suppliers. Have we forgotten that water runs downhill, wind-blown rain runs uphill, and moisture condenses on cool surfaces? Are we no longer aware that humidity is a real problem in hot, humid climates? Have we forgotten how to "shingle" surfaces to shed water?

Perhaps in earlier times there was a greater tolerance for the impact of infiltrated water and the condensation of moisture. It could be because water did less damage to the materials used in the past. When older buildings are renovated today, it is common to "discover" that special measures must now be taken to control humidity that is resulting from vapor transmission. It is also common to "discover" that years of moisture seeping into the exterior wall have rusted or rotted windows and doors and other wall materials, especially in older wooden or masonry structures. Moisture often infiltrates old exterior masonry walls and resides within, doing so little visible damage that it is tolerated. Have you ever noticed a "musty" smell in an older building, perhaps like your town's city hall? That "musty" smell can get you sued in a modern building.

Today's buildings tend to be built of materials less resistant to the presence of moisture over extended time. Thin sheets of gypsum or plywood serving as substrates behind thin veneers of cement plaster, stone, or masonry simply do not perform well when assaulted by the continuous presence of moisture. So called "barrier" systems composed of coated foam sheets or wood composites that are intended to completely stop water or moisture from infiltrating the exterior envelope rarely survive nature's continual onslaught.

The art of detailing and correctly installing flashing to control water is mandatory for both constructors and designers if this problem is to be overcome. Even so, it seems that flashing design and construction are not well understood by everyone these days. A better understanding of working with available materials can benefit all involved in the design and construction industry.

This article will address some common issues concerning the exterior wall. We have chosen to focus on this element of the building envelope because of the many problems that arise from misunderstandings, misapplication, and poor workmanship. We will explore actions to take and issues to consider including the possibility that secondary water management may be an idea whose time has come. And in keeping with the spirit of our articles, we will relate some opportunities for giving *Shelter* that are available to the architect as the exterior wall is designed and constructed.

## Building envelope basics

It is important that the following basic issues be considered by designers and builders:

> **1. Water runs downhill.** As simplistic as it is, it often appears that this fact of nature was not a consideration in some building designs. It rains, it snows, and sooner or later water begins its journey downhill. Designs must be created and buildings built mindful of the reality that water will penetrate openings *that it can run down into*. If you have a design that places a material other than roofing, waterproofing, or flashing in a horizontal plane, then you must carefully consider the design and treatment of that material. Although the material may be typically configured in a horizontal condition, like concrete, metal, or skylights, where and how water runs off of it onto lower surfaces must be thoroughly explored. You must always ask yourself or the contractors the question, "What will happen if water does get through this material or assembly?" You must also ask the corollary question, "Should there be a means to get water that migrates across or through this material or assembly back outside again?"

**2. Moisture tends to condense on cool surfaces.** Water enters a building even before leaks from rain or snow can arise. That is because water is in the air. This is a complex subject involving weather, humidity, vapor transmission, and vapor retarders, and it transcends the scope of this essay. Nonetheless, designers and builders must have a basic understanding of vapor transition and condensation. Everyone must understand that water vapor "drives" from warm temperatures toward cooler temperatures. Bootleg whiskey runners have developed their finest products from this concept. If moist warmer air comes in contact with a surface whose temperature is at or below the dew point, then moisture will condense on that surface. If that surface is a material that is not designed to withstand encroachment and assault by water, then it will be damaged. Generally, in the winter in most locations, vapor will drive from the interior to the exterior. Conversely, in the summer, it will drive from the exterior to the interior most of the time.

An excellent reference check is a simple calculation performed by a mechanical engineer, commonly called a "vapor drive analysis." This calculation can help foster an understanding of what portion, if any, of the exterior wall assembly may be subjected to condensation and under what conditions. While the analysis is typically targeted at extreme conditions to which the building is not constantly subjected, nonetheless, the information gained can facilitate the determination of a vapor retarder location and the selection of materials that will not be damaged by transient water on surfaces where condensation will likely occur.

By definition, the permeance of an adequate vapor retarder should not exceed 1 "perm." Many designers and builders are confused by the dynamics created when vapor retarders are placed in the exterior wall. Not too long ago, prompted by energy-saving concerns, design priorities called for placing an impermeable vapor retarder as close as possible to the interior face of the exterior wall, allowing water vapor in the wall to dry to the exterior. In recent years, this wisdom has changed, suggesting that in some climates it is more appropriate to place the vapor retarder closer to the exterior surface, allowing moisture to dry toward the interior. Moreover, thinking today has evolved to the point that no vapor retarder at all is the recommendation in some climates allowing the wall to dry in both directions. Model building codes that require vapor retarders currently are undergoing study to reflect these changes of wisdom.

Vapor retarders may consist of plastic sheets or fluid-applied materials specifically designed and selected for that purpose. Vapor retarders can also be inadvertent, as was the case several years ago when it was discovered that vinyl wall coverings and some types of paint were effectively creating a vapor retarder on the interior face of gypsum wall board installed on an exterior wall.

**3. Buildings leak.** Many also believe that buildings do not leak, and they believe that if they do leak, it is because someone has made a mistake.

The reality is that materials combined to form an exterior building wall are vulnerable to movement, neglected maintenance, degradation, and substandard workmanship, and leaks can eventually occur even if the water is not evident in the interior space. It is wiser to recognize and acknowleged the fact that buildings either do, or will, leak than to remain silent and allow innocence to foster unrealistic expectations.

### A case for secondary water management: Would you put a screen door on a submarine?

So, the reality is that buildings leak. There is no such thing as a perfect weather "barrier" design except for a balloon. That's because it is hard to get water to leak into an inflated balloon. However, most building types cannot successfully be constructed like a balloon. Exterior wall designs that anticipate no moisture intrusion into the building naturally prove unsuccessful when leaks actually occur. A more successful exterior wall design is one that anticipates leaks and manages the moisture by directing it back to the building exterior before it can reach vulnerable interior materials and cause harm.

**Standard of care.** When an exterior wall with no secondary water management system fails and a claim is brought against the architect, plaintiff experts will likely suggest that the absence of a secondary water management system is a violation of the Standard of Care. The Standard of Care for architects may vary in some respects from state to state, and its application in a particular case will depend on the unique facts of that case. All that notwithstanding, the definition included in the Glossary of *The Architects Handbook of Professional Practice*, 14th edition, reflects basic elements generally accepted around the country: "Standard of care: usually defined as what a reasonably prudent architect, in the same community at the same time, facing the same or similar circumstances would do. It is the measure by which behavior is judged in determining legal duties and rights." Designing an exterior wall as a weather-barrier system without secondary water management should not be regarded as a de facto violation of the Standard of Care, because architects and builders all over the country routinely design and build exterior walls in this way. Nonetheless, inclusion of this feature will provide added protection against water that will inevitably penetrate into the wall.

**Forms of secondary water management.** Secondary water management can take many forms. It can be a "drainable" EIFS (exterior insulation and finish systems) in lieu of a barrier system. In a cement-plaster stucco wall, it can be a continuous weather-barrier membrane and flashings installed beneath the stucco veneer. In a masonry veneer wall, it can be through-wall flashings designed to intercept any water that leaks through the veneer. It can also be windows, doors, or other exterior opening systems capable of collecting and managing water through the head, sill, and jambs.

### Types of window systems

For purposes of simplifying the discussion of different aluminum and glass systems in this article, Jerry M. Johnson of Curtainwall Design and Consulting, Inc., Dallas, addresses them in three generic categories:

1. **Storefront systems.** These generally have little or no performance characteristics relative to managing secondary water and are only designed to "support glass." Basically, all companies provide these systems. They are best used for one- or two-story projects, preferably where they are covered by an overhang, or located in interior conditions. Sill pans, internal deflectors, and weep holes can provide some water management. However, for the most part, they are considered to be a barrier system.

2. **Window wall systems.** Window wall is used in "strip" windows and at "punched" windows. These are a more advanced engineered system that incorporates secondary water and air infiltration management. Unfortunately, during "value engineering" discussions, storefront systems are often proposed as a substitution for a window wall application, because they are less expensive. The key to obtaining the better system is through the specifications. It has been a while coming, but most of the major manufacturers now provide high-performance systems with secondary water management built in. Our preference is to call a product "window wall" only if it has high-performance (rain screen, air, and wind) and secondary water management.

3. **Curtainwall systems.** The ability to manage water and the resistance to infiltration rises dramatically with curtainwall (construction vernacular for a wall that spans two floors). By distinction, two-floor-high installations can and have been done with simple storefront systems. A curtainwall is a system that incorporates the rainscreen principle and/or a pressure-equalized chamber and effectively manages both air and water infiltration. Most of the "off-the-shelf" systems can be adapted to the rainscreen system but not the pressure-equalized chamber. Curtainwall includes "captured" (two-sided and four-sided structural silicone glazed) systems, "stick" (framed on site) systems, "unitized" (shop-glazed and field-set) systems, and panelized systems.

## Doing your homework

Some fundamental questions must be answered before designing and building an exterior wall because of the effect of varying conditions that affect the wall's behavior and performance.

**Climate conditions.** Where will the building be located? Will it be in an area where a hot, humid climate or a cold climate prevails? Does it rain a lot or is it arid? Certain wall systems and materials may not be appropriate in certain climates. The location of the vapor retarder or the insulation in the wall cavity may differ from the locations of your previous projects.

**Topographic conditions.** Will it be possible to design the site drainage so that water flowing on the site does not encounter the exterior wall? Will waterproofing a portion of the exterior wall be required? Does a portion of the base of the wall need to step up to avoid contact with water on the ground?

**Building type and use.** A thorough understanding of the building type and use is important. From issues as straightforward as knowing you will waterproof an open parking garage differently than you will a hospital, to those as complex as the selection of permeable interior finishes located on the exterior wall, the building type and use impacts decision making. Below-grade structures have their own set of rules for exterior walls.

**Compatibility.** Careful consideration is necessary as to compatibility and integration of the different materials combined to form the exterior wall. Not all types of sealant are compatible, and some sealants are not compatible with certain materials. Materials that expand or contract moderately under varying weather conditions require special detailing when paired with materials that are relatively stable.

## Exterior wall fundamentals

### Flashing, barriers, and waterproofing

For purposes of this essay, *flashing* is considered to be a material, either rigid or flexible, that spans from the sheathing and extends through the exterior wall or veneer and terminates in daylight. The *weather barrier* and also *waterproofing* behind a veneer are materials that are generally not exposed to daylight.

### Veneer basics: masonry and stucco

For both masonry and cement plaster stucco, the exterior veneer that you can see is not necessarily a weather barrier. The weather barrier is typically located behind the visible exterior veneer. Masonry usually incorporates an open air cavity between the back of the masonry and the face of the weather barrier. With stucco, the finish layers are usually applied directly to the face of the weather barrier. Masonry and stucco must be viewed as the permeable materials that they are. Water penetration through stucco and masonry veneers can be significant, measured in gallons and not ounces. Some parties believe that properly installed and cured stucco cladding does not allow water penetration through the stucco. We believe that it is best to assume the worst, that there will be cracks and compromised areas of the stucco that will allow water to leak through to the weather barrier or sheathing.

For stucco walls, asphalt-saturated paper-backed lath is available on the market as a quick way to install both materials at the same time. However, it is our opinion that this paper-backed lath should not be the only continuous weather barrier due to the complexity of layering and installation and the risk of damage to the paper as it is installed. We concur with the manufacturers and industry associations that recommend two layers of building paper and believe this product should be installed over an additional weather barrier, such as grade "D" building paper, to create a "belt and suspenders" solution in a water-managed design. Also, the use of secondary moisture barriers can vary based on different types of sheathing. For example, the code requires two layers of grade "D" building paper, or the equivalent thereof over wood-based sheathings. (Note: The Portland Cement Association Web site and the *PCA Portland Cement Plaster/Stucco Manual* are excellent sources of information for detailing cement plaster stucco.)

It is common with both stucco and unit masonry to see attempts to repair leaks by applying sealant to the exterior veneer surface. If the failure symptom is water leaking into the building interior and damaging finishes, then the water has already breached the weather barrier behind the veneer. Applying sealant on the surface veneer will likely not cure the problem unless the veneer is totally "wet sealed." Such applications are difficult to achieve and have limited performance durations that require ongoing maintenance programs.

Moreover, the way to prevent water intrusion through veneer systems is to construct the supporting weather barrier to keep water out of the interior and to direct water that penetrates the veneer back outside. Care must also be taken when the veneer is installed so as not to compromise the substrate barrier.

In masonry veneer systems it is beneficial to detail head and sill through-wall flashing at exterior openings with the added protection provided by "end dams." An end dam is a folded-up or welded segment of flashing that prevents water from flowing out the end of the flashing and back into the wall cavity. However, if the sheathing, flashing, and weather barrier are properly designed and constructed, the absence of end dams should not cause damage.

It is also important in masonry veneer walls to prevent excess mortar buildup in the cavity behind the brick. When mortar builds up, it bridges the cavity and provides a direct path for moisture migration from the veneer to the weather barrier. MASTERSPEC requires that mechanical methods or masonry accessories for controlling mortar buildup be used during the installation of masonry. The Brick Industry Association thoroughly covers the subject of mortar buildup in the cavity in their Technical Notes.

Some designers have chosen to solve the wet cavity issue with the use of impermeable "peel-and-stick" waterproofing over the entire face of the sheathing that forms the interior surface of the cavity. They have also called for it to be installed beneath a stucco veneer. While this solution may effectively solve the water infiltration issue, it may also cause other problems, because it creates a very effective vapor retarder, and the location may not be appropriate in some climates or for some building uses. Although vapor retarder location requirements may preclude the use of peel-and-stick over an entire wall, the product can be effectively used at critical locations around openings and at ledges.

Today, it is widely recognized that an intact weather barrier that is capable of managing infiltrating water is necessary for a successful veneer system. It is also widely recognized that door and window head design and flashing around building windows and doors must perform acceptably. An aluminum window system that collects water in the window head but cannot direct the water back to the exterior is a serious problem in a veneer wall because the water will flow horizontally within the window head. If the window system cannot manage the water, the flashings around the window must prevent water from reaching internal window components. However, when flashings serve as the water management system, they must be carefully coordinated with the weather-barrier substrate in order to be effective. Architectural openings, such as doors, windows, or louvers, in the exterior veneer that are sometimes sealed at their intersection with the veneer for aesthetic reasons, but this sealant will not stop water infiltration through the veneer. Weeps and other pathways intended to allow water to flow out of a veneer wall may be "baffled," but they should not be sealed.

Masonry veneer/steel stud cavity wall designs are complex and more likely to experience problems that go beyond what appears on the surface. Accordingly, the Brick Industry Association, in "Technical Notes 28B," offers the following caution: ". . . many commercial brick veneer/steel stud wall systems have greater exposure to their environment than their residential counterparts. For this reason, it is important to closely observe proper design, detailing, and construction practices to ensure that expected and required levels of performance are met."

Christine Beale also cautions in her book, *Masonry Design and Detailing: For Architects and Contractors:*"Masonry veneers are designed as drainage wall systems because moisture will always be present, even with good design, good detailing, and good workmanship."

### EIFS basics

It has been well-publicized that EIFS systems have been the source of significant controversy, including extensive claims and litigation, in some areas of the country. Some EIFS experts advise that research and investigations have determined that the EIFS product is generally not at fault, but that bad building practices were found to be responsible for the failures. A review of manufacturer Web sites reveals that many companies provide barrier-type EIFS products. Even so, most manufacturers also now market a "drainable" EIFS system that has some capability of managing infiltrated water. Drainable EIFS systems offer the promise of an opportunity to construct a wall of greater weather-resistive integrity than barrier systems; however, the cost can approach that of cement-plaster stucco, which many practitioners consider to be a superior system.

**It's just a shot away . . .** The selection of the exterior skin system for a project is an important decision. It is a decision that should not only involve discussion of costs but also discussion of the owner's inclination for dealing with the cost of maintenance, durability, leaks, and repair. While the selection of or acquiescence to the use of barrier technology for any type of exterior wall to save money is not a breach of the Standard of Care, it is a decision that can have serious consequences. Some of the EIFS manufacturers' Web sites offer literature that will help you establish a list of pros and cons for comparing a barrier system to a drainable system.

**Informed consent.** We believe that the architect should be one of the parties explaining the consequences of such decisions to owners. This is because the owner's *informed consent* in selecting any sort of exterior wall barrier system with no secondary water management capability may assist in resolving claims that may arise down the line. Remember, if claims are filed when an exterior wall fails, you will likely be accused of negligence, rightly or wrongly, if you did not at least discuss the option of secondary water management. Discussions with owners should include potential consequences of their decisions, such as the lack of control over infiltrated water and the damages that can result.

**Owner and contractor influences.** Although the industry often looks to the architect when problems arise with exterior walls, the reality is that owners and contractors frequently exert significant influence over wall design. Owners often choose to let project costs determine the outcome when faced with budget problems. The word of a contractor who has used lower-quality exterior building systems on other projects may be regarded as more compelling than your concerns about the possible consequences of lower-quality products.

A good way to manage this situation is to research the lower-cost alternatives and then present a clear and concise written analysis of your concerns. If you have had an unpleasant experience with proposed lower-quality systems on a past project, you may wish to suggest that the owner contact the previous client and get the lowdown firsthand. In these situations, there is no more credible argument than the experiences of a past client. This will help the owner make informed decisions when considering cost reduction measures.

Even if you manage to preserve the quality materials and systems that you recommend, project success remains vulnerable to the contractor's actions. Should the contractor fail to prepare and effectively execute their work plan or fail to properly supervise, direct, and inspect the work, project success can suffer. Good designs and quality specifications will always be subject to the contractor's expertise and priorities in planning, buying, and placing the work.

## Gimme, gimme shelter

Delivering an exterior wall that does not cause damage when leaks occur ultimately comes down to whether or not the wall is constructed properly. Neither the AIA Owner-Architect Agreements nor the Standard of Care requires the architect to make continuous or exhaustive inspections to determine the quality or quantity of the contractor's work. Yet the degree of construction observation required if the architect were to absolutely determine if the wall is properly constructed would most certainly approach "exhaustive inspections."

An excellent recourse is to look to the control mechanisms provided in MASTERSPEC Section 014000, 1.3, DEFINITIONS, C. Mockups. It states that mockups are used: "to demonstrate aesthetic effects and, where indicated, qualities of materials and execution, and to review construction, coordination, testing, or operation; they are not samples. *[**Approved mockups establish the standard by which the Work will be judged.**]*" In Section 014000,1.6, QUALITY ASSURANCE, J, 1, "Build mockups in location and of size indicated or, if not indicated, as directed by Architect."

Additionally, in Section 014000, water testing of the mockup can be required as referenced in Section 1.3, DEFINITIONS, H. Field Quality Control Testing; "Tests and inspections that are performed on-site for installation of the Work and for completed Work." It is suggested that the mockup be required to pass a water test before construction of the in-place work can begin.

If these MASTERSPEC sections are used by the architect and adhered to by the contractor, the likelihood of an improperly performing exterior wall will be lessened.

Because mockups and testing cost money, an appropriate line item should be listed in the schedule of values. This is a good way to be sure that the contractor either performs the work or can be held responsible for not doing so. The exterior wall mockup is a popular candidate for the value analysis cut list, and contractors sometimes request to use the actual in-place exterior wall construction as the mockup. The problem that arises in addition to the loss of quality control is that the exterior wall will most likely be constructed on the project's critical path, and should there be problems with its construction, the subsequent demolition and rework could adversely affect construction completion. It is often difficult for an architect to convince an owner or contractor to remove and replace defective and nonconforming work when it significantly impacts schedule or cost.

Fulfilling the requirements of Section 01400 requires that a wall mockup design be prepared through a cooperative effort between the architect and contractor. The "preinstallation conference" required for building and reviewing the mockup will illustrate to all parties that the trades understand how their work will be incorporated into the construction and that the contractor has purchased the necessary expertise and services to get the job done.

The contractor's responsibility for planning and coordinating the work is acknowledged in *Guidelines for a Successful Construction Project,* a joint publication of the Associated General Contractors of America, the American Subcontractors Association, and the American Specialty Contractors. The publication addresses subcontractor coordination and offers guidelines for the preconstruction conference. It is available as a PDF online.

Important elements of the mockup include exterior openings, flashing, sealants, and the composition of the weather barrier and substrate. Although the architect cannot observe the entire construction of the wall when it is being built, the knowledge that the contractor and their subcontractors have actually planned and practiced constructing the wall will increase everyone's confidence that the wall is being adequately constructed.

Another way to increase the chances that the exterior wall is properly constructed is to recommend that the owner retain an exterior wall consultant to review the contractor's work and perform scheduled inspections during the construction phase. There are reputable firms available to perform this task, and they can provide reports of work progress.

With these safeguards in place, there is still no assurance that all will go well, and compromises in means and methods still can occur. If you become aware that poor workmanship exists in the wall system where leaks may occur, you should notify the owner and contractor in writing immediately and, if appropriate, call for special consultants or testing to determine the extent of the problem. A notice of nonconformance may not be sufficient for getting the contractor's attention and response. As previously stated, when work is already in place, there is often reluctance to remove and correct it due to the pressures of project completion and costs. Thoroughly document your concerns in writing and with photo images as a defense against fading memories of who caused the problem.

Possible next steps can include withholding your certification for payment for the nonconforming or defective work, including it on punch lists, and listing it as an exclusion in the certificate of substantial completion.

## You can get some satisfaction

Exterior walls seem to be more difficult to construct these days than ever before. Although an architect's wall details may have performed successfully for many years, after they have passed through the gauntlet of value analysis, endured the uncertainty of buyout, or undergone workmanship challenges, success may not be a foregone conclusion.

Giving shelter these days has a chance for an improved outcome if both the architect and contractor understand the basics of water management and wall construction, including the behavior of the materials that are used in today's market. The architect must also be aware of the influences of the owner and contractor on the delivery process and take appropriate project management actions.

The contractor must do an adequate job of incorporating exterior wall construction into the work plan, and the exterior wall mockup should be included in the project schedule, listed in the schedule of values, and properly constructed by the trades. Special inspection should be considered where appropriate, and MASTERSPEC Sections 01453 and 01454 should be faithfully enforced.

Finally, the architect must not be persuaded to take a benign position on suspected defects when told, "It's OK, anyway, it's already built." or "We've always done it this way before." Invasive testing or specialized consulting should be considered if defects are evident and the contractor is not responsive. It is pay now or pay later, because invasive testing and specialized consulting will certainly be required after the wall has failed and a claim is filed.

Whether modern problems with exterior wall quality are the fault of poor workmanship, poor design services, poor maintenance, or poor manufacturing, the adverse impact is the same. The design and construction industry must make stronger efforts to improve this chronic problem that constitutes such a significant portion of claims. When litigation involving water infiltration arises, maintenance, products, workmanship, and design issues are all often involved.

The cost of construction is reaching record levels, and less expensive materials and cheaper buyout of trade responsibilities will remain an influential part of project delivery. Architects must practice effectively and use the tools available to us if we expect to provide shelter.

And, as you ponder if those clouds on the horizon will bring a storm, don't forget to be careful out there.

# Lemons to Lemonade: Benefiting from Mistakes

W ith the objective of learning from our mistakes, we address our fallibility as architects and the lessons that can emerge from our imperfections. The case studies in Part II bring home the reality of imperfections in our practice and the risks that accompany them. The operative phrase for this article is "learn from your mistakes."

## Part I

Risk management, as applied to project management, is a subject worthy of endless observations and discussions. In this book, we have reviewed a number of significant issues, and we sincerely hope that they have been useful in your architectural practice.

In this article, we examine the importance of learning from our mistakes and improving our practice so that we can apply effective solutions to future work. Learning from our mistakes is essential for professional growth. However, learning does not always come naturally or with ease.

When Frank Lloyd Wright was asked which of his buildings was the most beautiful, he reportedly replied, "The one on my board right now." Obviously, Mr. Wright felt that each of his designs was better than the one before, with the apparent assumption that his skills and knowledge improved with each project. Likewise, our objective should be to take our experiences—however rewarding and delightful, or painful and challenging—and use them to improve our basic skills with each project experience.

## "Experience is simply the name we give our mistakes"

This well-known quotation by Oscar Wilde captures the essence of how we learn. We spend a significant amount of our time attempting to avoid mistakes with seminars, research, professional articles, and discussions with our colleagues. We ardently strive to maintain our corporate knowledge, our detail libraries, and our professional references so that we can try to avoid getting it wrong the first time.

Although it may sound like an oxymoron, mistakes are in fact an integral part of the standard of care. Every practitioner makes mistakes, and AIA documents such as G701, Change Order; G716, Request for Information; and G710, Architect's Supplemental Instructions, are examples of tools that anticipate these naturally occurring events. Reality dictates that mistakes will always occur no matter how hard you try to avoid them. An ambitious goal to pursue is the elimination of repetitive errors. If we could do only that, within a short time we would be experiencing only original, never before experienced mistakes. Realistically, this may never be achievable; nonetheless it is a prudent career objective.

There are many approaches when designing and detailing any built condition; some ways are better than others, some ways are just plain wrong, and no way is absolutely perfect. Nonetheless, experiencing the wrong approach can provide benefits, but only if we learn the correct way during the process. If we can gain from each misstep, over time we can realize a progressive improvement in our talents and in our products of service.

Every project in architecture is in some way a new adventure because no two projects are exactly the same. Most clients do not wish to commission a building exactly like the one across the street. Accordingly, our quest for originality includes continuously attempting new actions and endeavors, and, as Albert Einstein said, "A person who never made a mistake never tried anything new."

## An attitude of gratitude

The lemonade development process may require an attitude adjustment. No one wants to take time to wallow in their failures, and our tendency is to ignore them or to correct them and move on as quickly as possible. But in our haste to resolve, we miss opportunities to study and learn. Although we should seek to avoid mistakes, we should be grateful that with them comes the positive experience of knowing what not to do in the future. Knowledge is power.

We should embrace these opportunities and take measures to retain the valuable information that accompanies them. For the small office this could be a journal entry or memos to the project file, and for the large firm it could involve a more complex process of feedback to other service groups, and possibly could include company-wide policy changes in the delivery process.

Mistakes are an integral part of professional practice, and we will be making them as long as we practice architecture. But if we discipline ourselves to be students of our mistakes and practice accordingly, we can improve the services that we provide.

## Don't forget the past

The Chinese proverb "Fool me once, shame on you; fool me twice, shame on me" asserts the premise that we only make mistakes a second time because we allow ourselves to, and our unpleasant experience adequately enables us to avoid a repetition. Nonetheless, repetitive mistakes continue to haunt us even with best efforts.

The process of gaining experience involves learning what we should or should not do in our work, and the practice of architecture involves the prudent use of millions and millions of pieces of information. It is a daunting task to remember all of our bad experiences and apply the corrective lesson in the future.

Since there are so many "lessons learned" to retain, it is advisable to keep some type of record. In Chapter 12, "Construction Phase–Office," and Chapter 13, "Construction Phase–Site," in *The Emerging Professional's Companion*, the suggestion is given to compile and maintain a personal notebook for construction contract administration activities. Construction contract administrators are encouraged to keep copies of letters and completed AIA documents as examples of effective services and actions. As you gain practice experience, your notebook will grow and become an effective reference for your construction phase work.

In addition to keeping project records or making sketches of interesting details, a journal is an excellent tool for making contemporaneous notes about mistakes as you become aware of them. For example, on a job site you might observe how an interior acoustical ceiling detail exhibits flaws where the ceiling intersects a curved wall. The best time to brainstorm a better way to detail it next time is while you are standing there looking at the condition. A photograph and some handwritten notes or sketches can help fix the solution in your mind.

The most popular form of record keeping for architects is old drawings and specifications. Our files tend to bulge with projects that we cannot bear to discard because of their handy use as a reference for current work.

Record keeping at the firm level may be accomplished in a somewhat different form. Some firms compile a guidebook that includes not only good practices but also the firm's specific approach to providing services. At a minimum, architects in a firm who perform the same tasks are encouraged to compare notes from time to time. Exchanging war stories can be quite effective for learning what not to do before it is done.

## Building the lemonade stand

If we expect to make gainful use of the lemons in our life, we must devise ways to process and incorporate them into our personal and professional activities. We cannot expect corrective professional behavior to occur naturally. In your personal practice, you can incorporate the process within your private realm of activities—at your workstation and proximate to your physical surroundings. In an architectural firm, the process must be more encompassing—contained in written policies and perhaps committee driven.

**Record generically.** Documenting our mistakes, while potentially beneficial, carries with it increased risk. Although the reality that plaintiffs' lawyers avidly feed on your "lemon" experiences tends to be more apparent in larger firms, impeaching yourself with your documentation as a result of your efforts to learn from past mistakes can easily happen. Therefore, you should record your mistakes generically so that they cannot be linked back to a particular project. If you retain information specifically referenced to a project on errors and omissions in your files and a lawsuit is filed, you could be providing damaging information against your position in the case. The discovery phase of a lawsuit includes the production of all existing project-related documents in your possession to the plaintiff. Not all lessons learned, like the ceiling example above, will rise to the level of a lawsuit. However, since we must continuously improve our services in order to survive, the fear of being attacked by a zealous lawyer in a legal action must not dissuade us from attending to our business and learning from our mistakes, large or small.

**Incorporate mistakes into available "lessons learned."** The next step is to incorporate these documented experiences into your services process. This can be accomplished in a variety of ways. Some firms make read-only files of detail libraries and guideline drawings available at each workstation, and they are updated as details are refined through experience. Many firms provide seminars on specific topics or have outside consultants present them. Many product vendors are willing to buy your lunch at a "lunch and learn" as they tell you what to do and not do with their product.

**Use a checklist.** Another common method for distributing information is through a checklist. This not only informs and educates, but it also gives the user a method of tracking progress. AIA Document D200–1995, Project Checklist, is a convenient listing of tasks a practitioner may perform on a given project. Many firms become so frustrated when problems repeat that they establish office policies for a minimum level of design on a particular product or system. This could be things such as the quality of flashing, higher-quality roofing systems, or the inclusion of membranes in walls or beneath floors.

**Make a reference book.** Another approach could be to maintain a reference book of problems on each building type. Again, the entries should be categorized generically and not referenced to a particular project. Regardless of how you choose to retain a record of your historic missteps, you should administer them thoroughly and faithfully. We addressed the challenges of mentoring and the experience quotient in "Your Grandfather's Working Drawings" in Chapter 6, and maintaining a record of unsuccessful experiences will make a positive contribution to that effort.

## Part II

The best way to describe how to make lemonade out of your lemons is to examine what has been experienced in the past by others. The following case studies illustrate how problems and mistakes can be incorporated into the delivery of future projects.

## No substitute for experience

A small architecture firm designed several medical clinics for a repeat client. The client is a developer who is also an architect. All of the projects were fast tracked, with construction beginning before all construction documents were completed. As with most fast-track projects, there were some coordination problems, and changes were required in previously issued drawings as new drawings were issued. The client was experienced in these matters and understood the sometimes arduous nature of the fast-track process. The client budgeted for these predictable difficulties and, consequently, made no claims against the architect.

The architecture firm was interviewed by another medical group for a similarly sized project and was awarded the commission. The new project was also fast tracked, and the predictable difficulties occurred once again as the sequence of issuing partially complete documents unfolded. Unfortunately, this new client was not experienced in the rigors of fast track. The client did not budget for the anticipated problems and demanded that the architect pay for what they perceived to be errors and omissions.

After the issues were resolved, the firm conducted an internal post-project review session. The firm had delivered two very similar projects with similar construction challenges, costs, and schedules, but with very different outcomes. One project was successful with a satisfied client, and the other was mired in claims with an unhappy client. The firm focused on the idea that the major difference between the two projects was that one had an informed client and the other did not. The firm resolved that they would make efforts to inform future clients interested in fast track regarding the challenges that can be expected on fast-track projects, and present generic descriptions of past experiences in the form of case studies.

In addition, the architects initiated the following procedures for the delivery of all future fast-tracked projects:

- They will openly discuss with the client both the advantages and disadvantages of the fast-track process.
- They will send a letter to clients confirming those fast-track discussions.
- When changes are required to previously issued construction documents, the necessary changes will be reviewed with the owner and contractor in advance.

This firm took the initiative and analyzed project challenges to develop a process for avoiding those problems in the future.

The Construction Specifications Institute addresses project review and feedback in *The Project Resource Manual—CSI Manual of Practice* in Section 7.6.15, Review, Analysis, and Evaluation, on page 7.94. An example of CSI Form 16.0A, Feedback, is provided on page 7.95.

## Invoice solutions

An architect was having trouble getting a client to pay invoices promptly. After an internal review of overdue invoices related to several clients, the architect discovered that the most common reason for nonpayment was that the client was objecting to minor issues involving the architect's reimbursable expenses. In one extreme instance, a large invoice for professional services was held up for several months because of a dispute over a $13 long-distance telephone call, and in another instance, payment was delayed while the architect justified a meal for employees working overtime.

In an effort to avoid these delays with future payments, the architect decided to submit professional services and expenses on separate invoices, thus avoiding withheld payments on services. The architect also contacted the client's accounting manager to determine particular preferences for invoice format. This enabled the client to have a higher comfort level and decreased the amount of time required for review and approval.

Similarly, another architect had trouble getting paid when a phase of service was billed at 100 percent. Some clients felt that the phase had minor work remaining, as is often the case, and they were reluctant to pay in full. As a result, the architect changed billing procedures to bill only 95 percent of a preconstruction phase until the following phase was started. For example, schematic design was not invoiced past 95 percent, until the construction documents phase had commenced.

By making these minor adjustments based on feedback from clients, these two firms were able to improve their billing-to-payment aging cycle. Their positive actions not only increased their efficiency and profits, but it also improved client relationships.

## Problems are a two-way street

An architecture firm worked for several developer clients who routinely kept score of their view of the architect's performance. At the completion of each project, these clients would ask for a portion of the architect's fee to be discounted to account for costs the clients believed were incurred as a result of the architect's errors. The sums of money were small, and they were more of a frustrating nuisance than a threat to profits. The architects reviewed the situation and concluded that the claims made by these clients did not warrant an internal change in their delivery process. The claims were minor and clearly designed to obtain a discount in the architect's fee. Instead, the architect initiated noninvasive countermeasures designed to inform yet not provoke the client.

On future projects, the architects began keeping a contemporaneous timesheet record of extra services provided to the client for small scope changes and assistance for which the architect did not normally invoice. The architects considered these services to be their way of providing a little "extra value" to clients. These "qualified" services were added value that clients had begun to take for granted because they were given away without fanfare during the course of the project. Examples of these services include making design presentations to an owner's prospective tenants or making design changes or otherwise helping a contractor determine a solution to a construction error of a scope too small to be worth the effort and expense of billing. However, the total of these unbilled services was a more significant number.

When the client demanded a fee discount on the next project, the architect's qualified service records were presented to the client as "offset" to the client's minor claims asserted at the conclusion of the project. The architect explained that, if the owner wished to "count the marbles," then everyone's should be counted. These actions enabled the client to realize better the overall value of the firm's services, and, as a result, the fee disputes ended.

## Cultivate the citrus crop

The endeavor to make lemonade out of lemons will not be adequately successful unless the participants gain something from the process. Learning from mistakes is not easy, and it is not glamorous. It takes courage to face shortcomings, and it takes more courage to realize improvement. To benefit fully from these efforts, the following are suggested.

**Track success.** Keep records on what is being done within the firm or within your personal practice to realize improvement. Whether it is fewer claims, happier clients, better design execution, or faster payment, some notations on improving results is beneficial to all.

**Measure results.** When possible, measure the differences gained. Fewer RFIs, fewer change orders, and accolades from clients can serve to mark progress. Although project documentation is largely dependent on the contractor's organized behavior and the client's demands, make an attempt to measure the results of your and your firm's accomplishments.

**Recognize achievement.** Finally, it is important to put the spotlight on those who make measurable progress, even if it is only attitudinal. Recognize those who go beyond and those who master the ethic. This is a difficult part of architecture, and it is not easy or fun; yet it is just as important as creating the design concept. Recognition of those who enter the arena day after day with resolve and determination should be viewed as the talents that they are. Shine a light upon them and tell them, "job well done."

## The sugar in the lemonade

Our careers in architecture have given us many opportunities to make mistakes, and we have gained much valuable experience in that arena. We believe that if occasional missteps are not made, we are not performing on the leading edge and growing our skills. However, our concerns should not be about making mistakes, but instead we should concentrate on how we use these challenging experiences to improve our practice.

We have attempted to provide you with a reasonable view of risk management as it applies to the profession of architecture; from preventive measures, to an assessment of what went wrong, to how mistakes can be corrected and used as learning tools.

The *Fundamentals* are basic concerns that we must apply in guarding our practice. These include establishing a personal risk management program, pursuing a fair and balanced services contract, and being constantly aware of the dangers that lie in wait when we do not exercise good risk practices. Our *Clients* are our life blood, and we cannot keep our doors open unless they believe in us and desire our services. Moreover, we must consider their interests, and in so doing we should not only serve them but also share with them our knowledge and experiences to assist them with their risk management concerns.

The effectiveness of risk management practices is determined by our *Power and Proficiency* in delivering services. We must be effective, yet not overbearing in our risk applications, and we must be capable of identifying challenges and resolving them quickly. We must always be aware of our contracted authority, and above all, Grasshopper, we must administer our projects with the appropriate balance of calmness.

The *Essentials* in our program must include awareness and understanding of risk elements in our services, errors and omissions, betterment, nonconforming work, and contractor obligations. We must make *Applications* of risk discipline to construction phase activities such as project buyout, changes, submittals, site observations, and payment certifications. To fully appreciate the challenges and pressures of practice, we offer *The Architect's Lament* of days gone by. A look at our past, our pace, and the lost treasures of our art can provide us with valuable reference points for the future, regardless of our age or experience.

Risk management is relatively new ground in architecture, and its application can benefit from a careful *Introspection* of our identity, how we apply our skills, and how we produce original design in a risk-challenged world. These aspects of risk management run throughout our services, from early marketing to post construction. They go beyond our basic skills, involving our demeanor, our interactive abilities, and our state of mind.

Our desire for this book is to provide you with a valuable companion that will remain with you while developing your risk management approach. As you go forward, when you encounter issues and circumstances that threaten your practice, consult this reference and compare its messages to your situation. Use it as an aid in developing your ambidextrous project management/risk management style.

And as you go about managing project risk, above all, we must implore, please be careful out there.

# Index

Change review meetings, 153–154
Charles de Gaulle Terminal 2E Concourse, 226–227
Checklists, and learning from mistakes, 245
Chief draftsman, 190–191, 204
Claims
  and betterment, 108–109, 111
  definition of, 6–7
  documentation and, 13
  importance of responding to, 9–10
  and nonconforming work, 128
  and perceptions of architects, 215
  quick response plan for, 7–9
  relationships after, 11
  reporting to insurer, 7
  style of, 116–118
Client(s), 39–61
  advocacy for, 68
  care of, rules of, 10–11
  and construction contract administration, 95
  and contracts, 18
  expectations of, managing, 44–45, 67–68
  knowledge of, and relationships, 41
  and learning from mistakes, 245–247
  maintaining relationships with, 39–44
  and problem resolution, 86
  and project manager attitudes, 65–66
  See also Owner(s)
Climate, and building exterior walls, 235
Commanding, versus consulting, 75
Common authority, 70
Communications
  about nature of architecture, 211–217
  and client care, 10
  and client expectations, 46–47
  and design, 227
  management of, 5
  in problem solving, 84
  on staffing issues, 219
Compatibility, of exterior wall materials, 236
Compensation
  contracts on, 31
  for discrepancies, 103
  learning from mistakes in, 246–247
  substantial completion and, 183
Competition
  communication and, 47
  conceptual design drawings and, 132
Complete, term, 194

Completion
  term, 24, 99–100
  See also Substantial completion
Computer-aided design. See CAD
Concealed work, observation of, 171
Concept, term, 131
Conceptual design drawings, benefits of, 132–133
Condensation, 233
Conditions
  atypical, agreements on, 34
  contracts on, 31–32
Conferences
  and construction contract administration, 93–94
  pre-closeout, 172
  preconstruction, 52–53, 133
  preinstallation, 173, 226, 240
  See also Meetings
Construction administration, 88–98
  preparation for, 92–93
  proactive involvement in, 92
Construction contract administration (CCA), 88–98, 213
  definition of, 89
Construction drawings, 100
Construction methods
  authority for, 74
  conceptual design drawings and, 133
Construction phase
  architect's documents not used for, 130–138
  discovery of drawing discrepancies in, 101–102
  drawings in, 193
  observations during, 113–122, 166–174
Construction phase services, deletion of, 21, 28–29
Construction schedule, authority for, 74–75
Construction Specifications Institute
  on project review and feedback, 246
  Substitution Request, 148
Consultant(s)
  and certifications, 187
  documentation and, 13
  relationships after claim, 11
  separate, 49–55
  and workforce issues, 221
Consultant agreements, policy on, 35
Continuing education, 220
Contract(s)
  accepted, 18–29